COMPREHENSIVE READING INTERVENTION
IN GRADES 3–8

Also Available

Early Intervention for Reading Difficulties, Second Edition:
The Interactive Strategies Approach
Donna M. Scanlon, Kimberly L. Anderson,
and Joan M. Sweeney

Comprehensive Reading Intervention in Grades 3–8

Fostering Word Learning, Comprehension, and Motivation

Lynn M. Gelzheiser
Donna M. Scanlon
Laura Hallgren-Flynn
Peggy Connors

THE GUILFORD PRESS
New York   London

Copyright © 2019 The Guilford Press
A Division of Guilford Publications, Inc.
370 Seventh Avenue, Suite 1200, New York, NY 10001
www.guilford.com

Printed in the United States of America

This book is printed on acid-free paper.

Last digit is print number: 9   8   7   6   5   4   3   2   1

Library of Congress Cataloging-in-Publication Data

Names: Gelzheiser, Lynn M., author. | Scanlon, Donna M., author. |
   Hallgren-Flynn, Laura, author. | Connors, Peggy, author.
Title: Comprehensive reading intervention in grades 3–8 : fostering word
   learning, comprehension, and motivation / Lynn M. Gelzheiser, Donna M.
   Scanlon, Laura Hallgren-Flynn, Peggy Connors.
Description: New York : The Guiford Press, [2019] | Includes bibliographical
   references and index.
Identifiers: LCCN 2018022676| ISBN 9781462535606 (hardcover : alk. paper) |
   ISBN 9781462535552 (paperback : alk. paper)
Subjects: LCSH: Reading (Elementary) | Reading (Middle school) |
   Reading—Remedial teaching. | Response to intervention (Learning disabled
   children)
Classification: LCC LB1573 .G395 2018 | DDC 372.43—dc23
LC record available at *https://lccn.loc.gov/2018022676*

About the Authors

Lynn M. Gelzheiser, EdD, is Associate Professor Emerita in the Department of Educational and Counseling Psychology, Division of Special Education, at the University at Albany, State University of New York. Dr. Gelzheiser's professional career has focused on students with learning disabilities. Her research has examined both instructional and system-level variables that affect the reading and mathematics achievement of students in special education settings. Most recently, she has focused on the efficacy of the Interactive Strategies Approach—Extended for improving reading achievement, content vocabulary knowledge, and motivation in third- to eighth-grade struggling readers.

Donna M. Scanlon, PhD, is Professor in the Department of Literacy Teaching and Learning at the University at Albany, State University of New York. Her research focuses on the relationships between instructional characteristics and success in learning to read and on developing and evaluating approaches to preventing and remediating reading difficulties. Her work has contributed to the emergence of response to intervention as a process for preventing reading difficulties and avoiding inappropriate and inaccurate learning disability classifications. Dr. Scanlon is a developer of the Interactive Strategies Approach and the Interactive Strategies Approach—Extended.

Laura Hallgren-Flynn, MSEd, is a reading teacher in Guilderland Central School District in Guilderland, New York. She has worked as a part-time instructor in the Department of Literacy Teaching and Learning and as a research associate in the Child Research and Study Center, both at the University at Albany, State University of New York. In her work at the research center, Ms. Hallgren-Flynn has helped develop reading interventions and instructional materials for teachers, supervised intervention teachers, and provided professional development to preservice and practicing teachers learning to implement the Interactive Strategies Approach and the Interactive Strategies Approach—Extended.

Peggy Connors, MS, has been working in the field of elementary education since the 1990s. Her experience includes serving as classroom teacher, reading specialist, educational research assistant, teacher educator, and, most recently, independent literacy consultant. Mrs. Connors has been associated with research studies on the Interactive Strategies Approach and the Interactive Strategies Approach—Extended conducted at the Child Research and Study Center, University at Albany, State University of New York.

Preface

There has been a substantial amount of research demonstrating the merits of different approaches to fostering reading comprehension among intermediate and middle grade students in intervention settings. To our knowledge, there is no research, other than our own, that explicitly assesses the value of the approach that we have taken in this book and in the research that preceded this book. Our approach *simultaneously* focuses on helping readers who have limited oral reading accuracy skill to:

- Become more proficient word solvers.
- Build their sight vocabulary.
- Become more active in meaning construction.
- Develop topic and genre knowledge in order to enable meaning construction and the development of relative expertise related to specific topics.

Our research has evaluated this comprehensive and integrated approach to intervention (Gelzheiser, Scanlon, Vellutino, & Deane, 2017; Gelzheiser, Scanlon, Vellutino, Hallgren-Flynn, & Schatschneider, 2011). Thus, we have not evaluated the individual elements of the intervention that are discussed in detail in this book, and do not know the relative contribution to student progress made by each facet of the intervention. We provide the reader with the logic for each element of the intervention plan as well as its grounding in the research literature.

We encourage teachers of intermediate and middle grade readers with limited word identification skills, whenever possible and as appropriate, to incorporate all elements of the intervention in their work with students for whom word-reading accuracy remains a concern. We make this recommendation based on the enthusiasm for the comprehensive approach expressed by the experienced teachers who have used the intervention described in this book, and on the improvements in both word identification skills and comprehension that intervention participants have demonstrated.

We also suggest that, as students are developing their reading accuracy, they read texts that allow them to learn meaningful science and social studies content. This approach allows teachers to address multiple learning goals, and offers a way to connect intervention with the general education curriculum.

Acknowledgments

Every teacher's understanding of teaching and learning is constantly developing. Each student a teacher encounters and each lesson a teacher conducts offers the teacher insights into the great mystery known as *learning*. This book is a humble effort to share what we, the teachers who have written this book, have learned about teaching and learning.

Much of what we understand about learning comes from the reading intervention students we have taught and observed. Each student has given us a unique window into the challenges posed by learning to read, and we thank them for sharing that window. We have also learned from our teaching efforts (some successful, and some still needing to be improved), and again we thank our students for their responses that shaped our understanding of how to address their unique challenges.

As researchers, we have had the special opportunity to acquire understanding about teaching and learning by observing and instructing teachers as they conducted intervention with their students. While it is not possible to enumerate what we have learned from these teachers, we can acknowledge our gratitude for all they have taught us. Our initial development of the Interactive Strategies Approach—Extended (ISA-X) was informed by the rich contributions of Michelle Bonczkowski, Pat Caccamo, Lynn Connor, Michele Cosselman, Robin Delaney, Kiera Hovey, Judy Kapila, Lauren Kvam, Kelly McGillycuddy, Alison Klein Slater, Ruth Ward, and Beth Wilson. Our study of the efficacy of the ISA-X was possible because of the generous efforts of Emily Pohl Anderson, Teri Burns, Maureen Butler, Deb Conti, Christine Guarnieri, Katrina Keith, Kate Lamica, Susan Lynch, Melissa Manning, Heather Swiecicki, and Bill Wendelken. It is fair to say that a considerable fraction of this book is what we have learned from our time with them.

Our research on effective reading intervention was possible only because of the investment of tax dollars. We are grateful for this support and hope that, through this book, the investment will yield better outcomes for readers who are experiencing word-reading difficulties. Specifically, the ISA-X research was supported by the Institute of Education Sciences, U.S. Department of Education, through Grant Nos. R324A110053 and R324A070223 to the Research Foundation of the

State University of New York. The earlier Interactive Strategies Approach (ISA) research was supported by grants from the National Institute of Child Health and Human Development (Grant No. R01HD42350) and the Institute of Education Sciences, U.S. Department of Education (Grant No. R305W060024). The opinions expressed in this book are those of the authors and do not necessarily represent those of the funding agencies.

Many talented colleagues have contributed to this work in diverse ways. We are grateful to Frank Vellutino for his role in the creation of the ISA and for his ongoing wisdom and support. We thank Anita DeSarbo, Diane Fanuele, Nicki Foley, Suzanne Moore, and Sheila Small for their careful attention to the details of data collection; they enabled us to focus on reading intervention. They also coordinated the efforts of dedicated teams of assessors and research staff whose careful work we gratefully acknowledge. While we are not able to identify by name each person who has contributed to this work, we are well aware of and thankful for their commitment to the improved lives of readers.

Contents

Part III. Meaning Construction

Guide to the Reproducible Materials

All the reproducible materials associated with this book are listed below in the order in which they are mentioned in the text. Those that appear in the book are identified by figure number and page number. Those that appear only on the book's companion website are indicated as *website only*. All the materials listed here are available online for purchasers of the book to download and print (see p. x for details).

PART I

The Foundations of a Comprehensive Approach

CHAPTER 1

Introduction

In this chapter, we explain our purposes for writing this book. Briefly stated, our major and ultimate purpose is to improve the oral reading accuracy and reading comprehension performance of intermediate and middle grade students who have yet to learn to read grade-level materials with enough accuracy to enable comprehension. Because improved comprehension is the end goal, we begin with an illustration of the factors that influence reading comprehension and share our view that there is a need for comprehensive reading intervention for the readers upon whom we focus in this book. These students need to improve their reading accuracy because it is an important prerequisite for reading comprehension. We introduce an approach to comprehensive reading intervention, the Interactive Strategies Approach—Extended (ISA-X), and discuss its premises as well as research evidence of its effectiveness. We conclude with a brief overview of the organization of the remainder of this book, which fully describes the ISA-X as it applies to readers who have difficulties with word identification.

Rationale: What Is the Purpose of This Book?

While our purpose in writing this book is to help students become stronger readers, the intended audience for this book is, of course, the teachers who provide the needed intervention. Every day, reading intervention teachers welcome intermediate and middle grade students into their classrooms who are not yet achieving the needed level of accuracy, and they often find it challenging to effectively address this aspect of reading development. We (the authors of this book) too have provided intervention to intermediate and middle grade readers. We have also had the privilege of studying reading intervention as researchers and scholars and have spent many, many hours observing and discussing intervention with practicing teachers. Through this combination of teaching, researching, observing, and collaborating, we—and the teachers with whom we have worked—feel that the approach to instruction/intervention that we have developed holds promise for helping students who have struggled for years. In this book, we share some of the lessons we have learned (actually, we share *a lot* of what we have learned) in hopes that our learning and experiences can, in turn, help teachers to become more effective in helping readers to accelerate their growth in literacy learning.

Reading is a complex process. A good deal of this book discusses that complexity in order to help teachers better understand it. This way, as they work with their readers, they can better discern the source(s) of their students' difficulties. Teachers will also have new instructional techniques to draw upon as they plan for and deliver responsive instruction that moves students forward.

Preservice and Experienced Teachers

Our goal in writing this text is to provide information that is useful for both preservice teachers and experienced professionals. As a result, for seasoned professionals we may come across at times as seeming to state the obvious, although perhaps our careful attention to the needs of preservice and beginning teachers will be of value to seasoned professionals in mentoring relationships. However, based on our work with numerous teachers over many years, we also know that seasoned professionals are likely to learn a great deal as well—perhaps even more than teachers just entering the profession—because seasoned professionals are likely to see immediate application for many of the approaches to instruction that we describe.

Teachers reading this book are on a learning journey. We anticipate that teachers will find the journey to be worthwhile, because teachers who are more knowledgeable about the reading process and about their students are better equipped to provide instruction that moves their students forward. Experienced teachers who have learned about the approach described in this book report that they have found it to be different from the ways in which they had been accustomed to teaching because it focuses on enabling students to become strategic, independent readers. Teachers who have implemented the ISA-X are enthusiastic about the effect that promoting independence has had on their students' sense of confidence/competence and their reading accuracy and, most importantly, their reading comprehension.

Our goal in this book is to share instructional techniques that we have found to be effective in accelerating students' reading growth and to, thereby, contribute to efforts to reduce the number of students in the intermediate and middle grades who do not read well enough to meet national standards for reading comprehension (National Assessment of Educational Progress, 2015). If students reach high school and have yet to learn to comprehend text sufficiently well, they are at increased risk for a range of negative outcomes, including dropping out (Hernandez, 2011), having limited employment options (Miller, McCardle, & Hernandez, 2010), and being incarcerated (Greenberg, Dunleavy, & Kutner, 2007).

As every reading intervention teacher who teaches them knows, intermediate and middle grade students are a varied lot (Buly & Valencia, 2002). By the time students have reached the intermediate grades and beyond, they have participated in years of reading instruction. Each student has learned some things from this instruction, but not others. While the goal for all students in intervention is improved reading comprehension, the route to this goal is different for each reader. Because each is unique in his or her knowledge and skills, different readers have different goals to be addressed so they can better understand what they read.

In this book, we address intervention for one subset of intermediate and middle grade readers: those who find it challenging to understand what they read, at least in part, because they have yet to learn to read words with the level of accuracy and fluency that is expected for their grade placement. These are readers who need to develop their sight vocabulary and the word-solving skills that enable readers to grow their sight vocabularies.

The term *sight vocabulary* is used to describe words that the reader has stored in memory sufficiently well that they can be read accurately and with seemingly little to no effort. The size of the reader's sight vocabulary is one factor that influences reading comprehension.

We describe ways that teachers can help intermediate and middle grade readers to build their sight vocabularies. Yet this book is about more than how to develop word-reading skills, because many interrelated factors influence reading comprehension. We have found that many readers who have a limited sight vocabulary have come to perceive reading as being about accurate word identification rather than about understanding the meaning of the texts they read. As a result, they may be unaccustomed to attempting to understand the texts they read and they may not have developed the knowledge and vocabulary that would have accrued had they been more focused on meaning making as they read.

A Surprising Fact

The number of words in a proficient reader's sight vocabulary is huge. The exact number is, of course, unknown for any individual, but scientific estimates vary between about 40,000 and over 80,000 words. The vast majority of these words are not explicitly taught to readers but are instead learned because the reader can effectively puzzle through the identity of unfamiliar words while reading.

Based on our research findings, we believe our perspective on instruction for students who have yet to develop sufficiently large sight vocabularies is useful. Teachers often ask us whether they should continue to spend time addressing intermediate and middle grade students' reading accuracy. They are concerned for several reasons. For example, because these students have not benefited sufficiently from previous decoding instruction, teachers fear that further progress is unlikely and thus wonder whether it is time to move on. Additionally, teachers may find themselves encouraged to "be on the same page" as general education literacy instruction, and to support the general education program that typically stresses comprehension for intermediate and middle grade readers.

Our perspective, as detailed in this book, is that a limited sight vocabulary is such a major barrier to comprehension that it must be addressed by instruction if such readers are to progress. Further, we are confident that progress is possible when students receive accuracy-focused instruction that is closely linked to reading in context. We describe an approach to accuracy instruction in which students see a clear connection between the decoding and word-solving knowledge they are learning and the reading of meaningful text. In addition, we describe a comprehensive approach in which students' motivation for reading, reading skills and strategies, vocabulary and comprehension, and knowledge development are addressed in integrated lessons.

Phonics Instruction and More for Readers Who Struggle

The National Reading Panel (NRP; 2000), in its review of the research on reading instruction, concluded that in the early primary grades (K–1) phonics instruction has a significant positive impact on children's success in learning to read if the instruction is systematic and explicit. The NRP was not able to identify any particular phonics "program" that was definitively better than others that were available at the time of the review. The NRP also concluded that phonics instruction in later grades has little to no reliable impact on reading success. In 2016, the International Literacy Association's Literacy Research Panel published an advisory related to dyslexia and instruction for students who encounter serious difficulties with developing oral reading accuracy (*www.literacyworldwide.org/docs/default-source/where-we-stand/ila-dyslexia-research-advisory.pdf*). Their conclusion related to instruction for readers in the intermediate grades and beyond was similar to that of the NRP's but was more nuanced. The advisory states, "Reviews of research focusing solely on decoding interventions have shown either small to moderate or variable effects that rarely persist over time, and little to no effects on more global reading skills" (p. 3).

While we agree with the conclusions of the advisory, not everyone shares our support for the report, as a Google search for *dyslexia research advisory* will reveal. Despite research findings that have accumulated across more than two decades, there are many professionals who remain strong proponents of specific types of highly scripted and often multisensory phonics programs as treatments for readers who continue to have difficulty with word-reading skills. As we discuss throughout this book, if students spend too much time receiving phonics instruction in programs like these, they have far less time to engage in meaning-focused reading. This pattern of instruction has the potential to send the wrong message about the purposes for reading and to limit students' opportunities to develop the motivation, language skills, and knowledge base upon which reading comprehension depends.

Understanding the Reading Process: Factors That Influence Comprehension

Comprehension is complex. Because they are proficient readers, this complexity is not always apparent to proficient readers, including teachers. To illustrate, we provide a concrete example in the section below. This example is intended to help teachers gain greater appreciation of the complexity of comprehension as they consider the process from the perspective of someone who is not a proficient reader.

Reading from the Perspective of Someone Who Is Not Proficient

Imagine that a visitor from Mars walks into a teacher's classroom. Through the miracle of modern technology, the two are able to communicate. The visitor picks up a book and asks, "What is this? How does it work?"

The teacher explains that a book is a record of ideas that a person, the *author,* has decided are important to communicate to many others. By using a process called *writing,* the author's thoughts are recorded for others to access when they use a process called *reading. Readers* are able to understand the ideas and thoughts that have been recorded in countless books by countless authors.

The teacher points out that some books are written because the author wants to share information about a topic or person. Other books are written because the author has imagined characters whose experiences will engage, entertain, and/or enlighten readers.

At this point, the Martian visitor is probably curious about how one can learn to read and gain access to all of this information and these stories. To help the visitor, the teacher describes, on a basic level, *how books work.* In English, every spoken word has one agreed-upon written representation (with a few exceptions) that consists of individual letters; there are 26 letters that can be used to write words. In a word's written representation, the letters often, but not always, correspond to the sounds in spoken words. The writer begins at the top of the page, and writes the words from left to right, continuing down the page, with a return sweep at the end of each line of text. Readers use their stored knowledge of written representations to access the author's words and message. A large part of the challenge of learning to read is learning to recognize the printed representation of thousands of spoken words.

The teacher picks up *Frog and Toad Together* (Lobel, 1971) to show the visitor how she identifies the words the author has written. But very quickly, it becomes apparent that identifying the words is just the first of many things that readers do. The visitor has questions about things in the book, although having had no experience with books and print, the Martian may not be able to articulate his questions using the words we might use.

"Why are there pictures along with the squiggles [print]?"

"Why are some of the squiggles in the book darker than others [bold print]?"

"Why is there one row of squiggles [title] on the outside of the book?"

"Why are these squiggles at the start of the book in a list [table of contents]?"

As the teacher reads, she realizes that there are things that readers do that are not obvious to her visitor. For example, the author assumes that the reader will use knowledge and make inferences and connections while reading. When the author writes, " 'I am sorry,' gasped Frog, 'but I could not catch your list' " (Lobel, 1971, p. 15), the author expects the reader to know the meaning of the word *gasp*, and to infer that Frog is gasping for breath because he has been running to catch the list that has blown away in the wind. The reader does not understand the author's message simply by identifying the words. "Reading," the teacher explains, "requires knowledge and thinking."

At this point, the reader of this text may be thinking (because reading is thinking), while it is entertaining to imagine a Martian who needs reading instruction, "What is the purpose of this vignette in a book about readers with who have yet to learn to read with expected levels of accuracy and fluency? What is the message the author wants the reader to infer?"

One purpose in sharing the vignette is to illustrate the factors that contribute to comprehension. These include motivation, the ability to recognize words automatically (both high-frequency words that may be taught directly, and words that the reader identifies by strategically using context and decoding knowledge), knowledge of word meanings, knowledge about the world, and engagement in meaning construction. In the upcoming chapters, we discuss each of these factors, and how each can be addressed in a coherent way in a comprehensive approach to reading intervention for the readers who are the focus of this book. Because reading involves many interrelated factors, it seems unlikely that learning about only one of them will result in optimal comprehension growth for an intervention student.

We, and the teachers with whom we have worked, have observed that the previous reading experiences of the students who are the focus of this book often result in gaps and limitations in these readers' motivation, vocabulary, and knowledge.

These factors constrain comprehension and take on increasing importance as students progress through school. Reading intervention often focuses on the traditional domains of accuracy and comprehension. Indeed, a recent study (Ciullo et al., 2016) of middle school students identified as having learning disabilities found that roughly 40% of instructional time was devoted to skills and knowledge related to comprehension (e.g., strategies, genre, fluency). Another 20% was devoted to reading and understanding literature or informational text, with only 5% of time devoted to phonics and 8% to vocabulary development (the remaining time was devoted to writing, management, and other miscellaneous tasks). In contrast, this book is organized around the belief that motivation, vocabulary, and knowledge development are fundamental targets of intervention, in addition to instruction designed to directly foster accuracy and comprehension.

Instructional Decision Making: An Introduction to the ISA-X

Themes and Goals

We designed the ISA-X to reflect our belief that teachers may best assist intermediate and middle grade readers with diverse needs if they have greater expertise related to the complexity of the reading process and how a *comprehensive* array of instructional tactics can be used to foster reading growth. We also take the position that it is helpful if teachers instructing intermediate and middle grade readers start with a working hypothesis about what each reader still needs to learn to promote comprehension, and use that hypothesis to design instruction that is *responsive* to each reader's specific needs, while respecting the strengths that the reader may have. As they interact with students, teachers' ideas about how to best respond may develop and/or change.

Further, our objective was to create an *approach* to intervention, and not a scripted program. This approach relies upon knowledgeable teachers who attend to their students in order to make numerous decisions as they plan, deliver, and reflect on instruction. Therefore, this book is designed to help teachers become more knowledgeable about the reading process and about ways to approach instruction to more effectively support their students' growth as readers.

There are several reasons that we have opted to develop an approach rather than a program. The first is detailed in the next chapter—the idea that there is no "one-size-fits-all" intervention. Programs are limited because they require that teachers fit students into the instruction, instead of designing instruction that fits students.

Flexibility is another advantage to learning about an approach, rather than a program. In conducting research on the ISA-X, we have elected to use one practicing teacher per school, who was placed on special assignment in order to learn about the intervention and allow us to collect data about its effectiveness. Teachers who have participated in ISA-X research and then subsequently returned to their regular teaching assignments report that, no matter what reading program or approach is in place in their school, they are able to use some or much of what they learned during their involvement with the ISA-X. If their school requires teachers to use specific intervention programs, these teachers have a greater understanding of the importance of enabling their students to become strategic, independent readers. As a result, we have found that the students of the former ISA-X teachers showed greater gains in comprehension across the school year than do students whose intervention teachers had not learned about the ISA-X (Gelzheiser et al., 2017). We hypothesize that having learned the approach, teachers were able to adapt and improve the intervention they offered when they returned to their typical teaching context.

Finally, we have opted to rely on teacher decision making because we believe that it promotes teacher thinking in a way that a program does not. In proposing an intervention approach that relies on teacher decision making, we acknowledge that *there are no perfect lessons* and that even the most proficient teachers make decisions that they may later see as less than ideal. Teachers can never have perfect insight into their students, and have to think quickly, so they make the best possible choice under given circumstances. But there is value in missteps. Every less than optimal decision is an opportunity for a teacher to reflect and to continue to learn. This book is ultimately about learning, trying, reflecting, and then learning from experience.

In the ISA-X, we have found it helpful to design instruction around instructional goals. As described in the next chapter, the overarching goal for intervention students is to become *independent readers* who have acquired knowledge and strategies that will help them to solve puzzles (like unfamiliar words or challenging ideas) that they may encounter as they read. We organize much of the rest of the book around more specific goals that are intended to help teachers plan responsive and targeted instruction. These student-focused goals are identified at the beginning of Chapters 3–13. We organize our approach to intervention around goals for students because we want teachers to design instruction that is goal oriented rather than activity oriented. However, our experience has revealed that, in order to address some of these instructional goals, some preservice and inservice teachers themselves need to develop additional foundational knowledge related to certain aspects of the reading process. Therefore, some of the chapters address increasing teachers' knowledge rather than instructional practices.

As they plan instruction, we encourage teachers to ask themselves, "In what way will this instructional activity enable the readers to move forward toward attaining particular goals?" Throughout this book, we describe ways that teachers can observe, listen to, and assess students in order to identify what individual students are ready to learn as this will inform where to begin instruction toward given goals.

Note that these goals are written using professional vocabulary that may not be familiar to every teacher. Both the vocabulary and the goals are explained in greater detail in the chapters that follow—this chapter is just an overview. We have also included a glossary at the end of the book with the intention of enabling teachers to readily access the meanings of terms that may be new to them.

ISA-X Goals for Students

Motivation: Students will develop the belief that reading is an enjoyable and informative activity that is not beyond their capabilities. This belief will result in greater meaning-focused engagement in the reading process.

Word identification strategies: For the purpose of enabling comprehension, students will build their sight vocabulary through the interactive use of word identification strategies to puzzle through and learn unfamiliar words encountered while reading.

High-frequency words: Students will add high-frequency words to their sight vocabularies.

Decoding elements[1]: Students will learn information about decoding elements that they can use for strategic word identification to support word learning and, thereby, reading comprehension.

Comprehension: Students will use information and ideas in the text and background knowledge to actively construct understandings of the texts they read.

Knowledge: Students will learn science and social studies content encountered while reading and will use this knowledge to foster reading comprehension.

Vocabulary and language: Students will learn the meanings of new words, grammatical structures, and expressions encountered in both instructional interactions and through their reading; the expansion of these language skills will, in turn, foster reading comprehension.

Fluency: Students will read grade-appropriate text accurately with appropriate speed and with phrasing and intonation that conveys the intended meaning.

Intervention Session Format

After teachers have spent a little time getting to know their students and have made decisions about what students are ready to learn, the ISA-X intervention takes the following form. A typical intervention session begins with a statement of the day's agenda, followed by brief teacher-led instruction that is provided to one or all of the students in the group. After the mini-lesson, the bulk of the

---

[1] We use the term *decoding elements* to refer to aspects of the writing system that are explicitly taught, such as the two sounds for a vowel letter, or the pronunciation of a letter combination such as *aw* or *tion*. The term *decoding* refers to the process of reading. Of course, the elements taught are expected to be applied in the process of writing as well. This is sometimes referred to as *encoding*.

intervention session comprises reading and discussion of text selected to align with readers' readiness to learn. The session ends with the opportunity for students to reflect on and respond to what they are learning, often in a brief written response.

As determined by the decisions that the teacher has made about instructional foci for students, the lesson may introduce a word identification strategy, provide some students with high-frequency word practice, or involve an activity to develop knowledge of specific decoding elements. Throughout, we encourage teachers to help students to see the relationships between what they are learning and improved comprehension. The lesson may involve all the students, if they are at similar points in development. Alternatively, when a teacher is leading a lesson some students may participate in another activity such as rereading. Throughout this book we provide illustrative sample lessons and provide a rationale for each step of instruction.

The bulk of the intervention session involves students in purposeful reading and discussion of texts. These books are selected with the skills and goals of the readers in mind, and may vary from group to group, and in some cases, vary by student. As students read and discuss these books, they have the opportunity to practice the strategies and reading knowledge they have acquired, and the teacher has the opportunity to listen to them as individuals and to note progress and instructional needs so as to plan future lessons. As students read and discuss, the teacher's language promotes motivation for reading. Intervention sessions may conclude with a brief written response by students about what they have read, or what they have learned as readers. Chapter 14 provides guidance on ways to use reading, discussion, and written response with intermediate and middle grade readers.

Session versus Lesson

Many teachers use the term *lesson* to refer to the time when they are engaging with a group of readers. In this book, we use the term *session* instead and we reserve the use of the word *lesson* to refer to the time during the session when the teacher is actively providing instruction.

Because we see vocabulary and knowledge as fundamental to comprehension, one important feature of the ISA-X is that students read books that are related to some of the science and social studies content they are learning in the general education setting. Multiple books are read about each topic. Readers' developing knowledge and vocabulary supports the process of making the inferences that enable comprehension. This aspect of the intervention is described in more detail in Chapter 11, and a sample thematic unit is provided in Chapter 16.

Throughout each session, teachers use instructional language that focuses on the process of reading as illustrated in Figure 1.1. Rather than introducing a book by saying, "The title of this book is . . . ," a slight change in language can make explicit the reading process: "The author often chooses a title that tells us something important about the book, so readers pay attention to the title. I wonder what the author wanted to tell readers when he [she] chose the title for this book. . . . " Teachers do this because many intermediate and middle grade readers have a limited understanding of what readers do to understand books—similar to the Martian we described earlier. Throughout this book, we provide examples of instructional language designed to promote understanding of the process of reading.

We learned about the need to use language that is very explicit about what readers do by interviewing students. We include this example, in part, to illustrate what we mean when we suggest that teachers listen to students, and then teach in a way that addresses the points of confusion that have been revealed. We asked students:

"In your opinion, what does a good reader look like? What do readers do?"

"In your opinion, what does a good reader think about?"

"What does it mean if someone is an 'independent reader'?"

"What would you like to do better as a reader?"

Listed below are some informative responses from third- and fourth-grade readers in intervention to the question "What do readers do?"

- Readers won't be fooling around.
- Readers make sure they read everything correctly.
- Readers look at the pictures to know what is going on.
- Readers concentrate on what they are reading, and are not worrying about others.
- They don't get distracted.
- They sound out the words.

Teaching about Reading	Teaching about This Book
"Readers use the chapter title to help them to know what the chapter will be mostly about, or what they will learn by reading the chapter. Let's read the chapter title and see what we learn from it."	"Read the chapter title first."
"You checked the pictures to help you identify that puzzling word. That's what readers do."	"Nice job of checking the pictures."

FIGURE 1.1. Choosing language that conveys the process of reading.

- They like to stretch out the words they don't know.
- They read quietly, without bothering someone.
- They pay attention, and look back if they make mistakes.
- I don't know.
- They read to their parents.
- Readers read hard books.
- Readers listen to whoever is reading.
- They read chapter books.

A modified version of this interview (corrected for what, in retrospect, was a poor choice in wording for the first few items) is available in Figure 1.2 and on the website for this book (see the box at the end of the table of contents).

Research on the ISA and the ISA-X

In a first research study, the ISA-X was found to be effective when it was used in one-to-one instruction with fourth graders who had individualized education programs (IEPs; Gelzheiser et al., 2011). Specifically, students who participated in the ISA-X intervention showed more growth in reading comprehension, word-reading accuracy, basic reading skills (decoding of nonsense/pseudo-words), and content knowledge than did similar students who did not participate in the intervention. One-to-one ISA-X intervention was also used successfully with grade 7 special education students (Gelzheiser, Scanlon, & Hallgren-Flynn, 2010).

In a second study, we (Gelzheiser et al., 2017) tested the efficacy of the ISA-X with readers in grades 3 and 4 who were receiving remedial or special education reading services. All of the students had comprehension needs; about half also needed to learn to read more accurately. Eleven public school teachers participated in initial professional development and then ongoing coaching. They provided roughly 50 intervention sessions to groups of three students.[2] Sessions lasted 40 minutes. To evaluate the effectiveness of the intervention, we also recruited a comparison group that received the instruction and intervention that was normally available to them in school. For students like those who are the focus of this book, the intervention group students made substantially and significantly greater gains in their basic reading skills and accuracy in reading continuous text. The intervention group students also demonstrated greater gains on a measure of reading comprehension than the comparison group. These effects were modest but significant, and greater than those reported for other interventions evaluated by other researchers (see Wanzek et al., 2013, for a review). The intervention also resulted

---

[2] The research design specified the number and duration of intervention sessions as well as the group size. In a typical intervention setting, we anticipate that the amount of time devoted to intervention and the size of the group may be different from what was used in the research. Further, we anticipate that the intervention would be continued until students meet benchmarks.

"WHAT IS READING?" INTERVIEW

Student's Name _____ Date _____

Purpose: This assessment is designed to provide teachers with an initial understanding of their students' view of both the reading process and themselves as readers. The results of this assessment can be used by teachers to identify what students still need to learn about reading and themselves as readers. Then teachers can plan instruction and/or motivational language to address those needs.

Say: "I'm going to ask you a few questions on your thinking about reading. Since we will be spending time together learning more about reading, I'm interested in your thoughts. There are no right or wrong answers to these questions—I just want to know your thoughts on reading."

(Note: It may be helpful to audio record the interview as a way of capturing and reflecting on student responses. This will free the teacher from writing the student's full response and allow the teacher to convey true interest in the student's response.)

In your opinion, what would someone who is good at reading be doing while he or she is reading?

In your opinion, what does someone who is good at reading think about while he or she is reading?

(continued)

FIGURE 1.2. "What Is Reading?" Interview.

What does it mean if a reader is independent when he or she is reading?

Is there any part of reading that you would like to learn more about? Do you have any goals as a reader?

Analysis and Next Steps

If the student seems to understand that reading is thinking and involves activities such as carefully attending to the author's words and ideas, reading with a purpose, asking questions and making predictions, and doing the thinking that may be necessary in order to make their understanding of the text coherent:

- The student is likely an engaged reader.

If the student characterizes reading as saying all the words accurately and does not mention understanding the meaning:

- The student may need instruction to foster understanding that comprehension is the goal of reading, as detailed in Chapter 15 of this book.

If the student does not characterize an independent reader as one who can solve his or her own challenges encountered while reading:

- Teach what it means to be an *independent reader* (see p. 23).

If the student has personal reading goals:

- Whenever possible, help the student to see that progress is being made toward those goals.

FIGURE 1.2. *(continued)*

in students making significantly greater gains on measures of content vocabulary and word identification strategy knowledge.

Part of the research involved observing the instruction given by intervention teachers who were providing the ISA-X as well as the instruction given by other intervention teachers in their schools. These observations showed the ISA-X teachers to be more responsive to students' needs than other teachers. Overall, the Gelzheiser et al. (2017) study results suggest that a responsive approach to instruction will have positive effects for intermediate and middle grade readers who have word identification difficulties that impede comprehension. In the next chapter, we discuss approaches to providing responsive instruction that promotes students' independence as readers.

One feature of the ISA-X research that should be acknowledged is that teachers received extensive individual coaching as well as group professional development to learn to implement the approach. One reason that this book is so detailed is that we recognize the importance of providing teachers with ample guidance as they are learning about the approach.

Research Based versus Research Tested?

This book is one of a handful of texts that describe a *research-tested* reading comprehension intervention for intermediate and middle grade readers who have yet to become proficient with word identification. For such students, instruction in word identification skills and strategies, coupled with appropriate guidance in meaning construction and extensive amounts of appropriately challenging reading, has the potential to enable them to learn to comprehend grade-level text. To determine what effects the ISA-X might have, we conducted two research studies, one that involved implementing the ISA-X with fourth- and seventh-grade special education students in a one-to-one context (Gelzheiser et al., 2010; Gelzheiser et al., 2011), and the second with third- and fourth-grade remedial reading and special education students in a small-group context (Gelzheiser et al., 2017). Additional research support is provided through studies of the Interactive Strategies Approach (ISA), an intervention for primary grade students that was the basis for the ISA-X. The effectiveness of the ISA was documented by testing the intervention in one-to-one (Vellutino et al., 1996), small-group (Scanlon, Gelzheiser, Vellutino, Schatschneider, & Sweeney, 2008; Scanlon, Vellutino, Small, Fanuele, & Sweeney, 2005), and classroom settings (Scanlon et al., 2008).

In contrast to the research-tested ISA and ISA-X, many reading interventions include specific practices and tactics that have been researched—however, such *research-based* interventions have not been researched as a whole. Because the ISA-X has been research tested, we have greater confidence as to what it can potentially accomplish.

Organization of This Book

In this book, we detail the ways that teachers can address comprehension directly, and also how intervention can address factors that support comprehension: motivation, word identification strategies (which enable word learning), high-frequency word knowledge, decoding knowledge, world knowledge, vocabulary, and reading fluency. The logistics of negotiating written text require that each of these contributors to reading accuracy and comprehension be relegated to its own chapter, although within each chapter we discuss how the components are interrelated.

The organization of this book should not be interpreted as suggesting that intervention should address only one of the identified goals at a time. Instead, as we illustrate in Chapter 2, sessions address multiple instructional goals in a way that responds to individual student needs.

This book is organized into three major parts. In Part I, we describe the foundations of a comprehensive approach to intervention. Part II is designed to help teachers better understand how word learning occurs, and to plan and implement instruction that promotes word learning. Part III is focused more directly on comprehension. Again, the purpose of these chapters is to increase teachers' understanding of comprehension and how to develop readers' comprehension while still maintaining a focus on building readers' ability to quickly and accurately identify words in texts.

As we describe in Chapters 3, 11, and 12, intermediate and middle grade readers' motivation, knowledge, and vocabulary are foundations that support comprehension. Because many of these readers have had experiences that have reduced motivation, and have resulted in more limited opportunities to acquire knowledge and vocabulary through reading, these are likely to be goals for almost any reader in intervention. These components of comprehension may not be addressed with lessons per se, but rather through the language that teachers use in their modeling and feedback, the texts that they select for students to read, and the opportunities they provide for students to discuss and reflect upon what they are reading and learning. Fostering students' motivation, knowledge, and vocabulary is a part of the fabric of every ISA-X intervention session, although the topic may not appear as an item on a lesson plan.

Part II of this book (Chapters 4–9) describes instruction designed to improve students' ability to identify words accurately and fluently. For the readers who are the focus of this book, limited reading accuracy is a barrier to comprehension. We do not mean to suggest that accuracy is a sufficient goal. Instead, we encourage teachers to understand accuracy and fluency to be important facilitators of comprehension,[3] and to portray to their students the ideas that accuracy

---

[3] Of course, comprehension is also an important facilitator of reading accuracy in that understanding of the text being read provides supports for limiting the potential identities of unknown printed words and confirming the accuracy of hypothesized word identities.

instruction is a route to comprehension. For all students, we encourage teachers to include the opportunity to read, construct meaning with, and discuss continuous text in every instructional session.

For the readers who are the focus of this book, instruction would typically include explicit teaching of and practice with strategies to help readers identify unfamiliar words (described in Chapters 5 and 6), high-frequency words (described in Chapter 7), and/or decoding elements (described in Chapters 8 and 9). These goals are related. In our approach, the purpose of decoding instruction is to support a strategic approach to word identification and word learning. Learning new decoding elements provides the reader with knowledge that can be used to more accurately and effectively apply a strategic approach to word identification. High-frequency words are taught and practiced because automatic identification of these words provides support to the reader who is using strategies for word identification that rely upon context.

This book provides an approach to instruction that integrates the learning and application of decoding elements, the ability to accurately and quickly identify high-frequency words, and the knowledge and use of strategies for word identification in context. The ultimate goal is to build readers' ability to read text fluently, which in turn enables them to devote most of their thinking to the process of comprehending the material they read.

Part III of this book addresses meaning construction. In Chapter 10 we describe comprehension and its components. Chapters 11 and 12 address the acquisition of knowledge and vocabulary to support comprehension and reading accuracy, and Chapter 13 considers the elements of fluency instruction and assessment and the relationships between reading fluency and reading comprehension.

Most of the chapters in this book are written to guide teachers as they provide instruction and engage students in practicing and consolidating what they are learning. The level of detail provided around decoding and word solving should not obscure the fact that most of the time in an intervention session should be devoted to reading and discussion, and not to explicit instruction related to word solving. As described in Chapter 14, reading is the instructional activity that addresses all goals simultaneously, and discussion too can be used to address many instructional goals. For these reasons, reading and discussion, rather than teacher instruction, are, in ISA-X intervention sessions, the lengthiest parts of intervention.

In Chapter 15, we describe how teachers can use noticing and naming to enhance comprehension while maintaining an instructional focus on accuracy. Finally, Chapter 16 illustrates how many of these instructional objectives can be addressed in the context of a thematic text set. As students read texts about a science topic, in the example provided, we illustrate how they can be assisted in developing knowledge, vocabulary, accuracy, and comprehension.

Summary

In this chapter, we introduced the ISA-X and provided a rationale for comprehensive intervention for readers in grades 3–8 who still need to build their sight vocabulary and word-solving skills. In the next chapter, we discuss the importance of responsive instruction for these readers.

CHAPTER 2

Responsive Instruction
for Student Independence

Teaching to foster student independence is one of the distinguishing features of the ISA and ISA-X. We begin this chapter by defining responsive instruction and student independence, and provide a rationale for why responsive teaching that promotes independence may be useful. We describe continua of reading accuracy and comprehension, and how these can be used to plan instructional content that is responsive to the needs of different readers. After describing some of the factors that influence how independently a student can think and solve problems, we detail some aspects of responsive teaching that promote student independence.

Rationale: What Is Responsive Instruction,
and Why Is It Important?

In this book, we use the term *responsive instruction* to describe a process in which a teacher collects information about what an individual reader already knows how to do and what that reader is ready to learn. That information is used by the teacher to set instructional priorities and to select appropriate learning activities and reading materials for the reader. Responsive instruction includes monitoring the student's progress toward attaining the objectives that the teacher has set and revising and updating these objectives as appropriate. This view of responsive intervention is similar to the process described in the Individuals with Disabilities Education Improvement Act (IDEIA; 2004), which recognizes the right of all learners to receive instruction that appropriately addresses their individual needs.

We also use the term *responsive instruction* in a second way, to describe the "in-the-moment" decisions that teachers make as they respond to and support learners. In their interactions with intermediate and middle grade students, intervention teachers offer challenge so that students grow, and support so that students have positive and meaningful reading experiences. In this chapter, we detail ways to appropriately balance challenge and support for readers, with the goal of promoting students' abilities to read and learn independently.

As we noted in the previous chapter, each reader in grades 3–8 presents a unique set of characteristics, because each reader has learned some things but not others in the years of reading instruction that occurred previously. Because of their unique characteristics, it seems unlikely that a single program of instruction could be successful with all intermediate and middle grade readers, and research confirms this supposition. When teachers use a "one-size-fits-all" program in an effort to improve older readers' comprehension, it may result in little to no improvement, at least as indicated by performance on standardized tests (Wanzek et al., 2013). Even when older readers are selected for intervention because they all have the same type of instructional need (e.g., they all need to improve reading accuracy), uniform or scripted instruction has often not produced the desired improvements in comprehension (Vaughn et al., 2011; Wanzek & Roberts, 2012).

In contrast, research has shown that helping teachers to learn a responsive approach has positive effects on comprehension. Several investigations of responsive teaching for intermediate grade readers have resulted in significant effects on students' reading comprehension (Connor et al., 2011; Coyne et al., 2013; Gelzheiser et al., 2011, 2017; see also Simmons, 2015).

In this book, we advocate a responsive approach; we seek to enhance teachers' knowledge and skill related to reading processes and instruction so that they may better respond to readers. We suggest ways that teachers can observe and listen to students as they read, in order to identify students' abilities to apply word identification strategies as they puzzle through words they cannot readily identify. In later chapters and on the website for this book (see the box at the end of the table of contents), we include more structured interviews and assessments that can be used to identify students' interests, their understanding of the reading process, and where they stand with regard to basic reading skills. For each observation tool or assessment, we provide suggestions as to how the findings can guide the development of appropriate instructional plans to help the students attain the goals listed in Chapter 1.

To facilitate responsive planning, we encourage teachers to record observations of their students during each lesson. These ongoing observations allow teachers to determine the focus and support that will be appropriate in future instruction.

In responsive instruction, teachers plan differentiated instructional content that responds to students' current reading skills. Individual students may be taught different skills, strategies, and information. They may engage in different kinds of practice activities and read different texts. For purposes of clarification, we describe students' needs relative to continua for reading accuracy and comprehension. This is discussed in greater detail later in this chapter.

Rationale: What Is Student Independence, and Why Is It Important?

In this book, we use the term *independent reader* to describe someone who:

- Is alert to situations in which a problem has arisen (e.g., a word has been misidentified).
- Has tools and knowledge that are useful for tackling puzzles or challenges encountered while reading (e.g., words that the reader doesn't recognize).
- Has the inclination to solve these puzzles without support from the teacher or peers.
- Spontaneously and willingly does the thinking that is needed when puzzling words or ideas are encountered in text.

Many intermediate and middle grade readers in intervention are not independent readers. Thinking is difficult, so students may avoid it (Willingham, 2009). If readers have previously encountered too many challenges while reading, this can convince them (and perhaps their teachers) that they can be successful only if they rely on teacher support.

Of course, the intervention teacher is available to provide support for only a limited part of the day. If during intervention students develop the motivation to read and tools that they can use independently to solve words and understand puzzling ideas, then they are positioned to continue to grow as readers throughout the day and, ideally, eventually they will no longer need intervention services. However, if students do not become motivated to read and do not develop the confidence that they can address word identification and comprehension challenges on their own, this growth may not occur. Throughout this book, teachers will see reference to developing student independence. Fostering independence involves providing students with the skills and strategies that will enable them to be independent thinkers as they read, and then providing appropriate opportunities for students to practice their new ways of thinking.

To promote student independence, teaching changes as students develop proficiency. When readers are in the *acquisition stage* and just learning a new skill, a new way of thinking, or new knowledge, the teacher provides explicit modeling and a purpose for what is being learned. This initial phase is brief; most instruction involves the teacher gradually reducing the support provided to students as they progress through *consolidation* of the skill. This reduction in support is often called a *gradual release of responsibility* (Pearson & Gallagher, 1983). The amount of support a teacher provides responds to what students know and can do independently.

Student independence and teacher support may vary depending on the challenge presented to students at a particular moment. At times during the consolidation stage, the language or ideas in what students are reading may be more challenging, so the teacher may need to step in temporarily and assume more responsibility, or even provide more teacher-led instruction if needed.

Reading Puzzles

Readers may encounter several different types of puzzles to solve while reading. A reader who can readily identify only a limited number of words will frequently need to solve the puzzle of the identity of an unknown word. In Chapters 5 and 6, we describe how to teach students to independently solve these puzzles by using strategies that we refer to as *word identification strategies* (the reader will find these listed in Chapter 5, Figure 5.1).

Written materials often offer clues from the author that the reader must puzzle over to discern their meaning. For example, in a chapter called "Dragons and Giants" in *Frog and Toad Together*, Frog and Toad decide to test themselves to see whether they are brave. They encounter a snake, an avalanche, and a hawk. Each time, the author has them say, "I am not afraid!" but also describes them as "shaking," then "trembling," and finally, "they ran all the way to Toad's house." Toad hides under the covers, and Frog shuts himself in the closet, and "they stayed there for a long time, just feeling very brave together" (Lobel, 1971, p. 51). A reader who independently notices these conflicting clues and makes appropriate inferences will feel a sense of accomplishment and have learned a wonderful lesson about human nature. In Chapter 15, we describe how to help students to more independently engage in thinking about text.

A puzzle that the reader can solve with some effort leads to a feeling of accomplishment. However, putting effort into a puzzle and being unable to solve it can lead to discouragement. As detailed in Chapter 3, appropriate challenge during reading will encourage students to see themselves as readers and thinkers. If the teacher does too much of the thinking about a text or a word for the students, it will not promote students' sense of themselves as effective thinkers (Johnston, 2004).

In this text, we use the term *puzzle* deliberately, and avoid language such as "being stuck on a word." Solving a puzzle is enjoyable, while encountering a hard word and being stuck may be discouraging. In our work with teachers, we have also encouraged them to try to avoid using words like *tricky* and *hard* in referring to challenging words or passages in text because for some students, knowing that the teacher perceives a word or passage to be tricky or hard, may lead them to not even bother trying to solve the puzzle.

Understanding the Reading Process: Factors That Influence Student Independence

Human minds, when engaged in thinking, problem solving, and comprehending spoken or written language, have a certain amount of capacity that limits how much information can be processed at one time. Mental capacity can be allocated flexibly, but the mind can do only so much and no more. If a reader is asked to process too much information, and the demands exceed the limit of the reader's processing capacity, the system may function less well or shut down altogether.

The electricity available on a given circuit breaker is a useful analogy to the limits of mental capacity. Electricity can be allocated flexibly—that is, it can be used to run a toaster or a hair dryer or lights. But there is a limit to the capacity of a circuit breaker. Running the toaster, hair dryer, and air conditioner all at the same time will probably overload the system, causing the circuit breaker to trip and all the appliances to shut down. Similarly, people's ability to think will become overloaded or shut down if they are asked to do a task that is too complex for them and/or involves processing too much information at one time, especially information that is not well understood.

"Information overload" is especially common when learners are acquiring a new skill, strategy, or knowledge. This is because conscious, deliberate, and effortful mental activity uses up much more capacity than a skill or activity that has become fluent and automatic. Teacher support during the acquisition of a new skill, strategy, or knowledge helps to prevent information overload. It is often not possible for students to independently do something that they are just learning.

As skills and strategies become practiced and, ultimately, automatic, they require little mental capacity to perform. For example, when a student no longer has to puzzle through a word to identify it but can identify it automatically, reading that word requires little capacity. Practice to the point of automaticity has the effect of increasing the readers' available capacity because less thought needs to be devoted to the previously deliberate skill. This newly available capacity may then be allocated to other aspects of reading, such as constructing meaning. As a reader's proficiency with a newly learned skill or strategy increases, less teacher support is needed, and more independence can be expected of the reader.

Student independence is enhanced if teachers *respond to the unique needs of students in intervention by teaching for success*. The teacher can prepare students to be successful as they read by teaching them appropriate ways of working together in the group, providing them with resources that support independence, communicating how the instruction in the intervention setting supports the general education curriculum, and engaging them in lots of reading and thinking in which they can succeed. These practices are discussed in greater detail later in this chapter.

Instructional Decision Making: Planning Differentiated Content That Is Responsive to Readers' Current Abilities

In learning about the ISA-X intervention approach, teachers have found it useful to organize the diverse capabilities of intermediate and middle grade readers along two independent continua: reading accuracy and comprehension. Students' positions along these continua give teachers some general instructional priorities and help teachers to decide how to allocate instructional time in a way that will maximize learning. Of course, along the continua individual readers will vary widely. The purpose of the continua is to provide some general patterns that we have observed in work with readers and that teachers may find useful, while acknowledging that each student is unique.

The Accuracy Continuum

At one end of the continuum for reading accuracy are some intermediate and middle grade readers who are extremely limited in their ability to identify words fluently and accurately. Our research samples included some third, fourth, and even seventh graders who could not accurately read text that a typical beginning first grader is expected to read. For these students, instructional goals included daily instruction and practice in word identification strategies. They also had goals to learn to quickly and automatically read the most commonly occurring words, often referred to as *high-frequency words*, and to acquire knowledge of decoding elements. Chapters 4–9 provide detailed guidance about addressing the accuracy skills of such students. In the ISA-X research, because of their extreme accuracy difficulties, these readers did not participate in formal comprehension instruction, although comprehension was addressed throughout as students were reading and discussing the meaning of a variety of texts.

At the opposite end of the accuracy continuum are readers who can readily identify most of the words in grade-level texts, but who do not yet meet standards for comprehension. Our research sample included many students who qualified for intervention because of their comprehension scores, but whose reading accuracy was at or above grade level. The needs of these readers are not addressed specifically in this book, although teachers may find that Chapters 3 and 10–12 on motivation, comprehension, knowledge development, and vocabulary provide useful instructional guidance for these readers.

Many of the intermediate and middle grade readers we have encountered fall somewhere in the middle of the accuracy continuum. They have acquired some, but not all, of the decoding knowledge that can support strategic word identification. They know some, but not enough, of the high-frequency words, and often they are not fully strategic in how they use their knowledge to identify unfamiliar words. Some of these readers need additional reading practice so that they use their knowledge and strategies more fluently and build their knowledge of the writing system in so doing. Assessment and observation, as described in Chapters 6, 7, and 9, can allow teachers to determine the strategies for word identification, high-frequency words, and decoding knowledge that each reader has not yet learned, and then to target instruction and practice so that it addresses these gaps. A focus on developing these word-level skills will be a daily feature of instruction for these students, but depending upon the unique pattern of students' knowledge and skills, the teacher may choose to alternate among strategy, high-frequency words, and decoding elements instruction instead of addressing all of the areas daily. These readers may also benefit from instruction focused on comprehension skills and strategies, depending upon where they fall on the comprehension continuum described below.

A student's position on the accuracy continuum should change as he or she is provided with responsive instruction. Using what they observe during oral reading and in discussion, teachers can update their instructional objectives on an ongoing basis. As a student progresses on the accuracy continuum, the number of occasions and the amount of time devoted to accuracy instruction would decrease.

The Comprehension Continuum

At one end of the continuum for reading comprehension are some intermediate and middle grade readers who are much better at reading the words than in constructing meaning from text. Our research samples included some third, fourth, and seventh graders who demonstrated comprehension of text only when the text was two or more grade levels below the level at which they could read text with accuracy. This book does not address comprehension instruction for readers with this profile, although Chapters 3, 11, and 12 on motivation, knowledge development, and vocabulary are relevant to such readers.

At the other end of the continuum for reading comprehension were students who were active thinkers and problem solvers in relation to the meaning of what they read. Many of the intermediate and middle grade readers in our research sample made appropriate inferences and thoughtful observations about what they were reading; these were students who required intervention only because of limited reading accuracy. These students had already learned most of the content and routinely engaged in the ways of thinking discussed in Chapter 15, and so explicit instruction for these students mainly focused on developing reading accuracy and engaging them in as much reading as possible. Early in the intervention, teachers were encouraged to have students read as much as possible so as to enable them to guide the development of the readers' word-solving strategies and skills.

Many of the intermediate and middle grade readers we have encountered fell somewhere in the middle of the comprehension continuum. They demonstrated some, but not all, of the ways that proficient readers think as they read. Chapter 15 provides guidance on fostering these readers' thinking, while maintaining a focus on developing reading accuracy. These students may be in need of some accuracy-focused instruction, depending upon where they fall on the accuracy continuum.

A student's position on the comprehension continuum should change as he or she is provided with responsive instruction. Using what they observe during oral reading and in discussion, teachers are encouraged to update their instructional plans on an ongoing basis. As a student progresses on the comprehension continuum, the number of occasions and the amount of time devoted to comprehension fostering instruction will decrease as it becomes habitual for the student to focus on meaning construction while reading.

Figure 2.1 illustrates how the ISA-X lessons might vary, depending upon students' accuracy and comprehension skills. These lessons assume a group of three students, as was used in the ISA-X research.

	Students with Very Limited Accuracy	Students with Moderate Accuracy and Moderate Comprehension Needs
Rereading	Two students reread texts that provide practice with a specific decoding element while the teacher reviews high-frequency words with the third student.	All students silently reread an informational text with the purpose of sharing additional information they learned by rereading.
Teacher-led instruction	The teacher provides an activity to develop knowledge of a new decoding element to all students.	The teacher provides an explicit introduction to marking important information in the text to all students.
Reading and discussion	Before reading novel text, students are reminded to apply the word identification strategies they have been taught.	Before reading novel text, students are reminded to apply the word identification strategies they have been taught and to mark new information they encounter in the text.
	Students read a new book that allows them to practice the newly learned decoding element, and a book related to the content theme that includes some unfamiliar words so that students can practice the word identification strategies they have been learning.	Students read several short books related to the content theme. These books are relatively challenging, to provide students with opportunities to apply their word identification strategies. Students mark new information while they are reading.
	The teacher observes and provides support and feedback about strategy use.	The teacher observes and provides support and feedback about strategy use.
	Students take individual turns reading orally to the group; later, they read orally to a partner.	Students read orally to a partner and read silently.
	The teacher encourages students to comment on one major idea of the text. Students are encouraged to reflect on strategy use.	The teacher encourages students to comment on the major ideas of the texts. Students are encouraged to reflect on strategy use.
Written response	Students briefly note one fact they learned from the theme book.	Students write a short paragraph about information they found interesting in the reading.

FIGURE 2.1. Sample lesson formats for two different reading groups.

Instructional Decision Making:
Providing Teacher Support That Fosters Student Independence

Overview

To efficiently promote student understanding, instruction needs to be explicit as students are acquiring new knowledge. As students begin consolidating their skill or understanding, instruction provides carefully structured support and practice that allows students to act more independently. Student learning culminates with opportunities for students to perform independently and reflect on what they have learned. What follows is a summary of how instruction and the level of teacher support varies with the phase of student learning. It is based on a detailed description provided by Meichenbaum and Biemiller (1998).

Careful observation and record keeping by the teacher will reveal students' phase of learning, which can be used to adapt instruction accordingly. Knowing how instruction changes with student competence can help teachers to plan and teach more effectively and responsively.

Acquisition

When students are first acquiring new knowledge or a new skill or strategy, they can be described as being in the *acquisition phase* of learning. Assessment or observation by the teacher can be used to decide whether a skill, strategy, or concept is not yet known by students. Often, intervention students in the intermediate and middle grades have gaps in their knowledge, so explicit and comprehensive lessons may be required to fill those gaps. In other cases, somewhere in students' educational careers they have acquired some knowledge of an element, topic, or strategy, but they have not consolidated that knowledge. Learners who have some knowledge are in the consolidation phase, and instruction can begin with a brief review followed by consolidation activities, rather than an extended acquisition lesson.

The acquisition of new skills and strategies places heavy demands on the readers' thinking. Teachers are encouraged to set priorities for the learning of new content, and to carefully pace that instruction so that learners are not overwhelmed.

Explicit Introduction

During the acquisition phase of student learning, the teacher's role is to provide an explicit introduction, while the students' role is to listen and begin to learn. The most efficient introduction is highly explicit and the result of careful planning on the part of the teacher. When skills and strategies become automatic (as they are to the teacher), it is sometimes difficult to make them explicit. Planning provides the teacher with the opportunity to carefully consider the demands of the skill or strategy to be learned, and to identify ways to make them accessible to the student. In subsequent chapters, we provide many examples of explicit introductions, with the expectation that these can serve as models for other lessons that teachers plan on their own.

A teacher introduction during acquisition provides precise information about *what* the reader is learning to do. It also specifies *when* this new skill or strategy will be used and *why* it is useful (Duffy, 2009; Pearson & Gallagher, 1983). For example, in introducing a strategy, the teacher is encouraged to point out to students when and why the strategy will be helpful. The teacher introduction also includes a demonstration that shows students *how* to execute the strategy or thinking. Demonstration might include an explanation of how to do a particular thing. Further, when students are first learning a strategy or a way of problem solving, it is often useful for the teacher to share his or her thinking using a *think-aloud model* of the strategy's application. In a think-aloud model, the teacher provides an example of the kind of thinking and problem solving that he or she would like the reader to use (Duke, Pearson, Strachan, & Billman, 2011). Examples of think-aloud models are provided in the acquisition lessons throughout this book.

Precise Language

Some ISA-X teachers have found it helpful to script out what they want to say in an explicit introduction. Others preferred to list the key phrases and examples that they planned to use. The website for this book (see the box at the end of the table of contents) includes templates that teachers can use as they write their own explicit introductions for some of the types of lessons illustrated in the text. In any case, instructional language will be most helpful to students if it is both precise and accessible (understandable) to students.

Consolidation

After an acquisition lesson has been taught, there may be some students who can start to apply the new knowledge with limited independence. However, most students, especially those in intervention, need additional support if they are to learn to use new ways of thinking or strategies independently. They benefit from teaching that allows them to *consolidate* and *reflect* on what they are learning.

Practice

If a skill or strategy is truly new to the learner, or when the learner has some knowledge of the strategy but does not use it consistently, then guided practice in the use of that skill or strategy is often required before it becomes a part of the repertoire of things the student can do independently. During the early part of consolidation, students are more dependent upon the teacher to carefully guide selection and execution of the strategy. With regard to strategies, as students demonstrate their understanding, teacher support and prompting should be gradually reduced, allowing/encouraging the student to act more independently. Students take on (and teachers release) the roles of *selecting* and *executing* the strategy.

By practice, we mean multiple opportunities for the student to use a particular strategy during reading, or multiple opportunities for students to apply a particular decoding element or read new high-frequency words in both isolation and while reading connected text. If a teacher has introduced a strategy such as *check the pictures* to help identify an unfamiliar word, then the student should read a text that includes several challenging words for which identification would be assisted by implementation of that strategy. Or if the student has been taught a new decoding element, practice activities can be planned, including having the student read text containing several instances of that decoding element. Similarly, vocabulary words need to be encountered and used several times and in different contexts if it is expected that the student will fully learn their meaning.

In our experience, in order to consolidate new learning and function independently, students in intervention may require more practice than their peers who are achieving on grade level. For that reason, we suggest that the bulk of teaching time be spent on consolidation, rather than acquisition instruction. Responsive teaching includes observing and making notes about the extent to which students have consolidated what they have been taught and the degree of support needed by the student. A teacher may need to continue to provide practice (or possibly reteach) if students are not yet accurate and independent in utilizing newly taught skills or strategies.

Structuring Practice for Success

When students are first practicing a new skill or strategy, they will be more independent if the teacher reminds them to use the skills and strategies they have recently learned just before they begin reading. This *preset* can be as brief as noting the importance of using what they are learning—that is, talking about why students will benefit from using the new strategy or knowledge.

We recommend that when students are first practicing a new skill or strategy, they be provided with *resources* such as a strategy list or a key word to help them remember a decoding element. We provide examples of such resources throughout this book. These resources are designed to allow the student to independently select a strategy or remember the sound of a letter or letter combination, rather than relying on the teacher, or the student's already taxed memory, for the information. During consolidation, the preset might remind students that they have resources in front of them that will be helpful as they are reading.

Such initial reminders and resources are often sufficient to encourage students to problem solve independently, and may reduce the need for the teacher to "jump in" with reminders and support while students are reading. This book provides several examples of consolidation lessons with presets and resource support.

Once students have become more accomplished with their new learning, the need for teacher presets and student resources will be reduced. Students can be encouraged to remind themselves of ways that they have learned to be independent, and resources can be moved off the table and onto a bulletin board where they are still available if needed.

Resources for Groups with Very Different Needs

Some teachers have found it useful to have a different resource display for each group of students with whom they work. They do this by using a trifold presentation display (available at office supply stores) for each group.

On occasion during consolidation, the teacher will need to provide support to students as they read. The goal is always "just enough" support. Practice tasks should be structured so that the student is successful, but since the goal is student independence, the teacher is encouraged not to promote dependence by being overly involved in the student's problem solving. As students are first learning a new strategy, the teacher or another student may direct the reader to try a specific newly learned strategy (i.e., the teacher selects the strategy and the student executes it). But most of the support during consolidation includes less direct approaches that release the responsibility to the student to *select* and *execute* the strategy:

- Waiting for the reader to solve the word.
- Reminding readers to use resources such as a strategy list.
- Using open-ended prompts to problem solve (e.g., "What could you do to figure out this word?").

During consolidation the amount of support needed will vary depending on the context. If the language or content in a text (or part of a text) is more challenging, students may become overloaded and it may be appropriate for the teacher to step in, temporarily.

The Importance of Wide Reading

The amount of reading that students do is an important determiner of their success as readers. Reading widely is an important way for students to consolidate reading skills and strategies. Wide reading will foster independence if teachers provide students with extensive opportunities to read appropriately challenging texts and gradually provide them with full responsibility for puzzling through unfamiliar words and for making sense of what they read when the ideas in the text are more complex. To foster independence during wide reading, once they have been taught, teachers encourage students to use strategies to identify unfamiliar words, to try to resolve the problem when they encounter words for which they don't know the meanings, and allow students to take responsibility for gathering evidence to support their interpretation of text meaning.

The major activity during consolidation is providing students with ample opportunity to read and thus practice their newly learned skills and strategies, and to be engaged in meaning making as they read. For this reason, we recommend that at least half of an intervention session be devoted to reading and discussion of text, and with the further expectation that the majority of that time will be spent reading, not discussing. Time spent reading was the best predictor of growth in both accuracy and comprehension in the ISA-X research (Gelzheiser et al., 2017). The more students read, the more opportunity they have to consolidate the skills they have been taught, and to fluently apply what they are learning. This, in turn, enables them to add new words to their sight vocabularies through effective word solving and to build new knowledge related to the topics they are reading about. Chapter 14 provides guidance for teachers on how to maximize reading time.

Reflection and Independence

As students learn new strategies for identifying unfamiliar words or solving comprehension problems, it is useful for them to talk about those strategies and to link the strategies to their success. Full learning involves students reflecting on how they have solved puzzling words and ideas. A student who can name or recite the strategies may or may not yet connect these with the ability to problem solve. The goal of this aspect of instruction is student awareness of the *tools* they have in their repertoire.

Understanding the Reading Process: Factors That Influence Student Reflection

Meichenbaum and Biemiller (1998) make the interesting observation that, of all the students in a class, it is the lowest-performing students who are offered the fewest opportunities for reflection. Proficient students who finish their work promptly may have a bit of time to look back at what they have done. They may also be asked to assist another student, and engage in reflection as they explain the task or guide the other student. In contrast, students who work more slowly and deliberately often do not complete the work in the allotted time, and so have few moments for looking back. Less proficient students are seldom asked to assist other students, and thus miss those chances for reflection as well. Meichenbaum and Biemiller hypothesize that one of the reasons that some students fall further and further behind is that reflection is missing from their school experiences. Therefore, they encourage teachers to provide systematic opportunities for all students to make connections between the academic work they do and the progress they make.

There are several reasons why students reflections are a useful part of instruction as they are learning new skills and strategies. One is that if students are to be able to solve word identification puzzles independently, they need to have conscious access to a repertoire of strategies, and they need to know what these strategies help them to do. Once learned, the reader can then draw upon this conscious knowledge while reading independently.

Another reason that reflection is helpful is that it enables students to attribute success in reading to strategies that are under their control. If students believe that success in reading is the result of tactics that they use and control, they will be more motivated to engage in reading because they have a sense of efficacy and accomplishment. We discuss this idea more fully in Chapter 3.

Teachers can encourage reflection by using explicit language that connects strategy use to student success when they notice and name[1] what students do. A statement like "You tried different sounds for some of the letters and you read past the puzzling word to get a better idea of what would make sense, and that helped you to identify this word" is more likely to encourage reflection than is "Nice job using your strategies." The linguistic difference is subtle but powerful in the way that it guides student thinking.

Teachers can also encourage reflection by providing opportunities for students to think about what they have learned and how it is helping them. This reflection can be prompted by questions or comments like "What strategies helped you today?"

Skilled versus Strategic Reading

Proficient readers generally are not consciously aware of how they go about problem solving while reading. Rather, their cognitive resources are fully devoted to engagement in meaning construction. They are thinking about the text; they are not thinking about strategies—unless they encounter a particularly vexing problem that they cannot solve using their well-practiced problem-solving *skills*. Eventually, the objective of intervention is for readers to become so automatic in the application of the strategies they learn that word solving and comprehension would largely become *skilled* processes (which don't require conscious, strategic thought).

Instructional Decision Making:
Organizing an Instructional Group That Fosters Independence

How We Work Together

In a whole-class setting, for reasons of efficiency and safety, it is often necessary for the teacher to lead and for students to comply. Students may come to

---

[1]The phrase *notice and name* is attributed to Johnston (2004).

intervention having only experienced behavioral expectations that are designed to ensure that teachers maintain control over their classrooms. We recommend that in an intervention setting teachers consider expectations that are designed to promote a group that allows each student to grow as much as possible as a reader.

In a small-group setting designed to foster student independence, we have found it helpful to use expectations that stress student self-regulation and cooperation, and that encourage all members of the group to be actively engaged in learning. The goal of intervention is for each student to have ample opportunity to independently think when he or she encounters unfamiliar words or confusing ideas. If other students are silently engaged in parallel puzzling and solving, they too will learn.

In a small-group setting, peers can support a student who is thinking about a word or idea if they have learned to *wait while others think,* rather than calling out the answer. If the student runs out of ideas, a peer can show support if he or she *gives help when asked.* Peers can also *show interest and support for others* by acknowledging another's successful thinking or strategic action.

Peers can learn during another student's puzzling if they *listen to others* as they think about puzzling words or ideas. Peers can *choose to keep learning* if they reflect upon how they would solve the word or idea that is puzzling their peer. While reading independently, students can choose to keep learning if they stay fully engaged, and select another book to read when they finish early.

These expectations encourage students to take advantage of every opportunity to learn and to become more independent readers. They are designed to minimize student behaviors that might interfere with the learning of other group members: interrupting other speakers, calling out when a student is trying to identify a word, or not following along while one student is reading aloud. Figure 2.2 describes how the expectations might look during different group activities.

It is likely these expectations will need to be taught to the group, using the process of acquisition, consolidation, and reflection described in the previous section, as applied in the text that follows.

Acquisition

An overview of the expectations that the teacher will use and their purpose (to allow students to grow as independent readers) is a useful way to start. A written copy of the expectations should be made available and be clearly visible. As each expectation is introduced, it is helpful to ask students to share their ideas about what the expectation means—for example, what it means to "listen to others." If there are schoolwide behavioral expectations, the teacher can connect the expectations to those so that students understand that the desired behaviors are similar. For example, if a school expectation is to "be responsible," the teacher can explain that this is similar to the expectation to "choose to keep learning."

Expectation	During Word Identification	During Discussion
Listen to others	Follow along as others are reading and solving individual words in a small-group or partner reading settings.	Attend to others as they share their ideas during group discussion; think about what the speaker is saying.
Wait while others think	Wait patiently while another student in the group or pair is solving a word.	Allow members of the group time to think before and while speaking; wait for your turn to talk.
Give help when asked	When asked, suggest one or more strategies that another student might use.	If a student is confused and asks for help, a peer can suggest something that will provide clarification, such as a place to check in the text or a word meaning.
Show interest and support for others	Acknowledge the effort a peer has shown.	Acknowledge or disagree with an idea that has been shared by a peer; add to a peer's response.
Choose to keep learning	While someone else is trying to identify an unfamiliar word, think about strategies or resources that would be helpful.	Follow along when someone else is reading aloud; contribute ideas that help to build the group's understanding of the text.

FIGURE 2.2. How we work together in different contexts.

Consolidation

As the group is first learning the expectations, at the outset of the session, they should be reminded of them. Clear instructional language will help students to internalize and remember the expectations. Early on, before group members have learned the instructional language related to the ISA-X strategies, teachers might set the expectation of *listening to others* by saying:

> "Today we will be practicing 'listening to others.' That means that when someone is reading, the rest of us will listen and follow along. And, if we need to, we'll wait patiently while the reader figures out some of the words. Or if we are talking about what's happening in the book, we won't interrupt the person who is talking."

When students have begun to learn the ISA-X strategy language, the reminder to listen to others would be followed by:

> "That means we will be attending to how others are puzzling through unfamiliar words as they read."

> "Discussion is a good time to practice 'show interest and support for others.'"

Further, teachers will be most effective if they discuss only the agreed-upon expectations, and refrain from making comments that refer to other behavior systems—for example, stating "Eyes on me" rather than "Remember, we attend to the speaker to show that we are listening to others."

During reading, teachers can label any appropriate instance of the expectations. This is especially appropriate when behavioral expectations are being established.

> "Wow, we remembered to 'wait while others think' here. Everyone waited while Emily puzzled through that word."

> "Did you notice how Jessica and Trevon waited while Juan was looking for parts he knew in that word? They showed us what it means to 'wait while others think.'"

After reading, the teachers with whom we have worked found it helpful to provide students with feedback about their developing collaborative skills. Noticing and naming collaboration will create an environment in which it is clear that cooperation is valued. A teacher's feedback will be especially useful if it fosters student independence and self-efficacy. When a teacher says, "I like the way Jessica is listening to others," it seems as though the purpose of the expectations is to please the teacher. Instead, the teacher could convey that working together promotes understanding.

> "Juan was able to understand this idea because Jessica offered help when asked."

> "Our group was able to read and enjoy lots of books today because of the way we worked together."

It can also be useful to take a minute and have students share how the expectations have helped them to grow as readers. Students will be encouraged to act on the expectations if they hear a peer share, "I could really think about that puzzling word because I didn't feel rushed. I knew that others would wait while I was thinking." A teacher can prompt this with questions like:

> "Jessica, how did you feel when Juan said he agreed with your idea?"

> "Today we practiced listening to others. How did this affect our reading group?"

In our experience, it is motivating for students to understand how their behavior can contribute to their own and others' learning. In the next chapter, we discuss other approaches that teachers can use to promote students' motivation for reading.

Summary

In this chapter, we discussed the importance of responsive instruction for students in grades 3–8 who are participating in intervention. These students have participated in many years of language arts instruction and have learned some, but not all, of what has been taught. For these students, observation and assessment can be used to identify what they still need to learn, and then instructional time can be used efficiently to address those needs. We also described the importance of fostering students' independence as readers, and how using appropriate levels of teacher support can promote such independence.

In the next chapter, we address motivation for reading. For many intervention students, their experiences with reading have not encouraged them to see reading as valuable, or to see themselves as readers. Intervention can provide such disengaged/discouraged readers with experiences that will promote readers' motivation for reading.

CHAPTER 3

Motivation

STUDENT GOAL

Students will develop the belief that reading is an enjoyable and informative activity that is not beyond their capabilities. This belief system will result in greater meaning-focused engagement in the reading process.

In this chapter, we propose that promoting motivation for reading is central to intervention with intermediate and middle grade readers. We discuss the research support for this idea, and then detail instructional practices that teachers can use to create an engaging environment for reading as well as to promote readers' belief in their agency as readers.

Rationale: What Is Motivation, and Why Is It Important?

"Motivation is what gets one going, keeps one engaged, and moves one forward in any task that requires effort" (Scanlon, Anderson, & Sweeney, 2017, p. 55). Most students start school eager to learn to read, and believe that they have the ability to do so (McKenna, Kear, & Ellsworth, 1995). However, on average, the late elementary and middle school years are a period of declining motivation for academic achievement (McKenna et al., 1995; Wigfield, Gladstone, & Turci, 2016); this trend is particularly problematic for readers who have struggled with literacy acquisition. Avoidance of reading is a major problem for such students (Prochnow,

Tunmer, & Chapman, 2013; Wigfield & Guthrie, 1997). Since reading skills can be developed only if one reads, motivation is a critical issue for these readers. In fact, Guthrie and Klauda (2016) argue that "Reading motivation may stand as the strongest variable influencing achievement" (p. 48).

One reason that intermediate and middle grade readers may become reading avoidant is that they are often asked to read materials that are too challenging for them. As Schultheiss and Brunstein (2005) report, successful experiences lead to hopefulness and an inclination to seek further opportunities to solve similar problems, whereas repeated experiences with failure lead to expectations of further failure and therefore lead one away from engagement. Thus a major goal of intervention needs to be to ensure that readers encounter reading experiences in which they feel successful. The hope is that this will lead them to adopt (1) a view of reading as an activity to be embraced rather than avoided and (2) a view of themselves as capable rather than struggling readers.

Motivation researchers agree that observed motivation is a result of multiple, interrelated factors. This chapter is organized around two components of motivation that are frequently cited in the motivation literature and that are highly amenable to instructional influences: *value* and *self-efficacy*.

Motivation experts suggest that one question that learners ask themselves is "(Why) do I want to engage in this activity?" For some readers, their experiences have led them to see reading as something that is not valuable to them as a source of learning or enjoyment. Instead, reading may be viewed as confusing, or simply as work. Thus, one goal of intervention is to ensure that readers learn to value reading, because readers are more likely to engage in reading if it helps them to meet personal goals, and if they view reading as enjoyable or rewarding (Eccles & Wigfield, 2002). If intervention includes skill and/or strategy instruction, it is similarly important that readers understand the value of these activities in making reading more meaningful and enjoyable (Schunk & Rice, 1987).

According to Pintrich and Schunk (2002), a second question that learners ask themselves is "Can I succeed at this task or activity?" Individuals have greater motivation to engage in reading if they have self-efficacy—that is, if they *believe* that they can succeed, and if they attribute their success to their own efforts, rather than believing that success depends on factors beyond their control. For many readers in the intermediate and middle school grades who are continuing to find reading difficult, the experience of reading text that is too challenging has led them to question whether they have the ability to be a reader—that is, they lack self-efficacy (Paris, Wasik, & Turner, 1991; Unrau & Schlackman, 2006). Accordingly then, another goal of intervention is to help readers to develop the skills and strategies that will allow them to see themselves as effective problem solvers—that is, readers who have sufficient understanding of the process of reading to make reading seem less challenging. Readers who believe they are capable of succeeding at reading are more likely to engage in it and to progress as readers.

Instructional Decision Making: Developing the View That Reading Has Value and Purpose

There are many ways teachers can encourage readers to value reading. These include making reading an enjoyable and fulfilling experience, and linking reading to students' interests, students' experiences, and the acquisition of knowledge. The language that teachers use can also be a powerful tool in helping students to value reading.

Reading Can Be Enjoyable

Many teachers would describe themselves as individuals who love reading. What makes someone view reading as valuable and pleasurable?

Choice

Adult readers likely read books that they have chosen because they believe the book will be enjoyable or interesting. Or they may read a book because it will allow them to learn something for a profession or hobby they have chosen, or because the book group they have joined has elected to read the book. Also, if an adult reader starts reading a book and discovers that it isn't enjoyable, or isn't helping him or her to learn what he or she wants to learn, the adult may choose not to finish or to just skim the text. One reason that adults enjoy reading is that they have a fair amount of choice in what they read.

Providing students with choice of what to read has been found to both increase their motivation to read and yield gains in reading comprehension (Guthrie & Humenick, 2004). In the first ISA-X study, teachers worked with students in a one-to-one context, and offering students a choice of books to read was an important feature of the intervention. In the second study, which provided the intervention in a small-group setting, choice was offered in other ways. Intervention teachers incorporated choice in the group setting by (1) keeping a wide variety of books available for rereading, and allowing students to choose what they wanted to reread; and (2) when there were two similar books on a topic, allowing students to choose the text they wished to read and then share what they learned with other members of the group. Also, on occasion, students might vote on which text to read as a final book in a unit. Although voting meant that some students would be disappointed, it did mean that each student had a chance to express an opinion. Finding ways to provide choice is an effective practice for all readers, but especially important for those who have limited motivation for reading.

Having the group read a variety of types of books is another way that teachers can maximize the odds that at least some of the time, students encounter books that they would choose if given the opportunity. It is important to be mindful of the types of texts that students have available to choose from. For example, if a teacher enjoys fiction, he or she may assume that everyone else does also, and privilege his or her preference in the books that the group reads. Teachers are often surprised at how much students enjoy reading informational text. As we describe in Chapter 11, sets of thematically related books can be planned so that they include "something for everyone." A text set can include nonfiction and a variety of types of literature, such as graphic novels, historical fiction, folktales, and/or poetry.

Autonomy

An individual who has a sense of autonomy has a sense of control over his or her behavior and engagement. Instruction that allows for a reasonable amount of well-planned student autonomy has been shown to promote motivation (Van Ryzin, 2010). In the context of intervention, autonomy can be supported by providing students with some choice in which texts are read, as discussed above. In addition, students can be given some control as they share their thinking about the books being read. Teachers can support students' autonomy by asking open-ended questions and by making it clear that students are welcome (and expected) to share comments on and reactions to the readings without being specifically prompted to do so. Further, support for autonomy occurs when teachers show interest in students' thinking and responses:

> "What are your thoughts about this passage/book?"
>
> "The group and I are so interested to hear what you are thinking."
>
> "That's an interesting point; what makes you say that?"
>
> "Can you say more about your thinking?"

In contrast, if teachers largely control the discussion, routinely asking questions for which the teacher already knows the "correct" answer, and expects the readers to come up with the teacher's answer, students are likely to feel that they have no control of the situation. Moreover, such an interactional style is likely to create anxiety and/or anger among students who already have a history of reading difficulty. Thus, a steady diet of "correct answer" questions from the teacher has the potential to reduce students' persistence and motivation (Assor, Kaplan, Kanat-Maymon, & Roth, 2005).

Reading, Not Reading Lessons

No one has ever described the joy of reading lessons—it is reading that is joyous. Readers simply read and they may choose to share with others what they have learned or experienced, through casual conversation or a book group. But for the students we are focusing on in this book, reading lessons (and their associated tasks of answering comprehension questions, finding three supporting details, contrasting the point of view of two characters, etc.) are their only experiences with text. When these readers choose not to read, what they may actually be choosing to avoid is the "lesson" that has always surrounded reading for them.

A significant way that teachers can motivate readers is to structure intervention sessions so that they feel as much as possible like reading, not reading lessons. Teachers may find it helpful to see their role as promoting reading, rather than teaching a reading lesson. While the group is always engaged in constructing meaning with the book being read, that process appears conversational and motivating (for more details about a conversational approach, see Chapter 14).

Teachers can use language and behavior to convey the message that people read for fun. Teachers can simply share their *enthusiasm for reading,* and convey that to be a reader is to:

- Be enthusiastic about books you read.
- Become actively involved in books.
- Learn interesting things from books.

It is possible to help students to acquire these attitudes about reading through modeling and encouragement. To convey the message that reading is enjoyable, teachers can talk about books they have read and aspects of books that have influenced their lives. As they read with students, teachers can:

- Spend time enjoying illustrations.
- Laugh at a book, or cry.
- Share their natural reactions as a reader to characters, events, and information in books.

Language That Promotes the Value of Reading

Teachers' language conveys subtle messages that can encourage students to value or devalue reading. The teacher who says, "Let's get this reading done" presents a message that reading is something to be completed so that the group can go on to something better, while the teacher who says, "I can hardly wait to get to the end of this book to see what happens!" presents a message that encourages students to value reading.

Language can be used to convey to reluctant readers the idea that reading itself is a reward. Often, this message will need to be a central feature of teachers' initial contacts with students in intervention. For students who have years of negative experiences with reading, promoting the idea that reading is enjoyable may take time. Eventually, as students come to enjoy and value reading, they may take on the role of sharing motivational language about reading. When this occurs, the teacher, while continuing to be enthusiastic and to use language to promote reading, will be able to spend less time on motivation, and more time on discussing the text being read. Figure 3.1 contains some examples of language that can be used to *encourage readers to value reading,* and to motivate them, as well as language that might discourage students.

Language that conveys that reading is work or difficult will reduce student motivation and thus should be avoided. Similarly, when teachers talk about reading as though it has no intrinsic value, but instead is done to earn a reward (such as free time, a trinket, or even grades), they devalue reading. Teachers are often surprised to learn that in the ISA and ISA-X, students are not given rewards for reading. Reading *is* the reward!

For teachers who want to learn to use motivational language that promotes the value of reading, the intervention teachers with whom we worked found several tactics to be useful. Teachers found they could change their language if they:

- Audio recorded and then analyzed their language.
- Reflected on whether their language would be interpreted as promoting the value of reading.
- Scripted the language/statements they wanted to learn to use on lesson plans or prompt cards.

Relevance

According to McRae and Guthrie (2009), value and student motivation to read is enhanced when students see the relevance of what they are reading, and decreased when reading is perceived to be unrelated to students' knowledge, interests, or experiences. The instructional decisions that teachers make, as well as the feedback they give students, can promote or reduce students' perceptions of relevance.

Messages That Value Reading	Messages That Devalue Reading
"Today we get to read this book!"	"Today we have to read this book."
"Isn't it great that we had time to finish the chapter and find out what Ben decided to do?"	"We need to finish this chapter before we leave today."
"A lot of students have said that this book is one of their favorites."	"This book is required of all seventh graders."
"[Character name] is so much fun—don't you wish this story would go on forever?"	"We're almost finished with this book."
"It seems like you are really enjoying reading biographies."	"If you finish reading this biography, you get _____ as a reward."
"I bet you wish we had more time today, so we could see what happens next."	"We have to read before we can take a break."
"I can't wait to see how the story ends."	"We'll be done with this book tomorrow."

FIGURE 3.1. Choosing language that values reading.

Teachers can use their knowledge of students' lives and experiences to help students to see connections between themselves and what they are reading. If teachers are just getting to know their students, an interest survey can be helpful (see Figure 3.2). This survey can also be accessed on the website for this book (see the box at the end of the table of contents). We used this inventory, along with the "What Is Reading" Interview, Figure 1.2 on pp. 15–16, to learn about students' interests and goals as readers. We also found this useful in identifying whether students had a preference for fiction or nonfiction.

With knowledge about students' interests in hand, statements like those below can help students to better understand what they are reading and to see a connection between what they are reading and their own lives.

"Our school is near the [name] River. How is the river near us similar to or different from the rivers we are reading about?"

"The author told us that [character's] mother will not let him join with the bigger boys' activity. Has anyone ever had that experience? How did you feel? How do you think [character] is feeling?"

"[Character in historical fiction] is almost the same age as you are, and he is going with the militia. What would you do if you were [character]?"

Thematically Organized Texts to Promote Relevance

In the ISA-X research projects, students read books that were organized into thematically related sets that aligned with the science and social studies instruction in their general education classroom. (More information about the text sets is provided in Chapters 11 and 16.) A first advantage to these themes was that teachers could readily communicate to students that what was read during intervention would also build knowledge that they would find use for in their general education classroom. Further, because, within a thematic unit, the texts being read were all about the same topic, each text was relevant to students' growing interest and knowledge about the theme.

As a group begins reading a set of thematically related texts, the teacher can guide students to share learning goals for the unit. For example, the group might be reading with the goal of learning what everyday life was like during colonial times. As each individual text is read, it can be connected to the process of building knowledge that addressed the learning goal. A shared learning goal and related texts often prompt students to have a genuine or personal question about a topic, or a genuine purpose for reading a text. It is exciting when a text provides an answer to a student's question—and an unanswered question provides a reason (that created motivation) for reading more about the topic.

In selecting topics for thematic units, McRae and Guthrie (2009) advise teachers to include some themes that expose readers to diverse cultures. For some students, such themes are an opportunity to learn about cultures other than their

STUDENT INTEREST SURVEY

Student's Name _____ Date _____

Purpose: The purpose of this assessment is to enable teachers to begin to get to know their students as individuals. This should help teachers to engage their students and to make reading more meaningful for them.

Teacher: "I'm going to ask you about some of the things you enjoy, because this will help us learn together. If you don't want to answer a question, that's OK."

(It is not necessary to write down the student's responses word for word. Jot down key phrases. Making an audio recording of the interview will allow later reflection on the interview, as needed.)

How do you like to spend your free time?

Who are some of the people you spend a lot of time with?

Name a few of your favorite movies or TV shows. Why are they your favorites?

(continued)

FIGURE 3.2. Student Interest Survey.

What things do you like to learn more about?

Tell me about two books you've read in the last year. What did you like about them?

Analysis and Next Steps

Does this student show a preference for . . .

- Informational text and television?
- Fictional text and television?

Next step: Honor the preference, and encourage the student to value both kinds of text.

Does the student have interests that overlap with some of the thematic units?

Next step: Use this interest to motivate the student about the units.

FIGURE 3.2. *(continued)*

own. If themes are chosen to present cultures represented in the group, they present an opportunity to engage students who may not identify with the more typical texts.

Skill Instruction Is Relevant

Because it is apparent to them, teachers often assume that students understand that they are learning about strategies, high-frequency words, or decoding elements because such knowledge will ultimately allow them to better understand and enjoy what they read. However, if this connection is not made clear, and instruction in these areas is simply presented as tasks to complete, students may learn less (Vansteenkiste, Lens, & Deci, 2006) because students are less willing to devote effort to what they perceive to be meaningless tasks.

To increase the value that students assign to skill and strategy development, and to also increase how much students learn from these activities, teachers can briefly explain how this learning will enhance their reading. For this reason, each of the sample lessons in the upcoming chapters contains explicit teacher language that explains the connection between the instructional focus and the ability to read for understanding, learning, and enjoyment.

Rationale: What Is Self-Efficacy, and Why Is It Important?

Bandura (1997) defines *self-efficacy* as the learners' perceived capabilities for learning or performing actions at designated levels. One's self-efficacy can play a major role in how one approaches an activity or challenge. Those having a low sense of efficacy for a particular task or activity are apt to try to avoid it and, in doing so, have limited opportunity to learn the skill or how to effectively engage in the process.

Further, self-efficacy tends to vary considerably depending on the activity in question. For example, students in intervention might have a low sense of efficacy for reading and writing but a high sense of efficacy for activities in which they have experienced success. While success, or lack thereof, contributes to one's sense of efficacy, so too does the level of challenge encountered. Experiencing success on a task that is somewhat or even very challenging will do more to develop a sense of efficacy for that activity than success on a task that is very easy.

Instructional Decision Making: Developing Readers' Self-Efficacy

One's sense of efficacy is changeable. And when it comes to reading (and writing), teachers have a major role to play in the development of their students' self-efficacy. In what follows, we detail some of the ways in which teachers can support their students' development of self-efficacy for reading.

Reading Ability Can Change through Effort

Some readers may be reluctant to engage in reading because they have always struggled with reading and therefore come to the logical conclusion that they will always continue to do so. They are often convinced that effort will not make a difference, especially if they have tried and been unsuccessful in the past. The students who are the focus of this book have typically experienced 3 or more years of being unsuccessful as readers.

Recently, many educators have been made aware of the importance of effort through Dweck's (2007) notions of "fixed" and "growth" mindsets. According to Dweck's research, individuals who hold a fixed mindset believe that ability, especially their own, is fixed, and that effort can do little to change it. Thus, a student might think to him- or herself, "I'm not good at reading and I never will be." In order to avoid revealing limited abilities, the fixed mindset individual will avoid challenge that might reveal a lack of ability, and give up easily in the face of obstacles, because of the belief that effort doesn't make one more able. Thus, many intermediate and middle grade readers who have adopted a fixed mindset avoid reading and rely on assistance from others when they encounter problems. To a fixed mindset individual, feedback is often seen as criticism of his or her fixed and inadequate ability.

In contrast, an individual with a growth mindset believes that ability is not fixed, but instead can be changed and developed. This individual is more likely to have a desire to learn, and to embrace challenge and persist in the face of obstacles. For individuals with a growth mindset, feedback is an opportunity to grow and learn. Most importantly, effort is seen as the route to success.

Teachers can promote a growth mindset about reading by teaching students the important role that effort and practice play in reading ability. Teachers sometimes neglect to tell students in intervention that, with practice, reading will get easier. An analogy may help students understand how effort can serve to make a task that seems very challenging to eventually become manageable and even easy and enjoyable. For example, most students will understand that while initially it was difficult and frustrating to learn to ride a bike, with practice it becomes easy. Students who find reading challenging will find it motivating to learn that reading will not (necessarily) always be challenging.

As always, teacher language can make a difference. To promote students' understanding that effort will enhance ability, teacher feedback is most powerful if it focuses on effort, and not on ability. Figure 3.3 provides examples of teacher feedback that will promote or reduce a growth mindset.

Students need to engage in reading in order to get better at it. Teachers play a critical role in this, making sure that teacher-directed lessons and teacher talk are brief, so that time can be spent on what matters—reading. An important part of intervention is providing students with many (extended) opportunities to engage in reading, so that their ability to read will improve.

Promote Growth Mindset	Reduce Growth Mindset
"You were really strategic in figuring out that word!"	"You're so smart!"
"It took some careful thinking to figure out what was going on in this chapter!"	"You understood that perfectly."

FIGURE 3.3. Choosing language to promote a growth mindset.

There is an interesting connection between research on teachers' and students' views of ability. Research indicates that teachers who believed that students' abilities could change had students with higher motivation (Brophy & Good, 1970; Weiner, 1980). Intermediate and middle grade readers in intervention *can* become independent, successful problem solvers and readers. Teachers are encouraged to share this belief, and to plan and provide opportunities to ensure it will happen, because the more they believe and communicate that their intervention students will improve, the greater the likelihood that they will.

Independent Problem Solving

Self-efficacy develops in situations where students are engaged in a challenging activity and succeeding independently. That is one reason this book frequently refers to "promoting student independence." When students see themselves as independently able to solve problems they encounter while reading, a sense of efficacy for reading develops. In contrast, if readers are consistently dependent on assistance from the teacher or peers to solve problems, they will not develop the self-efficacy needed to be motivated to read. Independence is necessary, but not sufficient, for the development of self-efficacy.

In this book, we provide guidance (see Chapter 6) on how teachers can introduce readers to various strategies for word solving that will enable them to solve puzzling words they encounter while reading. We also describe how a gradual reduction of teacher support can enable students to become independent in utilizing these strategies. This means that as the needed skills and strategies for independent problem solving are learned and practiced with teacher support, the teacher gradually reduces support. The goals here are to:

- Allow students to do as much of the thinking as they have the skills, strategies, and knowledge for.
- Expect the student to judge whether or not problems have been adequately solved.
- As the teacher, refrain from confirming ("That's right!") or disconfirming ("Does that make sense?") when readers have the ability to do the confirming/disconfirming on their own.

The teacher's role is to show students how to use multiple sources of information to confirm for themselves that the puzzle has been solved.

Attribution[1]

Learners who struggle often attribute their difficulties to things that are beyond their control (e.g., they are learning disabled or "dumb," school is boring, the teacher doesn't teach well, the material is too difficult) and rarely attribute their difficulties to a lack of effort on their part. This is a bit of a vicious cycle because if one's difficulties are due to factors that are beyond one's control, it probably doesn't make sense to expend effort to try to overcome those difficulties.

Some of the factors that these learners point to are, of course, within the teachers' control (such as the level of challenge and interest), and those should be addressed as discussed in the next section. However, once those are addressed, students still may not make the kinds of gains they need to make in order to meet grade-level expectations if they don't expend the needed effort. But we can't just *tell* them to try harder! Rather, we need to show them how to try effectively, guide them as they learn to do so, and draw their attention to how their successes are attributable to their efforts.

The strategy lessons presented in Chapter 6 include discussion of ways that teachers can help students to attribute their success to the effort they are exerting and the strategies they are using. Teachers can foster these attributions by labeling for readers the word identification strategies readers are using, and the effect that these have on their reading. Comments like those that follow help students to be aware that the strategies they are using help them to grow as readers.

> "You figured out that word on your own because you used the strategies 'look for parts you know' and 'think of words that might make sense.'"

> "When you couldn't figure out that word, you read past it to get some more ideas about what word would make sense there."

Feedback can be especially powerful when a student has partially solved a problem. Noticing and naming (Johnston, 2004) the strategies that students have tried, or the thinking they have done, makes it far more likely that students will try another strategy or continue trying to understand a text than if the teacher does not acknowledge the effort students have already displayed. Thus, a teacher might say:

> "To figure out that word, you tried the strategies 'look for parts you know' and 'think of words that might make sense.' That has helped you to figure out part of the word. What other strategies can you try?"

---

[1]The discussion of attributions draws heavily on a summary of research in this area provided by Schunk, Meece, and Pintrich (2012).

As students become more adept at problem solving while reading, it is useful to encourage them to reflect on their effective strategy use and, on occasion, to reflect on how they have changed as readers. For example, a teacher might say:

> "When you were reading you puzzled over this word for a bit and then you said it. Tell me what you did to figure it out."

> "I noticed when you were reading this page silently that you got a puzzled look on your face and then you seemed to figure things out. Tell about your thinking on that page."

> "How do you think you have changed as a reader since we started reading together?"

Conversations such as these will help students to consciously attribute their success to their efforts and strategic thinking.

Challenge

Self-efficacy develops in situations where the individual *meets challenge with success* (Deci & Ryan, 1985). Some challenge is critical, because success at a task that is perceived as too easy does little to build self-efficacy. Yet if a task is too challenging, or if students do not have the strategies needed to address the challenges, students will avoid the task or engage in it and fail. Virtually everyone is at their best as a learner when the content to be learned is personally interesting and relevant, and when the learning challenge is sufficiently great to promote intellectual engagement but not so great as to seem undoable.

Students develop their self-efficacy as readers when they encounter problems that they can solve as they read. A major focus of this book is how teachers can provide students with strategies to solve problems, for two reasons. First, the strategies promote performance as a reader, and second, they help the reader to develop a sense of efficacy for reading. It is also important that teachers provide students with lots of opportunities to successfully use those strategies, so that the students learn the strategies and experience themselves as problem solvers.

"Just-Right" Text

If students read text that is too simple, there are no problems to solve and the reader's self-efficacy does not grow. However, readers' cognitive systems are limited in the amount of information that can be processed at one time during reading. If text is too difficult and the limits to the information processing system are exceeded, the reader will quickly become overwhelmed and unable to be strategic or understand the text. Self-efficacy will not grow if the text is too difficult.

Thus, effective reading material for students in intervention involves some, but not too much, challenge in terms of the words and ideas in the text. (We discuss this idea in more detail in Chapter 14.) Of course, the degree of challenge that a book offers is a function of the reader's background knowledge on the topic; the strategies that the reader can bring to the text; and whether the text is being read with teacher support, with a partner, or independently. Further, challenge will vary for each sentence within a book, depending on factors such as the support-iveness of the illustrations, the complexity of the syntax, and the number of new vocabulary words in the sentence. To promote students' self-efficacy as readers, it is necessary for teachers to preview all parts of every text that students will read in the intervention setting, and make their best possible judgment about the amount of challenge that the book poses for the readers in the group. In Chapter 6, we describe ways to support readers in moments when the challenge is too great.

KEEP IN MIND   When a student is not successful in reading, we need to look first at what we are asking him or her to read.

Some intermediate and middle grade readers in intervention may perceive "just-right" text as a negative statement about their abilities, and may instead reg-ularly express a desire to read text that is too challenging. Teachers can develop the reader's self-efficacy if they present these just-right texts as tools—that is:

"This book is a tool that readers can use to develop

- knowledge about the topic,
- vocabulary knowledge,
- sight vocabulary, or
- their enjoyment of reading."

Just-Right Text in Thematically Related Text Sets

A thematic text set can be organized so that students begin by reading more acces-sible books to develop background knowledge. We used this approach in our research, and illustrate it in Chapter 16. Once they had acquired helpful knowl-edge, students in the research projects then read more challenging and grade-appropriate books. As students learned this routine, they saw the usefulness of the simpler texts and looked forward to reading other books that were more grade appropriate.

Teacher Language

Most teachers are aware of the need to avoid language that suggests too much challenge: "That's a hard word" or "This book is too hard for you." Sometimes, it seems as though the opposite kind of language would be helpful. In trying to "encourage" students, a teacher may suggest that a task or book is not challenging.

There are two problems with such language. First, if the student perceives that the task presents no challenge, then the task will not help to develop the student's self-efficacy, since self-efficacy develops by successfully addressing challenge. Second, if in fact the "easy" task is experienced as challenging by the reader, this language devalues the challenge that the student is addressing. Students who encounter unfamiliar words in books deemed "easy" will lose self-efficacy, as they think to themselves, "If you can't figure out the words in an easy book, you must be really bad at reading." Examples of *language to avoid because it devalues the learner's effort* include:

"That's an easy word."

"You (should) know that word."

"We're going to start the theme with an easy book."

Developing Self-Efficacy by Creating a Sense of Mastery

When students do not see themselves as readers, realizing that they have successfully engaged in a lot of reading will help them to develop a sense of efficacy. Some milestones that teachers will want to enjoy with students include:

"You finished a whole book (or three books) in one session."

"You read a chapter book."

"You've read _____ books since school started."

"Your goal was to read [title] and you are doing it!"

Mastery in Thematic Units

Guthrie and Wigfield and their colleagues have conducted numerous studies of an intervention called Concept-Oriented Reading Instruction (CORI; Guthrie et al., 2004), which like the ISA-X, engages students in reading thematically related texts designed to build knowledge on a topic. In addition to the positive effects that CORI has shown on reading comprehension, they found that students' motivation to read was enhanced when reading and discussion occurred within thematic units that allowed students to build knowledge of a topic. They believe this to occur because, in a thematic unit, readers can be encouraged to set a mastery goal of becoming an expert on a topic and then read to attain that goal (McRae & Guthrie, 2009). Teachers using thematically related sets of texts should feel free to comment to their students, "You're becoming an expert on this topic!" and should expect students to eventually share the thinking, "I'm becoming an expert."

If students read unrelated texts instead of thematically related ones, Guthrie and colleagues conclude that "Student engagement is diminished whenever the topics change so rapidly that students are left with no clear conceptual reason to read the text" (McRae & Guthrie, 2009, p. 70). They theorize that reading a series of unrelated texts may leave students with less compelling goals, like saying the words correctly, or pleasing the teacher.

When reading thematically related texts, students' sense of mastery can be promoted by encouraging them to share their new knowledge of the topic with the group. Teachers may want to provide a central place where students can place "sticky notes" that summarize new knowledge about learning goals that the group is addressing. In our research, we also encountered numerous instances when intervention students shared what they had learned during the science and social studies instruction that occurred in their general education classrooms. Becoming sufficiently knowledgeable to share their expertise in class was a great way for previously unmotivated readers to develop self-efficacy.

Summary

In this chapter, we discussed the role that value and self-efficacy play in reading development. We considered how teachers can foster a sense that reading has value as well as the reader's self-efficacy, through careful attention to teacher language and matching the challenge of the reading task to the reader's current skills and abilities. Fostering motivation is particularly important for readers who may perceive themselves as less capable readers than their peers.

In the chapters that follow, we return to the idea of motivation. In the next chapter, we focus on the process of word learning, and how instruction may continue to build readers' motivation by building their ability to quickly and effortlessly recognize words.

PART II

Word Learning

In Part I of this text we addressed the foundational ideas of comprehensive, responsive, and motivating instruction. Part II is focused on knowledge and practices that teachers may find useful as they seek to help readers to readily identify words and to acquire the strategies and knowledge that will enable them to become more proficient word learners. It is organized around the following three student goals:

Word identification strategies: For the purpose of enabling comprehension, students will build their sight vocabulary through the interactive use of word identification strategies to puzzle through and learn unfamiliar words encountered while reading.

High-frequency words: Students will add high-frequency words to their sight vocabularies.

Decoding elements: Students will learn information about decoding elements that they can use for strategic word identification to support word learning and, thereby, reading comprehension.

As we discuss in Chapter 4, these goals are interrelated and their instruction is integrated.

Conceptualizing Word Learning

In this chapter, we provide an overview of accuracy instruction for intermediate and middle grade readers. This instruction is designed for readers whose lack of reading accuracy and fluency is an impediment to understanding grade-appropriate text. In this chapter, we provide a rationale for the approach to instruction that is described in more detail in Chapters 5–9.

Rationale: What Is Sight Vocabulary, and Why Is It Important?

A word that can be read accurately and automatically, with seemingly no effort by the reader, is known as a *sight word* or as a *part of the reader's sight vocabulary*. Reading comprehension depends upon fast and accurate identification of words (Samuels, 2006), for two major reasons. First, the accurate identification of the author's words is necessary to understanding the author's message. Second, a large sight vocabulary allows readers to devote most of their cognitive resources to analyzing and interpreting the meaning of the text being read (Tan & Nicholson, 1997). In contrast, a reader who must devote effort to identifying many words in a text has less mental capacity available to think about the author's message, so comprehension suffers. An important contributor to the development of reading comprehension, therefore, is learning to automatically identify most of the words that are encountered in texts.

One might ask, "What constitutes a sufficiently large sight vocabulary to support comprehension?" A competent middle school reader can quickly and accurately identify tens of thousands of words. Indeed, Nagy and Anderson (1984) estimated that the print that students encounter in school consists of approximately 88,500 distinct word families (their definition of a word family is a group of words with clear and predictable relationships between form and meaning; e.g., *assume, assumed, assuming,* and *assumption* would all be in a single word family). Nagy and Herman (1987) estimated that the typical fifth-grade student encounters 10,000 new word families in a year. Since a student just beginning to read can identify only a handful of words automatically, the task of building a sight vocabulary that may ultimately consist of such a huge number of words is a tremendous learning challenge.

Some intermediate and middle school readers who receive intervention have developed grade-appropriate sight vocabularies, but many have not (Valencia, 2011)—that is, for many readers, comprehension is limited because they have limited sight vocabularies. Word learning is an instructional priority for these readers. However, there is evidence that many intermediate and middle grade readers who need it do not receive such instruction (Bentum & Aaron, 2003).[1] Indeed, in our work, we observed great similarity in the word-reading skills among fourth- and seventh-grade readers in intervention, probably because students stopped making progress in developing a sight vocabulary. Little word learning instruction was provided to them in the intermediate grades and, we suspect, they engaged in far too little reading, which is the main way in which sight vocabulary is built (see Menon & Hiebert, 2011). These observations are consistent with those made by Ciullo et al. (2016), who found phonics instruction and independent silent reading to rarely occur in the middle school intervention classes they observed.

Not all interventions for fostering word learning have resulted in growth in reading comprehension, as illustrated in research by Vaughn et al. (2011) and Wanzek and Roberts (2012). Indeed, Wanzek and Roberts concluded, "there are no easy answers for effectively intensifying interventions for students who struggle with reading in the older grades, and continued research in this area is important" (p. 98). The word-learning instruction described in this book has been part of a more comprehensive intervention that was found to be effective in promoting growth in both word-reading skills and reading comprehension in two studies with intermediate grade readers (Gelzheiser et al., 2011, 2017).

While it is not possible to isolate from the overall intervention the "active ingredients" that accounted for word learning, there are three factors that we believe to

---

[1] There is also a recent trend to engage students characterized by limited reading accuracy in a great deal of rule-based phonics instruction as noted in Chapter 1. However, as noted there, to date, there is little evidence that such instruction has a positive impact on reading accuracy, fluency, or comprehension.

be essential to effective word-learning instruction for readers in intervention. First, the intervention we studied and describe in this book was designed based on our best theoretical understanding of *how word learning occurs,* as described in the next section of this chapter. Second, our intervention included substantial emphasis on teaching readers to use *word identification strategies* independently, with the goal of allowing word learning to continue beyond the intervention setting and after the intervention was concluded. Word identification strategy instruction is not often a feature of intervention for intermediate and middle grade readers. Finally, the intervention was *responsive*—that is, tailored to each individual student, rather than being the "one-size-fits-all" approach that characterizes many interventions for intermediate and middle grade readers. Each student has learned some but not all of what one needs to know to become an effective word learner. We believe that since instructional time is limited, it will be most effective if it is focused, for each reader, on addressing what that reader is ready to learn but has not yet learned.

Understanding the Reading Process: How Does Word Learning Occur?

When proficient readers have learned a word, they hold in memory a connection between the pronunciation of the word and its spelling (Ehri, 2005a). (The word's pronunciation is also connected to its meaning in memory.) Ehri suggests that "readers use their knowledge of the alphabetic system to create these connections" (p. 137). Specifically, a reader who analyzes all of the letters in words stores a complete representation of the letters in given words, which enables the reader to learn words and read with greater accuracy and fluency. In contrast, if readers encounter an unfamiliar word and identify the word using the context and a limited amount of the letter information, they may store only partial information about the word in memory. As a result, the next time they see the word, they may have insufficient information to recall it, especially if they encounter it in a different context. Such readers will often confuse words with other words that are visually similar (e.g., reading *cut* as *cat, from* as *for*). Researchers have concluded that systematic phonics instruction fosters reading accuracy and word learning (Ehri, Nunes, Stahl, & Willows, 2001), in part because it encourages readers to attend to all of the orthographic information in words (Adams, 1990).

Ehri (2014) refers to the process of making connections between the letters in a printed word and the sounds in a spoken word as *orthographic mapping.* Ehri describes how the mapping that readers do changes as they gain proficiency in reading. Beginning readers map words based on connections between individual letters and the sounds in a word (and sometimes only some of the letters). But letter-by-letter processing of longer words is time-consuming and demanding. There is evidence to suggest that, with experience, developing readers become able to "see" groups of letters (e.g., *-ing*) or little words (e.g., *ant*) and to connect these to their spoken forms (Adams, 1990). Attending to groups of letters (rather than individual letters) reduces the demands on the reader's working memory and makes it easier for the reader to learn to read longer words (Ehri, 2005a, 2014). Proficient readers, who will have acquired knowledge of common grapho-syllabic patterns, are likely to map in memory the sounds of letter groups or syllable patterns.

Word learning occurs if the reader stores in memory a complete representation of the word, and then repeatedly encounters the word, and continues to store full and accurate information about the word in memory. In Chapters 5–9, we discuss instruction that is designed to encourage readers to develop a habit of attending to all of the orthographic information in words, so as to foster word learning. Instruction addresses attending to both single letters and letter groups.

Relatively little is known about how many times readers must encounter a word before it becomes a part of their sight vocabulary, and the number of encounters likely varies depending on the learner, the word, and the contexts in which the word is encountered. It would be unusual for a word to be learned after just one encounter. Ehri and Saltmarsh (1995) reported that older readers in intervention needed more encounters with words to learn them than did younger readers with similar reading skills. Consistent with this, in our research, we found that intermediate and middle grade readers often required multiple encounters with words in order to learn to read them effortlessly. In this book, we emphasize the need for intervention to provide readers with opportunities to consolidate the skills and strategies needed for word learning through skill instruction and practice and through the reading of continuous text.

Understanding the Reading Process: The Components of Word-Learning Instruction

The task of learning to recognize, on sight, many thousands of words is a daunting one. What should instruction address to enable this to occur? We argue that building a sight vocabulary requires extensive amounts of reading in text that provides some but not too much challenge. To enable readers to meet those challenges, we encourage teachers to employ three interrelated instructional activities. These include an explicit introduction of and systematic opportunities to practice and consolidate:

- Word identification strategies (Chapters 5 and 6)
- High-frequency words (Chapter 7)
- Decoding elements (Chapters 8 and 9)

What follows is a brief introduction to instruction to promote word learning. Because there is insufficient time for teachers to directly teach the thousands of words that proficient readers ultimately know, in Chapters 5 and 6 we describe ways to help students learn to execute a set of word identification strategies that they can use to independently and accurately identify unfamiliar words while reading. The goal is for readers to fully analyze the words to be learned and store those representations in memory. In doing so, they have begun the process of learning the words. If readers continue to encounter and accurately read those same words, they will "teach themselves" the words—that is, learn them to the point that the words become a part of their sight vocabulary (Share, 1995).

The word identification strategies described in Chapters 5 and 6 include attention to the context in which the unknown word is encountered. In order to use the context effectively, readers need to be able to easily read the most frequently occurring words because they play an important role in establishing the context—that is, strategic word identification depends upon knowledge of the most frequently occurring words. If a reader has limited knowledge of the most frequently occurring words, instruction needs to support acquisition of these words. We recommend that instructional time be allocated to explicitly teaching the most frequently occurring words, and practicing them until they are a part of the reader's sight vocabulary. This is the focus of Chapter 7.

The word-solving strategies described in Chapters 5 and 6 also include attention to the alphabetic information in the unfamiliar word. In order to make effective use of the alphabetic information in a word, readers need to have control of the frequently occurring decoding elements in written language (i.e., the letters and larger orthographic units and the sounds they represent). If readers lack knowledge of useful decoding elements, we recommend that these be taught as a way to support and expand the reader's repertoire of decoding elements that will, in turn, enable the reader to more effectively apply word identification strategies. Instruction to support the development of knowledge of decoding elements is the focus of Chapters 8 and 9.

Ultimately, engaged reading is the most essential activity in word learning, because it provides students with a motivating and meaningful opportunity to encounter and learn words. As readers engage in meaning-focused reading of known words that are not yet automatically identified, these words become more automatic. As they use strategies to identify previously unknown words, they begin the process of learning those words. Readers experience a genuine reason for learning words by reading.

Instructional Decision Making:
General Guidelines for Teaching for Reading Accuracy

Responsive Instruction

A first step in fostering knowledge of word identification strategies, high-frequency words, or decoding elements is to identify, through observation and/or assessment, what readers already know, so that instruction can focus on what has yet to be learned. Instructional time is wasted if it is spent on things that readers can already do, or on things that are, as yet, too challenging for them to learn. Thus, instruction should be responsive to the learners' present abilities.

Ongoing monitoring of student learning is an important part of responsive teaching. To this end, it is useful to continually observe and record students' performance. These records allow the teacher to make appropriate decisions about the pacing and focus of instruction.

Provide a Rationale

Normally developing readers acquire knowledge of the high-frequency words, decoding elements, and strategies for identifying words at a young age. Older readers who have not yet learned these things may perceive instruction around these skills and strategies to be babyish, insulting, inappropriate, or aversive. In our experience, some readers resent it when teachers ask them to engage in learning the skills and strategies they need *if* teachers fail to provide them with a really good explanation of how the learning will benefit them.

Often, the reason for instruction in high-frequency words, decoding elements, and strategies for identifying words is not apparent to the student, even when it is clear to the teacher. We have found it helpful to consistently include in our lessons the explanation that learning these skills and strategies will, ultimately, make reading and understanding easier and more enjoyable. Older readers benefit from having a clear purpose for exerting the effort required to learn high-frequency words, decoding elements, and word identification strategies. Indeed, we found that the most effective teachers of the readers in our studies more frequently made explicit to their students that the purpose of learning these things was so that students could better understand and enjoy what they read (Gelzheiser et al., 2017).

Provide What, When, and How Information

Research on comprehension strategy instruction indicates that students are most likely to use strategies if the teacher (1) tells the student what the strategy is called, (2) states why/when the strategy is useful, and (3) shows the student how to use the strategy (Duffy, 2009; Pearson & Gallagher, 1983). In this book, we advocate adopting the same approach to teaching word identification strategies.

An integral part of this approach is the teacher sharing the kind of thinking that he or she hopes the students will do as they learn strategies for identifying words, build their knowledge of high-frequency words, and increase their skill with the alphabetic code. In comprehension strategy instruction, teachers share their thinking by modeling processes while thinking aloud about the process (Duke et al., 2011). We have found it useful to adopt the same approach in teaching students to be strategic in their attempts to identify unfamiliar words. Think-aloud models are a feature of the lesson examples provided in each chapter.

Gradual Release of Responsibility

The time that teachers have available to provide intervention is limited, while the number of words to be learned is large. To address this challenge, in the ISA and ISA-X, we have taken the approach that students need to become independent word learners. The teachers' initial role is to show readers how, when, and why to use word identification strategies, high-frequency words, and decoding elements. But then teachers must reduce their involvement if students are to become independent. Using an approach known as *gradual release of responsibility* (Pearson & Gallagher, 1983), teachers slowly increase the level of independence expected of students. During this process, teachers provide students with the time and the encouragement to do as much of the thinking or problem solving as possible, but are still available to share their thinking and support when needed.

Summary

In this chapter, we described what is known about how readers learn to identify words and add these words to the body of words that they can read with little effort. We introduced three components of instruction to foster word learning: word identification strategies, high-frequency words, and decoding elements. We also provided some general guidance as to how to maximize the effectiveness of instruction devoted to these components. In the next chapter, we introduce one of the most central features of the ISA: word identification strategies and their interactive use.

CHAPTER 5

Word Identification Strategies

STUDENT GOAL

For the purpose of enabling comprehension, students will build their sight vocabulary through the interactive use of word identification strategies to puzzle through and learn unfamiliar words encountered while reading.

Many readers in intervention are not strategic in how they approach unfamiliar words. They may lack knowledge of specific, helpful word identification strategies, or may not use all the information that is available to them to check and confirm their initial hypothesis about the identity of a word. In this chapter, we detail strategies that students can use interactively to identify unfamiliar words, with the goal of ultimately adding these words to their sight vocabulary. Some of the strategies use code-based information (the letters and spelling patterns in a given word) while others rely on meaning-based information (the context in which the word is encountered). These strategies should be used, conjointly, to hypothesize about and confirm the identity of unfamiliar printed words encountered while reading. Indeed, this is what we mean by interactive strategies use. The coordinated use of both code- and meaning-based strategies is essential in learning to read in a language such as English because the spellings of many words do not accurately signal their pronunciations (e.g., *was, they, of*). After detailing these strategies, we provide instruction in their use in Chapter 6. Both this chapter and the next are designed to assist teachers in helping students to meet the same instructional goal: building their sight vocabulary through interactive word identification strategies to support reading comprehension.

Rationale: What Are Word Identification Strategies, and Why Are They Important?

As described in Chapter 4, proficient readers can quickly and accurately identify many thousands of words; these words constitute their *sight vocabulary*. While some words are taught directly (see Chapter 7 on teaching high-frequency words), most of the words that ultimately become part of a reader's sight vocabulary are learned through effective and independent word solving while reading. Share (1995) referred to this process of building a sight vocabulary as serving as a "self-teaching mechanism." While many readers develop a self-teaching mechanism without too much explicit guidance, students who demonstrate reading difficulties in the middle elementary grades and beyond often do not demonstrate effective word-solving strategies and, as a result, have not built sight vocabularies that are sufficiently large to enable them to readily read and comprehend grade-level materials. In our work with readers who have a limited sight vocabulary, we have found it useful to explicitly teach strategies for word solving and to provide guided practice with the goal of gradually releasing all responsibility for word solving to the student.

Is It Only about Sight Vocabulary?

Proficient readers are so effective at word solving that they, for the most part, are able to read words they have never seen before with little or no hesitation. For example, they would typically be able to read words like *sloat, abbilain*, and *rebeedant* nearly as fast as the words *float, appellate*, and *redundant*. This is possible because, mostly through extensive reading, they have stored and know how to use many frequently occurring orthographic patterns.

Strategy Use Enables the Reader to Identify Unfamiliar Words

We use the term *strategies* to refer to tactics that readers can use when they encounter something puzzling when reading. In this chapter, we discuss the strategies readers can use to "solve" the puzzle of how to read some of the words they encounter while reading. The ultimate goal is that, through effective word solving and repeated encounters, readers will learn such words and add them to their sight vocabularies. Figure 5.1 provides a list of the word identification strategies (with some minor modifications) that have been explicitly taught in our studies (Gelzheiser et al., 2011, 2017; Scanlon et al., 2008). This list is also available on the website for this book (see the box at the end of the table of contents). The list is intended to serve as a resource that students reference to help them remember the strategies.

To figure out a word:

Check the pictures.

Think about the sounds of the letters in the word.

Think of words that might make sense.

Look for parts you know.

Read past the puzzling word.

Go back to the beginning of the sentence and start again.

Try different sounds for some of the letters, especially the vowel(s). Be flexible!

Break the word into smaller parts.

FIGURE 5.1. Word identification strategy resource. Reprinted with permission from Scanlon, Anderson, and Sweeney (2017, p. 250). Copyright © 2017 The Guilford Press.

What Is Interactive Strategy Use, and Why Is It Important?

While reading, a reader has several sources of information available when an unfamiliar word is encountered. For a typical reader, these may include:

- Knowledge of the most common sounds represented by individual letters.
- Knowledge of the sounds that correspond to frequently encountered spelling patterns (e.g., *ar*).
- Illustrations.
- Known words that can provide meaning or context for the sentence or passage.
- The reader's background knowledge.

If a reader cannot identify a word, he or she can draw on these sources of information for assistance. In our research, we have used the term *interactive strategy use* (Vellutino & Scanlon, 2002) to describe how the reader uses, as needed, multiple information sources in a mutually supportive manner to identify a word that is, initially, unknown.

When an accurate and independent reader (like the one in our example below) encounters but cannot identify a word in text, the reader generates a *hypothesis* about what that word might be by drawing on various sources of evidence as listed above. The reader "weighs the evidence" in support of the hypothesis and, if all goes well, ultimately *confirms*—that is, settles on—the identity of the word. The independent reader typically needs to use both the letters in the word, often referred to as "the code," and the meaning of the passage to be confident that the word has been accurately identified. Indeed, both sources of information may be necessary just to identify a word, since so many English words are only partially phonetically regular, and because frequently, letters may represent more than one sound. In fact, often, readers will use multiple code- and meaning-based strategies to identify and confirm a word's identity.

Below is an example of interactive strategy use that might occur while reading the beginning of the chapter titled "Night in the Forest" from *The Courage of Sarah Noble* (Dalgliesh, 1954, p. 1). Note that, along with the words quoted, the book includes a picture of Sarah asleep next to her father, under a tree with a musket that is resting on her father's knee. Another smaller picture of tree branches is also on the page.

> Sarah lay <u>on a</u> quilt <u>under a tree</u>. <u>The</u> darkness <u>was all around her, but through the</u> branches <u>she could see one</u> bright star. <u>It was</u> comfortable <u>to look at</u>.

Let's assume that the reader knows the 300 most frequently occurring words (those occurring in the passage are <u>underlined</u>), the common sounds for the vowels, and the most common sounds for the single consonants and the consonant digraphs (two letters used to represent one consonant sound). The reader has read up to the word *branches* but cannot immediately identify the word, although this is a word for which the reader knows the meaning. Use of word identification strategies such as "Think about the sounds of the letters in the word," "Look for parts you know," and/or "Break the word into smaller parts" might provide the reader with an approximation of the word /braaan/ /ches/ (perhaps with the last syllable pronounced like the game *chess*). Use of meaning-based word identification strategies such as "Check the pictures" and "Think of words that might make sense" would help the reader to adjust the pronunciation and accurately identify the word as *branches*. Thus, using both the code and meaning information interactively would allow the reader to independently identify the word. This accurate identification is a first step in learning to identify the word automatically, or, in other words, adding the word to the reader's sight vocabulary. Note that the reader may have been able to successfully identify *branches* using the context, including the pictures, and only some of the alphabetic information, as many students with limited sight vocabularies are inclined to do. However, by doing so, readers who take such an approach will have made little progress toward adding the word to their sight vocabularies.

Interactive Strategy Use Enables the Reader to Learn Words

In order for a word to be learned (i.e., stored in long-term memory), the reader needs to carefully analyze the word both in terms of its letters and the way the word is used in context (Cunningham, 2006; Martin-Chang, Levy, & O'Neill, 2007). Once a word has been analyzed and accurately identified by the reader, additional opportunities to read the word help to consolidate the reader's memory of the word. Interactive strategy use helps readers to learn words by encouraging them to attend to the letters and letter patterns in the word as well as the context in which the word is used. After this analysis, readers will find it easier to identify the word the next time they encounter it, and thus will have more cognitive resources to devote to comprehension of the text in which the word is encountered.

Other Approaches to Word Identification Fail to Enable the Reader to Learn Words

Readers may identify a word such as *branches* by relying in part on word-specific hints provided by teachers or others who are more knowledgeable than the reader (e.g., "They are a part of a tree," "There is the little word *an* in the word"). Sometimes, students have become accustomed to having the word's pronunciation provided for them. These approaches enable the reader to read the word in the immediate context. However, as described in Chapter 4, the reader must carefully store information about all the parts of the word to learn it to the point where it can be automatically identified. Unless the reader *chooses* to carefully attend to the letters in the word, a reader who relies on partial alphabetic information, word-specific hints, or having the word provided is unlikely to store sufficient useful information about the orthography of the word in long-term memory to enable automatic identification of the word upon future encounters.

Both Code- and Meaning-Based Strategies Are Needed

Given that written English includes both phonetically regular and irregular words, we have argued that it is useful to teach readers to use code- and meaning-based sources of information in mutually supportive ways (Scanlon et al., 2017; Vellutino & Scanlon, 2002) so as to enable readers to accurately identify a greater proportion of the unfamiliar words they encounter while reading. Gaskins (2011) concluded that learning only one strategy or one type of strategy will not adequately support the growth of word learning and sight vocabulary. Rodgers, D'Agostino, Harmey, Kelly, and Brownfield (2016) studied the support used by teachers who were providing reading instruction to at-risk beginning readers. They found that the most effective teachers prompted readers to take advantage of clues they were not using—that is, they prompted readers to strategically use the letters if they were relying heavily on the context, and prompted them to use context if they primarily used code information.

Instructional Decision Making: The Code-Based Strategies

This section provides specific information about the code-based strategies that teachers can teach to readers who have limited sight vocabularies. In Chapter 6, a sample introduction to one code-based strategy is provided. Teachers are encouraged to use this sample introduction and the templates available on the website for this book (see the box at the end of the table of contents) to create introductions for the other strategies. After a teacher has introduced a strategy, it is important to provide students with practice in using the strategy. Guidance on providing appropriate practice is provided in Chapter 6.

The code-based strategies taught and practiced in the ISA-X are:

- Think about the sounds of the letters in the word.
- Look for parts you know.
- Try different sounds for some of the letters, especially the vowel(s). Be flexible![1]
- Break the word into smaller parts.

---

[1]Readers familiar with the first edition of *Early Intervention for Reading Difficulties* (Scanlon, Anderson, & Sweeney, 2010) will note that the wording of this strategy has changed slightly in the current text and in the 2017 second edition of the *Early Intervention* text. This change was made both because we found that many teachers abbreviated the wording of the strategy, once taught, to "be flexible with the vowels," and because some teachers felt that the word *pronunciations* was too difficult for children to remember. Relatedly, we have made slight changes to the wording of a couple of the other code-based strategies based on teacher feedback.

In what follows, the utility of and challenges to the use of each of the code-based strategies is described. Ultimately, as students develop the necessary decoding knowledge to do so, we want them to develop the habit of looking all the way through words they are initially puzzled by and to use the letters (and eventually other familiar parts) to identify the words. It is important that readers understand that, by doing so, they will learn more words and more about words each time they read.

Each of the code-based strategies can be executed only if the reader has knowledge of the requisite decoding elements. In preparing to teach a specific application of a code-based strategy, it is important to consider whether readers know the needed decoding elements well enough to use them in applying the strategy and, if not, teach/review the decoding element(s) in preparation for teaching the new application of the strategy. Chapter 9 provides information about assessing and teaching the decoding elements. The decoding assessments will help teachers to determine how much knowledge students already have that will be helpful in using the strategy. If students still need to learn decoding knowledge, Chapter 9 provides guidance about how to efficiently teach students the knowledge that will help them to use the code-based strategies effectively.

Each of the code-based strategies can be used in more than one way, so each strategy is almost like several strategies. For example, one can apply the strategy "Look for parts you know" by looking for little words like *on* or word family/phonogram parts like -*ight*. This strategy can also be applied to vowel parts like *aw*.[2] Initially, a reader may have the knowledge needed to apply this strategy using little words only. Later, the strategy can be revisited and extended after the reader has been taught common phonograms or the frequently occurring vowel parts such as *aw*.

Because they can be used in so many ways, the code-based strategies appear complex. To manage instruction of these strategies, teachers are encouraged to begin strategy instruction at the level that the students' decoding knowledge allows. As the students' knowledge of the decoding elements improves, and as they become more efficient at using the strategy, new ways of applying the strategy can be encouraged. In this case, the teacher may need only to show students how the strategy can be extended to take advantage of their growing knowledge of decoding elements.

Think about the Sounds of the Letters in the Word

Utility

When using this strategy, a student works strategically through a word or word part, retrieving from memory the most common sound for each letter, and using those sounds to determine how the word might be pronounced. For the vowels, the most common sounds are the short vowel sound and the long vowel sound when

---

[2] We use the term *vowel part* to refer to vowel digraphs (e.g., *ay*), vowel diphthongs (e.g., *oi*), and combinations like *or* and *er*.

it occurs in a word that follows the silent-*e* generalization. Readers can use this strategy to identify and learn:

- Phonetically regular short words with blends or consonant digraphs[3] (*brave, chat, run, shine, snake, spin, wake, wide, wish, wrote*).
- Predictable parts of longer words in which the letters make their common sounds or contain known spelling patterns (*hopping*, *concrete*, *inside*, *letter*, *mistake*, *rabbit*).

Thus, for example, this strategy can be used to identify numerous words or word parts (*italicized*) in these sentences from *Frog and Toad Together* (Lobel, 1971):

Toad put the *list in* his *pocket*. (p. 8)
"*We will run* and catch *it*." (p. 14)
Frog *ate* one of the cookies. (p. 31)
"*But* we can *cut* the string and *open* the *box*." (p. 37)
"I *am* going *home* to *bake* a *cake*." (p. 41)

Students with limited sight vocabularies often think only about the sound of the initial letter and then guess the word often relying heavily on the use of meaning-based strategies (Ehri, 2005a). Other students may think about the sounds of the initial and ending letters in attempts to identify a word, rather than studying the word fully. Partial applications of the "Think about the sounds of the letters in the word" strategy may lead to accurate word identification in a particular context because the context serves to readily confirm the word's identity, but may not support word learning because the student has not analyzed and stored in memory a full representation of the printed word.

Students who are observed to think only about some parts of the word need to be taught explicitly to attend to *all* parts of the word. The activity described in Figure 5.2 can be used to illustrate the importance of considering all of the letters in a word. Instruction should begin with the teacher modeling how to think about all of the letters in the word. Then students can practice this approach in other contexts. If only partial analysis is the student's habit, then repeated practice that results in successful identification of the word will be needed to change the habit.

Following the example provided in Figure 5.2, the teacher and students together would reflect on how looking all the way through the word is often necessary for accurate identification and is necessary if the word is to be identified more readily on future encounters.

---

[3] We include consonant digraphs here, because most intermediate and middle grade readers can readily identify the sounds for these letter combinations. Some teachers prefer to consider a consonant digraph to be a "part," connected to the strategy "Look for parts you know," just as they treat a vowel digraph as a part. Either approach is fine but if students are receiving reading instruction in more than one setting, we encourage consistency across settings.

What the Teacher and Students Do	Text
In preparation for the lesson, the teacher writes a sentence, and for one word, covers all the letters except the initial letter.	"I have come home with a *t*. . . ."
With teacher guidance, students generate ideas about what the final word might be, using the context and only the first letter (*table, television, ticket*).	
The teacher adds the next letter to the unfinished word.	"I have come home with a *ta*. . . ."
Students generate ideas using *ta* (*table, tag, tablet*).	
The teacher adds the remaining letter to show that the word is *tan*.	"I have come home with a *tan*."
The teacher leads a reflection on the importance of attending to all of the letters in a word. "When we were basing our guesses about what the word might be on only the first letter or two of the word, we came up with ideas that didn't match the author's at all! We need to look all the way through the words to be sure that we are reading what the author said!"	

FIGURE 5.2. Teaching students to think about all the sounds in a word.

Challenges

For virtually every word, thinking about the sounds of the letters in the word will provide some clues about how the word will be pronounced. For this reason, many teachers and their students may overemphasize this strategy. We need to be sure to make students aware that there are many words for which this strategy, by itself, is insufficient to allow a word to be accurately identified. Consider this sentence from *Frog and Toad Together* (Lobel, 1971):

He <u>o</u>pened the d<u>oo</u>r and w<u>a</u>lked <u>ou</u>t into the m<u>o</u>rning. (p. 9)

None of the <u>underlined</u> vowels has the short-vowel sound or the long vowel sound as the result of the silent-*e* generalization, so thinking about the (most common) sounds of the letters in the words would not enable the reader to solve the word, and other strategies would be needed in order to identify these words. Teachers and students need to be mindful of the limitations of this strategy.

Look for Parts You Know

Utility

When using this strategy, a student strategically analyzes an unfamiliar word to see whether it contains a group of letters (a part) whose pronunciation the student can retrieve from memory—that is, the student knows the pronunciation of the part. Finding a part, rather than thinking about the sound of each letter, is a more efficient approach to word identification, and is especially useful when the reader is attempting to identify a multisyllabic word. This strategy may be helpful for words containing:

- "Little words" (_band, bat**on**, in**form**ation_).
- Common word families/phonograms (_ta**ll**, li**ght**_).
- Phonetically regular vowel parts (_**oi**_ in _spoil,_ _**er**_ in _letter_).

As soon as readers know any of these word parts, they can be taught to apply that knowledge strategically as they read. As readers acquire more knowledge of helpful parts, they can be shown how or be reminded to look for these parts when attempting to identify unfamiliar words.

For most students in intervention, the route to knowledge of word parts is explicit decoding instruction (as described in Chapter 9) and extensive reading. To ensure that students practice using the decoding elements they are learning, we recommend that the parts selected for instruction be drawn from texts that the students will read in the near future (typically in the same small-group session). After students have been taught a "part," they are encouraged to be alert for the part as they read new text, and to use a key word resource (see Chapter 9, Figure 9.5, p. 180) if they need assistance in remembering the sound. Doing so helps them to consolidate their knowledge of the specific word part. Teachers can select or create sentences for students to read to practice "attending to" the part that they are learning. Examples of such sentences are listed on the next page, and Figure 5.3 illustrates one teacher's materials. Many teachers like to personalize these sentences by using students' names in the sentences.

FIGURE 5.3. Sentence providing practice with the _ew_ and _aw_ parts.

When she walked into the room, [student] saw a very *bright light*.
At the zoo she *saw* the *hawk*'s big *claw*.

Challenges

There are times when a student will see a "part" that is not helpful; in these cases, the student should be taught to be flexible and to try other strategies interactively. Consider these examples from *Frog and Toad Together* (Lobel, 1971) in which the underlined parts might misdirect word-solving attempts:

Frog was sitting in the *theater*. (p. 52)
Frog was so small he could not be seen or *heard*. (p. 59)

Try Different Sounds for Some of the Letters, Especially the Vowel(s). Be Flexible!

Utility

In English, a letter (or group of letters) may represent more than one sound. For example, the letter *c* represents one sound in the word *cake* and a different sound in the word *city*. Sometimes a student's first attempt at pronouncing an unfamiliar word doesn't result in a real word that fits the context of the sentence. To enable students to word solve in these situations, we have found it helpful to explicitly teach students to try to pronounce the word using another sound that the letter or letter group may represent. This is a powerful strategy because it can be used in a variety of ways as listed below. This strategy is one that many intermediate and middle grade readers have not yet learned. When the strategy is taught and used effectively it can greatly increase a student's ability to identify unfamiliar words.

This strategy can be used with the letters and letter groups listed below. Each application of the strategy is described in some detail later in this section. Some students will learn just a few of these applications; others may learn more. Assuming they have the requisite knowledge of decoding elements, students using this strategy can systematically try:

- The long and short vowel sounds for vowels in one-syllable words (*top*, *bone*, *bold*, *give*).
- The long and short vowel sound for each vowel in words with vowel parts (*bean*, *feather*, *train*, *captain*).
- The alternate sounds for some vowel parts (*boot*, *foot*, *snow*, *cow*).
- The alternate sounds for some consonants (*city*, *cat*, *girl*, *gentle*).
- The alternate (silent) sound for some consonants (*know*, *ghost*, *wrestle*).
- The long and short vowel sounds for single vowels and vowel parts in multisyllabic words (*computation*, *providing*, *suggest*, *instead*).

This strategy can be taught as soon as the student knows two different sounds for a letter *and* can move flexibly between the sounds. Thus, if the student knows the long and the short sound for the letter *a*, then the student can be encouraged to "try a different sound for the letter" *a* in *have* if, upon first encounter, the word is pronounced in accord with the silent-*e* generalization. Similarly, if the reader knows both sounds for *c*, the strategy can be applied using that knowledge. As readers learn more decoding elements that have two or more frequent pronunciations, they can be taught and allowed opportunities to extend the strategy in additional contexts.

A Note about Vowel Sounds

It is not necessary for students to know which is the long and which is the short sound for the vowel letters. What's important is that students know the two most common sounds for each vowel letter.

Single Vowels in One-Syllable Words

If a student *knows the long and short sounds for the vowels, but does not move flexibly between the sounds,* it will be helpful to devote portions of a small number of lessons to Word Work (word building, word reading, and written spelling activities described in Chapter 9) to allow students to practice moving flexibly between the two sounds of a given vowel. As students practice building, reading, and spelling words that contain the long and short vowel sounds, they can be told that this will help them to readily remember the two sounds of the vowel so that, when they are reading and they come across a puzzling word, they can "Try different sounds for some of the letters, especially the vowel(s). Be flexible!" After students can accurately build, read, and spell words containing the long and short vowel sounds in isolation (for at least one vowel), an explicit introduction to the strategy should be provided. (Note that it will be useful to explain to students that the silent-*e* generalization taught and practiced in the activities as described in Chapter 9 does provide a useful clue with regard to how a word might be pronounced, but that the clue doesn't always work and so they will sometimes need to try both vowel sounds to see which one results in a word that makes sense in the context.)

Consonants

The letters *c* and *g* and the digraph *th* each have two common pronunciations (*city, cat*; *give, gym*; *this, thing*). The two possible pronunciations for *c* and *g* are typically explicitly taught. Once students know the two sounds for the consonant, they can be encouraged to use the strategy of trying different pronunciations if their first attempt at identifying a word doesn't result in a word that fits the context.

The two sounds for *th*, on the other hand, are not typically taught explicitly and, in our experience, many teachers don't realize that there are two common pronunciations, probably because the two pronunciations are so similar to each other (the only difference is that with one pronunciation the vocal chords vibrate—as in *this*—and with the other, there is no vibration of the vocal chords—as in *thing*). Certainly, if students find it difficult to identify a word because they are trying the wrong pronunciation for the *th* digraph, it would be appropriate for the teacher to provide feedback and guidance—for example: "I see that you remember that *t* and *h* together often represent the /th/ sound as in *thing*. But *th* can represent a slightly different sound as well—the sound that you hear at the beginning of the word *this*."

Words with Vowel Parts (Digraphs)

Many phonics programs suggest that students memorize the sound for each vowel digraph (two vowel letters that together represent one vowel sound). However, this isn't necessary for the vowel parts that are listed below. For these vowel parts, trying different sounds for each of the vowel letters within the vowel part will result in accurate identification of more words than the traditional approach that focuses on teaching one sound for the part. For example, although many phonics approaches teach students that *ea* represents the long-*e* sound, as in *leaf*; this is true only some of the time (Clymer, 1963). Similarly, students are frequently taught the ditty "When two vowels go walking, the first one does the talking," but this too is not very useful guidance because it is frequently not true. If students are instead taught "When two vowels go walking, someone says something," and encouraged to try the long and the short sounds for each of the vowel letters, they will be able to identify *heavy, heave,* and *great*. Words that include the vowel parts listed below can often be read using the strategy "Try different sounds for some of the letters, especially the vowel(s). Be flexible!"

ai	ea	ie	oa	ue
ay	ee		oe	ui
	eu			

If students are accurate in trying both sounds for the vowel in words with one vowel sound, an explicit strategy introduction should be provided to show them how to use the strategy with words containing vowel parts. Sample language for a teacher introduction is provided in Figure 5.4. This introduction can be embedded in a full lesson (see examples in Chapter 6) that includes opportunities for students to practice using the strategy with teacher support.

For students who need additional practice with this application of the strategy, sentences can be created to provide practice in trying different sounds for the vowels in words containing vowel parts in which one of the sounds of one of the vowel

What the Teacher Says and Does	Comments on Activity
Names and explains: "When you come to words you don't know, you've been practicing trying both sounds for the vowel to see which sound results in a real word. Today, I want to show you a new way to use that strategy. Lots of words have two vowel letters next to each other. When you see two vowels together in a word, usually only one vowel sound is heard. To figure out the word, you can try both sounds for each of the vowel letters to see which one makes a real word. Let me show you how this works."	Making clear connections between what the student already knows how to do and what the student is learning will help the student see how to apply the known skill in a new way.
Models: The teacher writes the word *thief* on the dry-erase board. "Pretend that I have just come to this word in my book and I don't know what it is but I know I can try the sounds for each vowel letter to see whether I can figure out the word. Because *i* is the first vowel, I am going to start with the two sounds for *i*." The teacher models pronouncing the word with long-*i* sound and then with short-*i* sound (*thife, thiff*). "Those don't sound like real words to me. I am going to try the two sounds for *e*." The teacher models pronouncing the word with long-*e* sound. "That's a word I know. This word could be *thief*. If I was reading it in a sentence, I'd be able to check to see if *thief* made sense in the sentence. If it didn't, I would try the other sound for the *e*. Then this word would sound like *thef*, which is not a word I've ever heard, so I'm pretty sure this word is *thief*." "Let's try it again with this word." The teacher writes *steam* on the board. "I am going to start with the two sounds for *e*." The teacher models words with long *e* and short *e* (*steam, stem*). "Wait a minute. Both of those are real words. To figure out which is right, I would need to see this word in a sentence." The teacher displays a piece of paper with the following sentence: I could see *steam* coming from the hot soup. "I am going to try both words in the sentence and see which makes sense." The teacher models reading *steam* and *stem* in the sentence. "Now I know the word is *steam*."	Being explicit about each step in the process helps students understand how to apply the strategy. In the second example, the teacher explicitly models how to use the strategy being taught in combination with other strategies because the context can be a necessary part of solving words with vowel digraphs.
Provides practice: "Let's practice this a few more times with these sentences." The teacher displays a few more examples to try together with the students. 1. Come for a ride in my *boat*. 2. We had a *great* time at the park. 3. *Spread* the cards out on the table. 4. We can go for a walk if the *weather* is good.	Trying two sounds for each vowel can be laborious at first. Guided practice gives the student the chance to build some fluency with the process. Some students may benefit from a few days of additional practice after the initial lesson.
Links: "So today when you are reading, you can use the strategy of trying different sounds for some of the letters in a new way. If you come across a word with two vowels together, you can try both sounds for each vowel to see whether that helps you solve the word."	Being explicit about how to apply what is being taught helps students transfer their learning to new contexts.

FIGURE 5.4. Introducing the use of "Try different sounds for some of the letters" in words with two vowels.

letters is pronounced. Note that some words (*throat, stream*) follow the "rule" that many students may have learned, and others do not (*thief, break*). Some words have more than one possible pronunciation—for example, *great* (which could be *greet*) or *mean* (which could be *man, men,* or *mane*). Sentences using these words will provide an opportunity to talk about the need to use context to make a final decision about the identity of the word.

Multiple Ways to Solve Words

The word endings *-ies* or *-ied* include two vowels together and can be identified using the strategy of "Trying different sounds for some of the letters." However, it is helpful to remind students that words containing these parts comprise a meaningful root word and suffix, and thus the word can also be identified by breaking the word into smaller parts.

Vowel Parts That Need Explicit Instruction

Students can also be shown how the strategy of "Try different sounds for some of the letters" can be used with vowel parts (such as *oo, ow*) whose pronunciation may not be accurately deduced by trying different pronunciations for each of the letters in the vowel part. Of course, the students should be familiar with both sounds for the parts. For *oo* and *ow*, students should be encouraged to use the key words to recall the possible sounds if need be (see Chapter 9). (Students generally readily adjust to the switch from being flexible with the sounds of individual letters to being flexible with the sounds of vowel parts.)

Multisyllabic Words

A three-syllable word with three vowel sounds has at least six possible different pronunciations. For most words with three or more syllables, students will find it helpful to "Look for parts you know," "Try different sounds for some of the letters," and use the meaning-based strategies to help to reduce the number of possible pronunciations.

As students gain proficiency with this strategy, it is helpful to point out that, in multisyllabic words, some vowels make the schwa sound,[4] rather than the long or short sound. This is another sound that can be tried as students implement the strategy of "Try different sounds for some of the letters, especially the vowel(s)."

---

[4]The schwa sound /uh/ can be heard at the beginning of the words *about* and *enough* as they are pronounced by most speakers of American English. The sound is the same as the short-*u* sound and most often occurs in the unstressed syllable(s) in multisyllabic words.

Break the Word into Smaller Parts

Utility

Multisyllabic words pose many challenges to readers. If readers break unfamiliar words into smaller parts, they can focus attention on just one part at a time, which reduces the demands of the task and increases the likelihood of accurate identification. Students can be taught this systematic approach for breaking words into smaller parts:

- Cover (known) parts of an unfamiliar word.
- Attempt to identify the part of the word that isn't covered, using other strategies.
- Read the word with the covered part(s) added back in.
- Check to see whether the resulting pronunciation is a word that fits both the meaning and the syntax of the sentence.

This strategy can be used in different contexts. Students can be taught how to break words into smaller parts when solving:

- Compound words.
- Words with inflectional endings (*-ed, -ing, -s*).
- Words with prefixes and (other) suffixes.
- Words with multiple syllables that do not include more than one meaningful part.

Because using the "Break the word into smaller parts" strategy requires some facility with several other strategies, this tends to be one of the last code-based strategies taught.

Compound Words

Compound words with familiar parts provide an excellent opportunity to introduce this strategy. Each part of a compound word is one or more separate syllables. These syllables may be indicated by two different consonants together that do not form a digraph and are parts of different syllables (e.g., *goodnight, maybe, breakfast*). In identifying a two-syllable compound word, the student can take the approach of covering up one syllable, determine the likely pronunciation of the other, and then, if need be, uncovering the other and determine its likely pronunciation. Then the two syllables can be pronounced together to determine whether a real word that fits the context has been identified. In the example below, the reader would cover *side*, identify *out*, uncover *side* and cover *out*, identify *side*, then uncover the whole word and read *outside*.

The children went *outside*.

Inflectional Endings

It is also useful to systematically break apart words with *-ing, -ed,* and *-s* suffixes. The teacher can demonstrate with words in isolation and then, when reading a text, students can be encouraged to:

- Cover the ending with a finger.
- Identify the root word.
- Read the word with the ending added.

Potential Impact of Dialect

Note that for children whose spoken language does not include standard use of inflectional endings, the strategy of "Breaking the words into smaller parts" may work a bit differently in that the existence of inflectional endings in written language may heighten their awareness of inflectional endings in the spoken language of others. Either way, knowing to cover up the endings has the potential to facilitate identification of the root word.

This process is simplest for *-ing*. The *-ing* ending is pronounced the same way in all contexts and so is the easiest ending for the students to learn. In the sentence below from *Frog and Toad Together* (Lobel, 1971, p. 13), the *-ing* ending is covered, the root word *blow* is identified, and then combined with the ending to result in *blowing*.

"My list is *blowing* away."

More Need for Flexibility

Words like *rating* pose a challenge because the root word is *rate* not *rat*. Students can be encouraged to be flexible, and try both sounds for the vowel. Of course, the word must be embedded in a sentence if the reader is to be able to determine the identity of the word.

The *-s* (or *-es*) used to mark plurals and progressives has different pronunciations depending on the sound that precedes the suffix. This suffix is pronounced as /s/ as in *cats* or *wants*, or as /z/ as in *balls* and *wades*, or as /ĕz/ as in *cages* or *patches*. In breaking apart words with this suffix, students can be encouraged to identify the root word, and then say the plural/progressive tense as it sounds in spoken language. In the example on the next page, the student would cover the *-s* ending, identify the root word *seed*, and then say the plural of the root word, *seeds*.

He watered his *seeds*.

The *-ed* used to mark past tense also has different pronunciations that depend on the sound that precedes the suffix. The past-tense marker can be pronounced /d/ as in *played*, /ĕd/ as in *wanted*, and /t/ as in *missed*. Here too, students can be encouraged to identify the root word, and then say the past tense as it sounds in spoken language. In the example below, the student would cover the *-ed* ending, identify the root word *trip*, and then say the past tense of the word, *tripped*.

But she *tripped* on her feet and fell smack on her ear. (Van Leeuwen, 1982, p. 9)

Words with Prefixes and Other Suffixes

To increase the independence with which readers identify unfamiliar words, we have found it helpful for students to learn common prefixes (*un-*, *re-*) and suffixes (e.g., *-ness*, *-ly*, *-ful*), consistent with recent findings on the important role that knowledge of meaningful word parts plays in literacy development (Carlisle & Goodwin, 2013; see Chapter 9), particularly for students with limited sight vocabulary (Bowers, Kirby, & Deacon, 2010). Chapter 9 provides more detailed information about teaching common prefixes and suffixes. Once they have learned these affixes, students can then be taught to cover common prefixes or suffixes and focus their attention on identifying the root word. Discussion of this process can emphasize that the meaning of the root word remains constant as prefixes or suffixes are added—but that the prefixes and suffixes modify the meaning and/or syntactic role of the word somewhat—depending on the meaning associated with the prefix/suffix. In the example below, the reader would cover *sad*, identify the *-ness* suffix, then cover it up and read the root word *sad*. The reader would then uncover and read the two parts together, *sadness*.

The boy was filled with *sadness*.

Word Parts That Are Not Meaningful

A syllable is a unit of pronunciation. Every syllable contains one and only one vowel sound, although that vowel sound may be written with more than one vowel letter. Usually, when two vowel letters are together in a word they represent just one vowel sound. Therefore, in attempting an unfamiliar word, it may help readers to look for the vowels in the word, recognizing, of course, that the silent-*e*'s will sometimes cause problems with syllables.

Readers may find it useful to group sounds around the vowels, thereby forming syllables. Thus, for the word *recognizing*, for example, looking for vowels allows the reader to accurately detect the syllables in the word (one for each vowel).

However, such an approach will not always work—for example, looking for vowels in the word *therefore* might lead one to expect three or four syllables (*the, re, fo, re*).

Many multisyllabic words are made up of syllables that do not have individual meanings. These syllables can often be found if the reader breaks the word into parts in the following fashion:

- For words with two consonants together, and vowels on each side, break the word between the two consonants and decode each syllable. Breaking between two consonants always works when the consonants are identical (*hap-py*), and often works when the consonants are different (*al-so*).
- For words with the consonant + *le* (C + *le*) syllable structure (e.g., *stable*, *stumble*), the *le* plus the consonant that precedes it forms a syllable. Students can be taught to notice the *le,* and if the preceding letter is a consonant, break the word into syllables just before that consonant, decode the first syllable, and then decode the C + *le* syllable by making the sound of the consonant and adding /ŭl/.

When a multisyllabic word is encountered while reading text, once an introduction to how to analyze multisyllabic words has been provided, it may be helpful to, on occasion, write the word from the text in isolation using larger font so that it is easier to illustrate for the students how to break apart the word. Of course, the word should then be checked in context to confirm its identity.

Instructional Decision Making: The Meaning-Based Strategies

This section provides specific information about the meaning-based strategies. In the next chapter, a sample introduction to one meaning-based strategy is provided. The website for this book (see the box at the end of the table of contents) includes templates that teachers can use to create their own introductions using the sample provided in Appendix 6.4 as a model.

Once a strategy has been introduced, it is appropriate to provide students with practice in using the strategy. Guidance on providing appropriate practice is given in the next chapter, in the section on strategy consolidation instruction.

Why Teach Meaning-Based Strategies?

Many English words are only partially decodable—for example, the *italicized* words in these sentences from *Frog and Toad Together* (Lobel, 1971) are not fully decodable given the phonics instruction often provided.

Frog and Toad went on a *long walk.* (p. 12)
"These must be the most *frightened* seeds in the *whole world*!" (p. 27)

Students who rely exclusively on code-based strategies will make errors when attempting to read unfamiliar irregular words like *walk* and *frightened,* especially if they have not had instruction that emphasized word families (e.g., *alk, ight*). Such errors will limit students' ability to build their sight vocabularies and are likely to result in frustrating and confusing reading experiences that, in turn, may cause students to lose motivation for reading. Thus, students need to have strategies that rely upon sources of information in addition to the code.

Further, the meaning-based strategies clarify for the reader that the ultimate goal of reading is comprehension. Instructional programs that overemphasize decoding may inadvertently convey the idea that the purpose of reading is only to accurately pronounce the words. Our experience with intermediate and middle grade readers suggests that this misconception and ensuing habit of passive reading is common and challenging to remediate.

Vellutino and Scanlon (2002) use the term *meaning-based strategies* to describe approaches to word identification that involve the reader in using the illustrations and/or context of the sentence and/or passage to assist in identifying unfamiliar words. Before readers can use these strategies, they must understand the illustrations and context of the text. In the examples above, *walk* makes sense in the context of the sentence; *frightened* follows four references to the seeds being afraid. Of course, if the reader encountered these same words in other contexts, other clues might be used to support identification and/or confirmation of the identities of the words.

Research shows that relying on the context alone is generally not sufficient for a reader to accurately identify and learn a word (Tunmer & Nicholson, 2011). Rather, meaning-based strategies help the reader to anticipate what the unknown word might be, thus limiting the number of possibilities for a given unfamiliar word (a process referred to by Ehri [2014] as *prediction*). Meaning-based strategies also allow readers to check their word identification by evaluating the fit between their hypothesized pronunciation of the word and the context of the sentence and/ or passage as a whole. The meaning-based strategies that have been explicitly taught and practiced in the ISA and ISA-X are:

- Check the pictures.
- Think of words that might make sense.
- Read past the puzzling word.
- Go back to the beginning of the sentence and start again.

In what follows, we explain the utility and interactive and confirmatory use of each of these meaning-based strategies, keeping in mind that an important goal of word identification strategy instruction is to help readers build their sight vocabularies as they read. Thus, while in some instances, an unfamiliar word can be identified solely on the basis of one or more meaning-based strategies, if the reader fails to use code-based strategies in conjunction with the meaning-based strategies, the word that is identified is not likely to be learned well enough to be identified more readily upon subsequent encounters.

Check the Pictures

Utility

In using this strategy, the reader checks the illustrations to see whether they provide information that is useful in identifying a puzzling word. This strategy is most helpful in texts that have illustrations that align well with the words.

The sentence below from *Frog and Toad Together* (Lobel, 1971) is accompanied by an illustration that shows Toad standing in front of his open closet, with the clothes visible. Checking the pictures could help a reader to identify the word *clothes,* especially when the picture is used in conjunction with sounds of (some of) the letters of the word.

> Toad took his *clothes* out of the closet. (p. 8)

In our experience, most intermediate and middle grade readers have been taught to consider the pictures. However, we have found some to be reluctant to use helpful illustrations, perhaps seeing themselves as "too old" to need this strategy. Even with older readers, it is helpful to review the value of this strategy in the reader's repertoire (and to extend it as necessary to include using the pictures and illustrations to support meaning construction).

Challenges

Some texts will have illustrations that are generally related, but that do not directly correspond with the text. For example, for the sentence "Frog and Toad went on a long *walk*" (Lobel, 1971, p. 12), the illustration shows Frog and Toad standing together. The illustration provides no support for the identification of the word *walk.* When this strategy becomes a focus of instruction, as for other strategies, teachers are encouraged to prompt use of the strategy when it is likely to be helpful to the word-solving effort. As students become more actively strategic, it will be important for them to learn that this strategy and others will be useful only some of the time, and that this is the reason why there are multiple things they can try as they are puzzling over unfamiliar words.

Think of Words That Might Make Sense

Utility

In using this strategy, the reader uses the meaning and syntax of what has been read to generate a hypothesis about what a puzzling word is, or to confirm the pronunciation of an unknown word that has been identified using one or more other strategies. So, for example, when the reader encounters "Frog and Toad went on a long *walk*," the reader can be encouraged to consider the beginning and ending sounds in the word *walk*, which are regular, and also to think of words that might make sense in the context. This strategic approach should enable the reader to accurately identify the word. The teacher and the student might then reflect on the use of multiple sources of information for word identification (reflection is described in the next chapter). The teacher might also encourage the students to look carefully at the irregular spellings in order to store useful visual information about the word in memory.

Guidance on Which Strategies to Try First

Note that many students who demonstrate difficulties with reading accuracy in the intermediate and middle grades have a history of overrelying on meaning-based strategies in word solving, and this may partially account for their limited sight vocabulary. Such students may not add words to their sight vocabularies effectively because they do not attempt to fully analyze the written representation of the words they are attempting to solve. Therefore, we advise that readers who demonstrate this inclination be encouraged to deploy code-based strategies as an initial step in word solving and use meaning-based strategies to confirm and/or redirect their decoding attempts.

Challenges

Readers will be most successful in using this strategy if they have a good command of English syntactic patterns. Students for whom English is a less familiar language may lack this knowledge. Further, when the book's syntax is literary, rather than conversational, this strategy will be more challenging to use. For example, many readers would be challenged by the syntax of this sentence: "The *shadow* of a hawk fell over them" (Lobel, 1971, p. 48). The syntax would make it more difficult for the reader to identify *shadow* by thinking of words that might make sense. Teachers should be alert to such possibilities and provide assistance. One approach would be to encourage use of another meaning-based strategy—such as "Read past the puzzling word." To support meaning construction and coherence of the text more generally, the teacher may need to rephrase the sentence into more conversational language—that is, "They were covered by the hawk's shadow." Having students then reread the author's sentence, in addition to supporting word identification, will also support the development of familiarity with literary syntax.

Read Past the Puzzling Word (and Then Come Back to It)

Utility

In using this strategy, the reader reads on, to the end of the sentence or beyond, and then returns to the puzzling word. The reader then uses the information gained from the additional context to inform the word-solving process. This strategy can be especially helpful when used early in a sentence or paragraph, when the reader has not yet acquired much of a sense of what the sentence or paragraph is about. However, this strategy is also useful if the puzzling word occurs later in the sentence when reading on into the next sentence will sometimes help to clarify what an unfamiliar word could be—enabling the reader to more effectively think of words that might make sense. Below are examples of sentences in which additional information, gained by reading past the puzzling word (*italicized*), would be helpful to the reader.

> Toad looked at the sunshine coming *through* the window. (Lobel, 1971, p. 63)
> He was *piling* the pennies into tall stacks.

Challenges

Sometimes what follows a puzzling word is another puzzling word or idea. In these instances, reading past is less likely to be helpful to the reader. Consider this example:

> He was on a stage, and he was *wearing* a costume. (Lobel, 1971, p. 52)

If the reader cannot identify *costume,* then reading past the puzzling word *wearing* will not be helpful.

Go Back to the Beginning of the Sentence and Start Again

Utility

In using this strategy, when the reader encounters a puzzling word, the reader rereads the entire sentence to help identify or confirm the word. The strategy may be especially helpful if the unknown word occurs near the middle or end of a sentence. Below is an example where rereading might help the reader to identify or confirm the *italicized* word.

> "That is a wall and that is a roof and that is a *chimney* on top." (Van Leeuwen, 1982, p. 51)

Challenges

Conversely, going back to the beginning is not likely to help the reader who is challenged by "The *shadow* of a hawk fell over them" (Lobel, 1971, p. 48). Yet some students will perseverate and continue to reread, without trying another strategy. This is yet another reason why interactive and confirmatory use of multiple strategies should be encouraged.

Summary

In this chapter, we described eight strategies that students can use when they encounter an unfamiliar word. These strategies are designed to help readers take advantage of both the print and contextual information available to them for solving words. By using these strategies interactively, readers can often identify words accurately and independently. This process, when coupled with wide reading, should allow readers to increase the size of their sight vocabularies.

In the next chapter, we present approaches that teachers may use to observe and monitor students' knowledge and use of word identification strategies. We also describe ways of teaching students to use the strategies they have not yet learned and how to guide students to use multiple strategies, both code and meaning based, in mutually supportive ways to solve unfamiliar words encountered in context. We also describe how to help students learn to independently and routinely select and execute strategies during word solving as this has the potential to allow them to independently grow their sight word vocabularies both in the intervention setting and beyond. The central rationale for promoting growth in sight vocabulary is, of course, ease in word identification that enables a focus on comprehension and knowledge development.

CHAPTER 6

Observing and Teaching Strategies and Interactive Strategy Use

STUDENT GOAL

As in Chapter 5, the goal is that students will build sight vocabulary through interactive use of word identification strategies to support comprehension.

In this chapter, we discuss instruction that can equip readers with a predictable and effective plan that will enable them to read, and ultimately learn, previously unfamiliar printed words while they are reading independently. We present ways that teachers can think about and instruct with the goal of fostering students' word learning through interactive and confirmatory use of word identification strategies. In our experience, many intervention students in the intermediate and middle grades are not strategic when they encounter puzzling words. Careful instruction and ample opportunity for students to practice the word identification strategies and their interactive use can change this and, thereby, enable students to learn the identities of previously unfamiliar written words as they read. Thus, we reiterate the goal that, for the purpose of enabling comprehension, students will build their sight vocabulary through the interactive use of word identification strategies to puzzle through and learn unfamiliar words encountered while reading.

Instructional Decision Making:
Observing and Monitoring Strategies and Interactive Strategy Use

In order to maximize the effectiveness of instructional planning, it is important that teachers determine which, if any, of the word identification strategies readers already know and use effectively, and which they still need to learn. Further, it is important to determine whether students are maximizing the likelihood of accurate word identification by using both code- and meaning-based strategies interactively. The most useful way to learn what word identification strategies readers are using is to observe and analyze their strategy use while reading. Observation would ideally occur during a planned "getting to know you" observation of an individual student during the initial phase of instruction, with one goal being to identify what the reader does upon encountering unfamiliar words.

Most intermediate and middle grade readers know some of the word identification strategies discussed in this book, although they may use different words to label given strategies. Instructional time need not be wasted on teaching strategies that students already use.

In Appendix 6.1 (see pp. 113–116), we provide procedures and guidelines designed to help teachers observe the word identification strategies that readers use as they read. While these procedures might initially be used during an individual "getting to know you" session, similar observations can and should be part of ongoing instructional interactions with a group of readers. Thus, these observations are not meant to occur as a distinct assessment, but rather, to be a regular, unobtrusive part of reading sessions. Figure 6.1 portrays one teacher's notes of the words that a student puzzled over, and the strategies (abbreviated) used by the student and the teacher.

As teachers begin to provide instruction in the word identification strategies, it is helpful to monitor which strategies are being learned, and whether the reader is

---

Adjustments to Strategy Language

If students have learned different names for a strategy, we encourage teachers to introduce the ISA-X name. There are several reasons for this recommendation. First is the age appropriateness of the strategy language that students know. In our experience, students may have been taught "cute" strategy names in the primary grades. The intermediate and middle grade teachers with whom we worked did not wish to use childish strategy language with older readers, and preferred the ISA and ISA-X strategy names for that reason. In this circumstance, the teachers explained how the new ISA-X language was connected to what students already knew, and used the ISA-X language. Students readily adopted this more age-appropriate language. Teachers also taught the new language because often some but not all of the students had other strategy names, so that everyone in the group used the same names for the strategies. Second, even if there is an alternate strategy name with which everyone in the group is familiar and comfortable, using the ISA-X name for the strategy is likely to result in the most consistent language by the teacher. Further, we felt, and the teachers agreed, that the ISA/ISA-X strategy labels are more explicit than other strategy names with regard to what the reader might do in attempts to solve unfamiliar words.

Word	Student		Teacher
shiny	TS SA	✓	
hole	DS	✓	
purple	SA RP	✓	
start	TS SA		LP(ar) ✓
park	LP	✓	
treat	TS SA		DS ✓

FIGURE 6.1. Example of teacher observations of strategy use during reading.

using both code- and meaning-based strategies. Observation continues throughout strategy instruction each day as students read. In this way, students' progress in learning the strategies can be monitored.

Figure 6.2 presents a word identification strategy "snapshot" that can be used to summarize readers' strategy use and the decoding elements for which the strategies are applied on an ongoing basis.

Understanding the Reading Process: Factors That Influence Interactive Strategy Use

In this book, we argue that it is critical for intervention to promote intermediate and middle grade students' abilities to identify words independently, through interactive use of word identification strategies. Learning to use strategies interactively requires certain conditions, which may differ from the instructional conditions provided in more traditional accuracy instruction.

Teach the Reader to Connect Strategy Use to Word Learning

Especially with older readers, we find it helpful to explain that when the reader carefully identifies an unfamiliar word, the next time the word is encountered, it will be easier to read. As the reader continues to read, it's likely that the word will be encountered in other contexts. Eventually, the reader will be able to identify the word without effort. The goal of strategy instruction is not strategy learning—it is word learning.

A Repertoire of Code- and Meaning-Based Strategies

Before they can use strategies interactively, students must have a repertoire of at least one code-based strategy and at least one meaning-based strategy that they can learn to use in a mutually supportive way. Most intermediate and middle grade students come to intervention knowing that it is helpful to check the pictures, and

Student's Name:	Dates					
Interactive strategy use						
Uses one or more strategies to generate a hypothesis about the word's identity.						
Is independently strategic in confirming the word's identity.						
Uses multiple strategies, usually both code and meaning based, to identify and confirm a word's identity.						
Code-based strategies						
Think about the sounds of the letters in the word.						
• Beginning sounds only						
• Beginning and ending sounds only						
• All sounds in the word or part						
Try different sounds for some of the letters, especially the vowel(s).						
• Single long and short vowel (*top, bone, bold*)						
• Vowel combinations that make the short or long vowel sound (*bean, feather, train, captain*)						
• Vowel combinations that have alternate sounds (*oo, ow*)						
• Consonants with alternate sounds (*c, g*)						
• Consonants that have a silent alternate sound (*k, h, w, p*)						

(continued)

FIGURE 6.2. Snapshot for word identification strategy and interactive strategy use.

Code-based strategies *continued*						
Break the word into smaller parts.						
• Compound words						
• Inflectional endings (*-ed, -ing, -s*)						
• Prefixes and suffixes						
• Multisyllabic words						
Look for parts you know.						
• Phonograms and little words						
• *ar, or*						
• *er, ur, ir*						
• *au, aw*						
• *ew*						
• *oi, oy*						
Meaning-based strategies						
Check the pictures.						
Think of words that might make sense.						
Read past the puzzling word.						
Go back to the beginning of the sentence and start again.						
Leave the box blank if the strategy is never observed. Code as T (taught session #); / uses with prompting but rarely uses independently; X sometimes uses independently; ✕ consistently uses independently.						

FIGURE 6.2. *(continued)*

to think about the sounds of the letters in the word. If so, they can be taught to use these strategies interactively.

In our work with readers in this age range, we've found it helpful to make students aware that there are two sources of information available to them to use in word solving: the letters in the word and the meaning of the context. We teach this because some readers have the habit of overrelying on only one of these sources of information, and they are often inaccurate in their word solving as a result. Some readers try to decode every word without thinking about the context[1]; others ignore most of the letters and produce words that might make sense. Both types of readers will frequently be inaccurate. A brief introduction to the two strategy types and the advantages of using both is helpful for these students, as are a couple of examples that illustrate how using *both code- and meaning-based strategies interactively* increases the odds that the reader will accurately identify unfamiliar words. As new strategies are taught, they can be labeled on the displayed strategy resource as code or meaning based.

One way to increase the likelihood that students use both kinds of strategies is to alternate between teaching code- and meaning-based strategies as the strategies are introduced. Alternating between code- and meaning-based strategies allows teachers to emphasize the need to use strategies interactively.

Teacher and Student Awareness That Independence Is the Goal

We have also found that some readers in this age range have learned to depend upon the teacher's assistance, and that some teachers have learned to view their role as helping students to understand the text that is immediately in front of them, rather than fostering more generalizable skills and strategies that help to foster independence. If students are asked to read text that is too difficult (which may occur in an effort to align intervention with general education expectations), dependence on the teacher is natural and unavoidable. With teachers and intervention students in the intermediate and middle school grades, it is helpful for teachers to:

- Explicitly teach students that they will learn how to identify and confirm words independently, and that once they have learned this, they will be expected to be (*get* to be) independent.
- Reflect upon whether the "help" they provide students will only promote understanding of the text being read, or whether it will promote student independence when reading other texts.
- Encourage strategy use in text that is of appropriate difficulty for the reader.

---

[1] Often these are readers whose prior intervention experiences have been heavily phonics focused.

Awareness of the Conditions Where Independence Is Possible

Learning to use word identification strategies interactively and independently takes time. Students need ample opportunity to practice the strategies in contexts where the strategies are useful and students are likely to be successful. Texts that have few unfamiliar words provide limited opportunity for strategy practice. Of course, texts with too many unfamiliar words are also poor vehicles for strategy learning, because in these texts, readers will be unable to use the meaning to confirm the identity of the unfamiliar words. Even in "just-right" texts, students may encounter words that they don't know the meaning of. Students have no way to confirm the accuracy of their word-solving attempts for such words, and so will need teacher assistance.

Interactive Strategy Use Is Learned in Text

In some reading programs, students are presented with a list of words, and asked to practice a strategy like "Break the word into smaller parts." While a word list might focus students' attention on a code-based strategy, it obviously does not allow readers to confirm that the word makes sense in context—that is, it does not allow for interactive strategy use. Thus, when a code-based word identification strategy is first introduced, the application of the strategy might be practiced with a few words in isolation. The next step would be to guide students to deploy the code-based strategies they are learning in the context of a sentence or two. For intermediate and middle grade readers, this is often accomplished by using a sentence that is constructed to make evident the utility of using the code-based strategy in combination with meaning-based strategies. In the same lesson, while reading a larger text, students would then be encouraged to apply the strategy in combination with other code- and meaning-based strategies as needed and appropriate to their current skill and strategy repertoire.

Initially, students will need some support from the teacher to select and execute newly taught strategies. With practice, students will become more independent, and the teacher can and should provide less support. Sometimes, in their eagerness to promote student independence, teachers reduce their support too quickly with the potential result that students don't experience the usefulness of the strategy (or strategies) and may therefore give up on them.

Instructional Decision Making: General Guidelines for Introducing Word Identification Strategies and Interactive Strategy Use

In our experience, many intermediate and middle grade readers do not have a history of explicit instruction in the use of word identification strategies and/or they have not internalized word-solving strategies that they can spontaneously and effectively deploy upon encountering unfamiliar printed words in context. In what follows, we provide general guidelines for introducing word identification strategies and their interactive use. We contextualize these guidelines with regard to how they are most likely to impact student use of word identification strategies. In subsequent sections, we provide lesson examples and discuss instruction that will allow strategy use to be consolidated.

Set Independence as a Goal

Some readers are dependent upon the teacher out of habit. Readers who look to the teacher when encountering an unfamiliar word, instead of tackling the word on their own, are dependent on the teacher. Students who identify a word and then look to the teacher for confirmation are dependent, not independent, readers.

If students are accustomed to being dependent on their teachers, it will be helpful for them to understand that now they will experience something different. Teachers can explicitly teach the idea of *independent* hypothesis generation and confirmation, and contrast that with *dependence* on the teacher. The teacher might say:

> "You will be learning strategies that you can use to figure out puzzling words all by yourself."

> "You will be learning to use strategies interactively, so that you can be more certain that you have figured out a word correctly. You won't need to look at me to see whether you have identified the word correctly."

Perhaps previous teachers have encouraged students' dependence in an effort to be "helpful." The idea of fostering students' independence is new to many teachers. If a teacher does not prioritize students' independence, he or she may inadvertently interfere with it. In situations where the student has the knowledge and strategies needed to identify and confirm a word, teacher moves that will *foster dependence* include:

- Providing the student with the pronunciation of unfamiliar words.
- Assisting the student as he or she attempts to identify a word.
- "Telling" the student that an error has been made by asking, "Did that make sense?" after a student misreads a word.
- Saying, "That's right" or "Uhuh" or in some other way confirming when a student has accurately identified a word.

The beginning of strategy instruction is also a time for teachers to examine their own behaviors. It is useful for teachers to ask themselves: "Do I promote dependence by providing words and/or hints that help the student to identify only *this* word (and, perhaps, only in this context), or by confirming accurate word identification?" If the answer is yes, for the purpose of promoting student independence, the teacher will need to change these ways of interacting around word solving by utilizing the instructional approaches described in what follows.

Teach Students What It Means to Confirm

When students have the ability to use more than one strategy, teachers can help them recognize how *using strategies enables them to be sure of a word's identity* (i.e., confirm). If a reader has the habit of relying on the teacher to confirm, or the habit of continuing to read on even when a word's identity is uncertain, this can be contrasted with the notion of using strategies to confirm the word, and of course, linked to the idea of becoming an independent reader.

A Note from Peggy

"Today I watched one of our fifth-grade 'toughies' solve the word—*circumstances*—with his strategies and the smile was priceless!"

Provide and Teach Students to Use the Word Identification Strategy Resource

Having a strategy resource means that the reader's cognitive resources can be devoted to making sense of the text, instead of trying to remember all the strategies. Learning a new strategy can use a tremendous amount of mental capacity. Learning to use the strategy resource (and key words for the decoding elements) allows more of the learner's capacity to be devoted to meaning making. Using the resource also allows the student greater independence from the teacher.

Students will need to be taught how to use the strategy resource that was presented in Chapter 5, Figure 5.1 (p. 68). The left-hand column provides a symbol that is intended to serve as a mnemonic for the strategy listed in the right-hand column. A part of introducing the strategy is teaching students what the mnemonics on the chart mean. Thus, for example, the student might be told that the little picture is a reminder that the pictures in a book might help readers to figure out what a word is. The word *fun* serves as the mnemonic for the "Think about the sounds of the letters in the word" strategy. A teacher might say, "*Fun* is used because you can figure out the word *fun* just by thinking of the sounds of the letters and it is *fun* to figure out words all by yourself." For the "Try different sounds for some of the letters, especially the vowel(s). Be flexible!" strategy, the teacher would point out that the line of vowels that serves as an icon for the strategy is bent to remind readers to be flexible. An example of teacher language for teaching students to use the strategy resource is included in Appendix 6.3 in the lesson for the strategy "Look for parts you know" (see p. 123).

> ### Strategy Bookmark
>
> In the ISA-X research projects, once students had learned how to use the strategy and knew most of the strategies on the list, we provided each student with the strategies printed on a bookmark—one bookmark to use in intervention, and another copy to use in the classroom setting. As each student read independently, he or she was expected to use the strategy list on the bookmark as needed.

Pacing

Generally speaking, a teacher should begin teaching the next strategy when students demonstrate that they are able to successfully use previously taught strategies with prompting. It is not necessary to wait until students are proficient in the use of one strategy before introducing another strategy. Students should be encouraged to practice the new strategy as it is introduced and guided to interactively use all of the other strategies that they know or have recently learned about.

Explicit Introduction

As described in Chapter 4, we advocate explicit instruction of word identification strategies. Explaining a strategy is challenging, because it is often hard for teachers to describe how to do something that they do without much conscious thought. To support teachers in preparing explicit introductions, we have provided example introductions to interactive strategy use, a new code-based strategy, and a new meaning-based strategy. These are provided in Appendices 6.2 through 6.4. The online resources for this book (see the box at the end of the table of contents) include templates that teachers can use to create their own strategy and interactive strategy use introductions for teaching the other word identification strategies.

Explain What Word-Solving Strategies Are

Before embarking on strategy instruction it is useful to help students realize what strategies they already know how to use as they may not think about their approaches to word solving as involving strategies. For example, the teacher might say:

> "When I listen to you read I notice that when you come to a word that you don't already know you try to think of a word that would make sense. [The teacher would name additional strategies that the students in the group seem to be using.] Those are all useful ways to try to figure out words that you don't already know. We are going to talk a lot about ways to figure out words; we'll call them word-solving strategies. We'll be talking about ways to use the word-solving strategies you already know in some new ways and we'll also talk about some word-solving

strategies that you may not have learned yet. I call them strategies because a strategy is like a plan for how to do something. We'll be talking about plans or strategies for figuring out words that you don't already know. We'll call them word-solving strategies. When you come to a word that you don't already know it is like a puzzle that you need to solve, and you can use your strategies to solve the puzzle."

Following this introduction of the idea of word-solving strategies, the teacher might introduce the strategy list depicted in Figure 5.1 (p. 68), point to and name the strategies that students are already using—at least partially—and then explain that students will, ultimately, learn to use all of the strategies.

In preparation for teaching individual strategies, teachers are encouraged to reread the strategy descriptions in Chapter 5 before beginning strategy instruction, so that they have a full understanding of each strategy. Once an introductory lesson has been taught, teachers should follow the guidance for effective practice as described later in this chapter, in the section on consolidation.

What the Strategy Is

If students learn a name for strategic activity, then they have self-guiding language to use when they encounter puzzling words. Teachers help students to learn the name of a strategy by *explicitly and consistently naming the strategy,* and then by encouraging the student to name the strategy.

For the strategy language to be internalized and used by the student, it needs to be used consistently and accurately by the teacher. When students are first learning a strategy, the teacher should name the strategy exactly as it is stated on the word identification strategy resource and the exact strategy language should be used repeatedly until students themselves can name the strategy exactly. If teachers rephrase the strategy names, they are likely to be less clear and less consistent than if they rely on the words on the strategy resource. It will take longer for students to internalize the strategy if teacher language is inconsistent. Once students have mastered the strategy name, the strategy may be discussed using a shorthand way (e.g., vowel flexing), as teachers remind students of how they might figure out an unfamiliar word.

When and Why to Use the Strategy

The "when" part of word identification strategy use is pretty straightforward—readers use the strategies interactively when they encounter puzzling words they cannot immediately identify. As students develop familiarity with the strategies, more detail about when they are useful can be provided. For example, long words lend themselves to "Break the word into smaller parts" or "Look for parts you know." If the first word in the sentence is unknown, it is often helpful to "Read past the puzzling word."

Provides feedback: "You took your time and really thought about the letters in the words _____, _____, and _____ so that you could remember the high-frequency words we practiced today."	Noticing and naming what students do with success increases the likelihood that they will apply their new learning in the future.
Corrects errors: "Remember to name the word each time you spell it, so that you can remember how the letters and word go together."	Providing corrective feedback helps students to further extend their knowledge base.
Provide additional practice with newly taught words following the guidance for consolidation of high-frequency words (Figure 7.4). This could occur in the same lesson during which new words are introduced if time permits.	

FIGURE 7.3. *(continued)*

Helping Students to Consolidate Their Knowledge of High-Frequency Words

If the student has a large number of high-frequency words to learn, teachers are encouraged to provide practice daily or even twice a day. Students with a smaller number of words to learn may need practice only every other day.

Figure 7.4 shows how to practice the high-frequency words. The lesson reminds students why these words are so important to learn. The student reads his or her set of words, and the teacher records the student's fluency and accuracy with these words.

There is no magic formula (or research base) for determining how many practice trials are needed before a student can be considered to "know" a word. If the student quickly and accurately identifies a priority word the *first* time it is presented across four to six consecutive practice sessions after the initial introduction, the word can probably be retired from practice or used as a "known" word as new high-frequency words are taught and practiced.

Practice with Tic-Tac-Toe

A tic-tac-toe game can be used to practice high-frequency words. The teacher and the student each have a different color marker. The student turns over one of the high-frequency words he or she is learning, reads the word, and then writes it in one of the tic-tac-toe squares, saying the letters and then the word as he or she writes. The teacher then takes a turn. The first player with three words of the same color in a row wins. Readers who have similar sets of high-frequency words to learn can also be set to play tic-tac-toe to provide additional practice to promote automaticity. In this instance, the words used should be those that readers can read accurately but not automatically. (Marking off a tic-tac-toe board with masking tape on a dry-erase board can eliminate time lost to making the grid.)

CONSOLIDATION OF HIGH-FREQUENCY WORDS FROM THE PRIORITY WORD LIST	
Teacher Activities before Instruction	
What the Teacher Does	**Comments on the Activity**
Prepares materials: The teacher gives each student a set of approximately 15 or 20 words to be practiced, some of which are words that are already known well by the student. Each word is neatly written on its own index card. All of the cards are the same color, as is the ink. When not in use, the word cards are organized in a labeled envelope or plastic bag. Prior to beginning the lesson, the teacher shuffles the student's cards so that readers don't rely on order as a clue to word identification.	Using similar materials for all the words encourages the student to attend to the words and the letters in the words and not to other clues. Shuffling the words ensures that word order doesn't serve as a clue for word identification.
Selects text: The teacher selects any text that will provide opportunities for practice of some high-frequency words. Students should be able to read selected texts at a fairly high level of accuracy. Students with very limited ability to read/identify high-frequency words may benefit from opportunities to read texts in which the words occur with unusually high frequency (such as *The Short Books* for students at a very early point in development or the books by Hillert or Hajdusiewicz mentioned previously).	The purpose of high-frequency word practice is to provide opportunities for students to become fluent in identifying high-frequency words. This will enable them to more effectively read and comprehend texts.
Materials needed: 1. Index cards (all of the same color) 2. Marker (always use the same color) 3. Paper or dry-erase board and markers for student to use to write the words 4. Labeled plastic bag or envelope to hold each student's cards after instruction 5. Priority Word List 6. Books of appropriate level of challenge (that can be read with 90–95% accuracy)	
Instruction Step 1: Your Pile/My Pile Practice (index cards with the words the student is practicing and some known words; keep dry-erase board and marker nearby)	
What the Teacher Says and Does	**Comments on the Activity**
Provides practice: "Now you get to practice your **high-frequency words** by playing Your Pile/My Pile. "I'll show you your high-frequency words one at a time, and if you read a word accurately and automatically (that means quickly), the word will go in your pile. If you hesitate or don't know the word, then it will go in my pile so we can practice it more."	Repeatedly reading the words correctly will allow the words to become a part of the reader's sight vocabulary.

(continued)

FIGURE 7.4. Sample consolidation lesson for high-frequency words.

Provides immediate feedback: The teacher names each word after the student attempts it.	When the teacher names the word, he or she provides an additional opportunity for the student to see the word and hear its pronunciation and, in instances when the word has been misidentified, the teacher is able to correct the error immediately.
Collects data: The teacher takes cards containing words that the student reads accurately and quickly and places them in the student's pile. Cards on which the student hesitates, self-corrects, or misidentifies the word are placed in the teacher's pile.	Recording what the student does as he or she does it helps the teacher decide: • What feedback to provide on the spot • The level of support or challenge to provide in follow-up lessons • How readily students are acquiring knowledge of high-frequency words
Provides feedback: "You thought carefully about the word _____ [name the high-frequency word] before you read it. Reading these words accurately will help you to remember them." "Because you did need to think about it, though, we'll put it in my pile—because you can still use more practice with it."	Naming the approaches that students are using successfully will increase the frequency of the behavior.
Corrects errors: "Remember that it's important to look carefully at all of the letters in the high-frequency word so that you read it accurately and remember it when you see it in the future."	Providing corrective feedback helps students to refine their approach to word learning.
Repeats Your Pile/My Pile: The teacher repeats the game if several words are in the teacher's pile following the first pass through the cards. The teacher plays Your Pile/My Pile for another round or more if time permits—using only the words in the teacher's pile. As in previous rounds, the words that the student identifies quickly and accurately go in the student's pile.	An important goal of Your Pile/My Pile is to promote automaticity. In a second pass (and subsequent pass if time permits) through the words, the student will have more opportunity to gain fluency.
Provides additional practice: The teacher repeats the game again if only one or two words end up in the teacher's pile. "_____ [word] needs a little more practice. Write _____ by saying it, saying the letters as you write it, and saying _____ again three times. Doing this thinking will help you learn the high-frequency word _____."	Written practice with high-frequency words provides the student with (several) opportunities to study the words and their internal structure. Writing them, naming the letters, and naming the word helps the student to establish a strong bond between the orthographic representation of the word and the name of the word.
Links: "Learning these words is going to help you as you read for understanding."	When the purpose for instruction is clearly stated by the teacher, it makes it easier for students to see how learning the high-frequency words will help them as they read.

(continued)

FIGURE 7.4. *(continued)*

After Instruction, to Prepare for the Next Lesson
(Priority Word List)

Instruction Step 2: Application
(text)

What the Teacher Says and Does	Comments on the Activity
Links: "Now you get to read a book. I'm sure you'll see many of your high-frequency words today while you are reading!"	The purpose of high-frequency word practice is to provide students with sight vocabulary that they can use when reading text. Often the book students read following this lesson will be a reread that they will engage in while the teacher provides lessons for other individuals in the group.
Records data: After the activity is finished, the teacher records a ✓ (checkmark) on the back of each of the cards that went into the student's pile on the **first** exposure during the activity: a ^ (caret) if the word is identified accurately but not quickly, and a – (minus) if the word was not identified accurately. [The latter markings can be made as the teacher puts the cards in his or her pile. The checkmarks can be added after the lesson.] This information is also summarized on the Priority Word List (Figure 7.2).	Keeping track of words that students are able to read quickly and accurately the first time they see them in a session helps the teacher to determine whether the words need additional practice in future lessons.
Reviews data and plans instruction: The teacher reviews the data collected about the student's fluency and accuracy, and decides upon next steps.	Most students will read the newly taught words accurately during the Your Pile/My Pile activity. Continue to provide practice with these words until the student has read each word fluently on the **first** exposure six times—meaning the student has six checkmarks on the back of the word card. Note that students will vary in terms of how many times they need to see words in this type of activity before it can be determined that they know the word well enough that it can be removed from the practice set (i.e., retired). So the criterion of six checkmarks can serve as a starting point and be adjusted across time for individual students. If a student is successful in quickly and accurately identifying his or her new priority words on the first exposure in three

(continued)

FIGURE 7.4. *(continued)*

	sessions in a row, three new priority words can be introduced. A few students will read the new words inaccurately during the Your Pile/My Pile activity. Carefully monitor these students' success in subsequent lessons, and consider reducing the number of new words that are introduced and increasing the number of practice sessions the student has.
Provides consolidation lessons: The teacher follows this template for subsequent consolidation lessons.	Repeatedly reading the words correctly will allow them to become a part of the reader's sight vocabulary.
Teaches new priority words: The teacher follows the format of the lesson in Figure 7.3 for teaching new words when students are ready.	Students need to have all of the high-frequency words in their sight vocabularies to be successful readers.

FIGURE 7.4. *(continued)*

We have found that, for most students, when the student has successfully read the words in three consecutive lessons, three more new words can be taught and added to the set of words the student is practicing. The number of words a student is practicing at one time should be a function of his or her performance on the initial high-frequency word assessment. In our experience, students who did not complete the first 100 words of the assessment were most successful if they practiced a relatively small set of 10–12 words. Students who ended the assessment on the second 100 words were able to practice 12–15 words; students who ended in the final 100 words practiced 15–20 words at a time.

Monitoring Students' Progress

Students' progress in learning the high-frequency words should be recorded in three ways. First, for any word that the student reads accurately and fluently during the initial practice with the words, the teacher can place a ✓ (checkmark) on the back of the card containing that word. A symbol such as ^ (caret) can be recorded if the word is recognized accurately but not quickly and a – (minus) if the word is not accurately identified or identified inaccurately and then self-corrected.

Second, this information should also be transferred to the Priority Word List (Figure 7.2), in the column used to record the words currently being practiced. Note that the list encourages the teacher to also record the date, so that the teacher knows how long a student has been practicing each word. This provides the teacher with an overview of the student's progress and an indication of whether too many or too few words are being practiced at a given point in time.

The teacher should also be alert to the student's accuracy in reading his or her high-frequency words in context. If a student is not reading a word known in isolation correctly in context, this may suggest a need for additional practice with the word.

Once a word has become automatic, the teacher can retire the word from practice, and indicate this by checking the "Retired" column on the Priority Word List. Retired words should be reviewed on occasion, by including them as known words in the student's set of words used for high-frequency word learning/practice. And if a student demonstrates uncertainty on words previously considered to be "known," those words should be included in future practice activities.

Where Do High-Frequency Words Go When They Retire?

When a word is retired from the priority list, it should be added to the Words We Know and Use chart (Figure 7.6) discussed in the "Spelling" section on pp. 154–155.

Adding Words to the Priority Word List

As students demonstrate mastery of the words initially included on their Priority Word List, the high-frequency word assessment can be revisited, and additional words can be added to the list. Students acquire the ability to read words in a variety of ways and many words are learned (if the student has developed an effective self-teaching mechanism) without explicit instruction. Therefore, it should not be assumed that words not previously known need to be explicitly taught. Indeed, it can be useful for teachers to make brief notes about words that pose difficulties for students as they engage in reading connected text and to determine which of those words should be given priority for instruction based on their position on the high-frequency word list.[2] Introduction of and practice with new words should follow the procedures outlined in Figure 7.3.

Responding to Students Who Learn High-Frequency Words Slowly

The instructional procedures described in this chapter, and ample time spent reading text of appropriate difficulty, will allow most readers who have limited reading accuracy to add high-frequency words to their sight vocabularies. Some students may progress more slowly. For students who repeatedly make errors with even

---

[2]Although it is a bit time-consuming, this can be facilitated by creating an alphabetical listing of the high-frequency word list and including the numerical position (e.g., 1–300) of the word on the high-frequency word list.

one of the high-frequency words, it is important to stop and think about why that might be happening, and to try a different approach. The more often a student reads a word incorrectly, the harder it will be for the student to add the word to his or her sight vocabulary. For these students, listed below are some suggestions that teachers have found helpful.

• Some students need more information about the utility of the high-frequency words before they are willing to invest effort in careful practice. For these students, it may be helpful to highlight the high-frequency words (using removable highlighter tape) in a text that the student is reading, as illustrated in Figure 7.5. Showing the student just how many words in a text can be read with knowledge of the high-frequency words may provide the student with motivation to learn the words.

• Sometimes students see fluency as the goal, and fail to understand that accuracy is necessary before fluency can be attained. This misunderstanding can be corrected if the teacher models, thinking aloud, the kind of careful thinking students need to do as they are learning the words. Then, before each practice session, the teacher can remind students that accuracy comes first, then fluency.

FIGURE 7.5. Student text with high-frequency words highlighted.

- Sometimes the source of the student's confusion is the word list he or she is practicing. If it contains several words that the student consistently confuses (e.g., *was, where, were*), all but one of the words should be removed from the list. The teacher can then reflect on the source of confusion (in our example, it seems as if the student is attending to only the first letter and perhaps the abstract nature of the words) and provide modeling and reminders designed to make the student more accurate.

- If the word that is confusing a student is one of the abstract function words, it may be helpful to provide the student with the word in the context of a sentence. The function word can be practiced in context, and then the sentence removed, and the word practiced in isolation.

Spelling

While this book does not address spelling instruction in great detail, high-frequency words will be used often by writers, and the accuracy with which students spell them will influence students' ability to read them with automaticity. As students are learning to identify and read the high-frequency words, it is helpful to set the expectation that these words, which occur so frequently in what students read, will also be beneficial in their writing. If students spell the high-frequency words in unconventional ways, their attempted spellings are likely to interfere with the development of fluency with identifying those words when reading. Further, it will be helpful to students to write these words accurately and automatically so that they can focus more on constructing their message when they write.

To assist students in spelling the high-frequency words conventionally, it is useful to create a Words We Know and Use chart such as the one shown in Figure 7.6. As illustrated, the chart can be attached to the sides of a file folder so that it can stand on the work space and students can readily access it. The website for this book (see the box at the end of the table of contents) contains a document that teachers can use to make such a chart.

Words that the students can read with automaticity but do not always spell conventionally can be placed on this chart for reference. In addition, words that are retired from the Priority Word List can be added to the chart as they are retired.

Students should be shown how to use the chart as a tool that enables them to spell conventionally when they write and should be reminded to reference the chart as needed. Telling students that they *get to* use the chart rather than telling them that they *have to* will make using conventional spelling seem like a bit of a privilege (at least for some students).

This chart is similar to a "word wall" but includes only the words that the student can read readily and, as a result, the student can rely on the chart for conventional spelling as he or she writes.

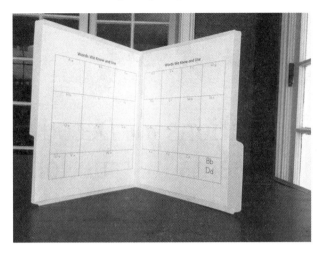

FIGURE 7.6. Words We Know and Use chart.

As students gain knowledge of high-frequency words and the chart illustrated in Figure 7.6 becomes overcrowded, students can be provided with resources such as *Words I Use When I Write* (Trisler & Cardiel, 1989) or *The Quick-Word Handbook for Beginning Writers* (Sitton & Forest, 1992). Making these resources readily available to students who struggle with conventional spelling and communicating that they *get to* use them to help them remember the spellings of words have, at least anecdotally, proven to be helpful in supporting students' spelling and writing.

Summary

In this chapter, we described how teachers can help students to learn to identify and spell high-frequency words. These words make up a large portion of the text students will read and write, so learning these words can support reading accuracy, comprehension, and composition. Knowledge of these words also supports students' ability to identify and learn words through interactive strategy use. Instructional time allocated to efficiently teaching and practicing these words is well invested.

In the next two chapters, we address another source of knowledge that will also support word learning, reading accuracy, and comprehension: knowledge of decoding elements.

CHAPTER 8

Foundations for Decoding Elements Instruction

STUDENT GOAL

Students will learn information about decoding elements that they can use for strategic word identification to support word learning and, thereby, reading comprehension.

Over the course of our research projects, we have learned that many teachers do not have the complete knowledge of the workings of the alphabet code and the English writing system needed to provide the comprehensive and responsive instruction that is crucial for students in need of intervention in the middle and upper grades. This chapter, therefore, departs from the organization and focus of the last several chapters. In the present chapter, we focus on developing greater expertise related to decoding elements among intervention teachers, thereby enabling them to (more) effectively plan and deliver responsive instruction related to the decoding elements that intermediate and middle grade readers may still need to learn. Specifically, the goal is for teachers to gain greater insight into the elements and complexity of learning about the alphabetic, orthographic, and morphological nature of written language. The development of this knowledge is, of course, in the service of enhancing students' learning about decoding elements, which they can use for strategic word identification to support word learning and reading comprehension. Instruction designed to help students accomplish this goal is the focus of Chapter 9.

Because this book is focused on instruction for intermediate and middle grade readers, this chapter and the next do not address some of the basic decoding-related skills that most of these students will have already learned. Thus, this book does not address phonemic awareness, or *initial* instruction of the sounds of consonants, consonant digraphs, short and long vowels, or word families/phonograms. A few intermediate and middle grade readers experience difficulty with such skills and, when they do, obviously, these skills need to be retaught and practiced. Instructional activities designed to promote these skills that typically develop in the early primary grades can be found in Chapters 5 and 8–10 of our companion book *Early Intervention for Reading Difficulties: The Interactive Strategies Approach* (Scanlon et al., 2017). Teachers who encounter students who need instruction in these basic decoding elements can consult that book.

What Are Decoding Elements, and Why Are They Important?

In this book, we use the term *decoding elements* to refer to letters and letter groups that are often used to represent a sound or group of sounds. Some intermediate and middle grade readers in intervention have a limited sight vocabulary (i.e., words that they identify effortlessly and in all contexts) because they have not acquired or consolidated sufficient knowledge of decoding elements to enable them to effectively puzzle through, and ultimately learn, the unfamiliar words they encounter while reading. There is ample research evidence and wide consensus that having a limited sight vocabulary prevents a reader from understanding and enjoying text (Adams, 2011; Foorman et al., 2016; Gough & Tunmer, 1986). As we described in Chapter 4, to fully learn a word, readers must carefully attend to the letters in the word, and associate that spelling with their memory of the word's pronunciation. Knowledge about decoding elements *helps readers to fully and efficiently analyze and learn words.*

In this book, we argue that, in addition to learning decoding elements, students must be taught to use their decoding knowledge strategically. Chapters 5 and 6 discuss word identification strategy instruction and detail word identification strategies that students can use to develop their sight vocabulary and comprehension. Effective use of these word identification strategies can lead to (rapid) growth in the ability to automatically identify previously unfamiliar printed words; this in turn supports reading comprehension. Decoding elements are important because they can *support the development and enable the use of the code-based word identification strategies.* Therefore, it is helpful if the instruction of decoding elements and word identification strategies are carefully integrated.

The decoding elements instruction described in Chapter 9 includes more than the sounds made by single letters. This is because letter-by-letter processing of longer words is demanding and inefficient. There is evidence to suggest that, with experience, developing readers become able to "see" groups of letters (e.g., *-ing*) or little words (e.g., *ant*) and to connect these to their spoken representations (Adams, 1990). Attending to these larger spelling patterns (rather than individual letters) reduces the demands on the reader's working memory and makes it easier for the reader to learn longer words (Ehri, 2005a, 2014). Thus, to use Ehri's (2014) example, a proficient reader would form connections between the spellings and the sounds of the syllables in a word like *ex-cell-ent* rather than mapping each letter to its corresponding phoneme. Learning to read spelling patterns that are irregular at the letter level, but that correspond to sound in a predictable way at the pattern level (e.g., *-ight, -tion*), may be particularly useful (Ziegler & Goswami, 2005). Of course, even these spelling patterns must first be analyzed letter by letter when the patterns are first encountered, in order for the pattern to be learned accurately (Gaskins, Ehri, Cress, O'Hara, & Donnelly, 1996). Readers need to learn, for example, that the spelling pattern *-tion,* when spoken, is typically pronounced as /shun/.

Ultimately, it is important for readers to learn that words containing the same sound pattern often share the same spelling pattern, and vice versa. When readers learn a number of common spelling patterns and have learned how spelling patterns can be generalized, they will be better prepared to efficiently analyze and identify words that they do not immediately recognize, and they will also be more strategic in their attempts to spell words.

KEEP IN MIND   The more reading students do, the more opportunity they will have to learn about the pronunciations of recurrent spelling patterns, which will, in turn, help them to become more efficient word solvers.

Understanding the Challenges of Developing Skill with the Alphabetic Code and the English Writing System

The Challenges of Some Letter–Sound and Pattern–Sound Relationships

In the next sections, we address some of the challenges posed in learning the sounds that letters and letter groups/spelling patterns represent. These challenges may be sources of difficulty for readers in intervention. If teachers better understand these challenges, they can better anticipate the level of difficulty that a word may pose to a reader and they will be better prepared to offer feedback and guidance that moves the reader forward.

Learning Challenges Posed by Consonants

Some Consonants Are Similar in the Way They Look, in the Sounds They Represent, and/or in the Names of the Letters

Most intermediate and middle grade readers know the sounds represented by the single consonants. An apparent exception is knowledge of the sounds associated with the lower-case letters *b* and *d* and, for some students, *p*. However, research

Terminology

Consonants and vowels play different roles in the English writing system. For example, every word—and in fact, every syllable—contains one and only one vowel sound. In contrast, a word or syllable can contain no consonants (e.g., the words *I* and *a*) or one or more consonants (e.g., *me, river, shriek*). Sometimes, students do not have labels for these two classes of letters and, as a result, our instruction can inadvertently confuse them. For example, when a teacher asks, "What vowel sound do you hear in the word *tape*?" if the student doesn't know what a vowel is, his or her answer will be, at best, random. Asking students, "Which letters are vowels?" will help the teacher to quickly determine whether students have the needed knowledge. And if not, simply telling them that *a, e, i, o, u,* and sometimes *y* are vowels and that all the other letters are consonants, and repeatedly doing so if need be, can help to avoid some potentially confusing and unproductive instructional interactions that might otherwise occur in relation to decoding elements.

has clearly demonstrated that this apparent exception is *not* due to limited knowledge of the letter–sound relationships for these letters (see Vellutino, 1987) but rather is due to the difficulty some children have in remembering which of the letters is the *b*, which is the *d*, and so on. The reason for this confusion is simple: The lower-case letters are identical in appearance except for their orientation, and their names have a strong phonological similarity in that the letter names rhyme (*bee, dee,* and *pee*). The fact that there are two sources of similarity for these letters probably explains why these letters are more often confused by students than are other letters that bear a comparable degree of visual similarity but whose names are not at all similar to each other (e.g., *n/u, M/W*).

KEEP IN MIND Students who confuse letters like *b* and *d* do so because they cannot remember which letter is which. Such confusions *do not* indicate a problem with visual perception as was once widely believed. Students with reading difficulties do not see the letters incorrectly—they simply do not reliably remember which letter is called by which name (Vellutino, 1987). This confusion generally begins in the early primary grades when students are learning about the names of the letters of the alphabet. The confusion arises because, until they begin to learn about print, most objects that children encounter are called by the same name regardless of how the object is oriented in space (e.g., a cup goes by the same name regardless of the angle from which it is viewed). Children who are accustomed to ignoring orientation as a distinguishing feature will sometimes have a hard time remembering to attend to it as they are learning letter names. As a result, they will sometimes call a *b* a *d* and vice versa. The more often they experience this confusion, the harder it will be for them to overcome their confusion because they are, essentially, practicing their errors. By the time they reach the intermediate and middle school grades, students who are still confusing these letters have "practiced" their mistakes for years and are likely to have considerable difficulty overcoming their confusion. (See Figure 9.2 in the next chapter for a useful resource that can help students to overcome this confusion.)

Another source of potential confusion for readers are letters that represent very similar sounds. For example, the sounds represented by the letters *b* and *p*, *d* and *t*, *f* and *v*, and hard *g* (as in *goat*) and *k* differ only minimally. The mouth movements used to form these sounds are identical with the only difference between the members of each pair being that for one member of the pair, the vocal cords vibrate during pronunciation, while for the other member of the pair, there is no vibration of the vocal cords. As a result of the similarities between these pairs of sounds, older readers sometimes substitute one sound/letter for the other member of the pair. This source of confusion is often most evident in their writing and is compounded by the fact that in everyday spoken English the distinctions made in writing are not always evident in speech. For example, a student who does not yet know the conventional spelling for a word like *little* is likely to spell the word with one or two *d*'s used to represent the second consonant sound—partly because that is the way that most people pronounce the word, but also because there is very little difference in the sound of *liddle* versus *little*.

Voiced and Unvoiced Consonant Sounds

When the vocal cords vibrate during the pronunciation of a sound, the sound is referred to as a *voiced* sound. Letters for which the vocal chords vibrate during pronunciation of the letter's sound include *b*, *d*, *v*, and hard *g*. If the vocal cords do not vibrate, the sounds are said to be unvoiced. The sounds for *p*, *t*, *f*, and *k* are unvoiced.

Sometimes Two Consonants Together Represent a Single Sound (Digraphs)

When two letters together represent a single sound, the letter combination is called a digraph. Consonant digraphs include *th*, *sh*, *ch*, *wh*, *ck*, *ph*, and *gh*. For many digraphs, none of the letters in the digraph represent their most common sound (e.g., in *th*, neither the /t/ nor the /h/ sounds are heard). The digraphs *th*, *sh*, *ch*, *ck*, and *wh* occur more frequently and are often known by intermediate and middle grade students in intervention. The less common *ph* and *gh* may require brief instruction. In instruction, digraphs are taught as individual decoding elements. A source of potential confusion for intervention students is the pronunciation of the *th* digraph—which actually represents two different phonemes—one that is voiced (as in the word *this*) and one that is unvoiced (as in the word *thing*).

Some Consonants Are More Challenging to Blend

In a consonant blend, the sounds of two or three consonants are blended together but the individual sounds of each of the consonants are still at least somewhat discernible (*cl, cr, bl, br, fr, scr, sm,* etc.). For this reason, in the approach we advocate, the blends are not taught as units, but rather, students are taught a process that uses the reader's knowledge of the sound made by the individual letters in the blend. We view this as a more efficient approach to teaching about consonant blends—rather than teaching about the many, many different consonant blends that appear in printed English—as we only need to teach students a process for blending consonant sounds they already know.

However, it is important to note that some blends are more difficult than others, so students may struggle with some, but not all, words containing blends. It is easier to teach about and to learn to read consonant blends that comprise sounds that can be elongated (stretched) without distortion (e.g., *s, m, n, f, r, l*) than to teach about and learn to read blends that include consonants that cannot be stretched, also known as the stop consonants (e.g., *p, b, d,* and *t*, as well as the hard *c* in *cat* and the hard *g* in *goat*).

For instructional purposes, it is easier to illustrate the process of consonant blending when the teacher can elongate each of the sounds in the blend (e.g., /fffffff/–/llllll/–/ame/) with the /fffff/ and /lllll/ each articulated as one continuous sound (/fffffllll/) than it is to illustrate the process when one of the sounds in the blend cannot be elongated (e.g., /bl/, /dr/, /gl/). This is so because, in saying the sound of a stop consonant in isolation, one often adds /uh/ so /b/ is pronounced /buh/. Thus, for example, when a teacher models the decoding of a *bl* blend, what the student will hear is /buh/–/lll/, which, if the student attempted to blend the individually articulated sounds, would sound like /buhl/ rather than /bl/ for the *bl* blend.

Thus, consonant blends that have a combination of stretchable and stop consonants (*pr, br, bl, cl, sc, st,* etc.) are somewhat more challenging because it is difficult to draw the student's attention to the stop consonant portion of the blend. Some of the most challenging consonant blends in the initial position are *dr* and *tr*. *Dr* and *tr* are challenging because the stop consonants *d* and *t* are not easily noticed in these blends due to coarticulation. Because of the way that the mouth naturally positions itself to make the /r/ sound as it is articulating the /d/ or /t/ sound, the sounds of the *d* and *t* are distorted. This is why a student might spell the word *drip* with the letters *jrip* or *jip* or spell *truck* with the letters *chrk*.

> ### Nasal Consonants
>
> A nasal consonant is one in which the air flows through the nose (nasal passage) instead of through the mouth. The sounds for *m* and *n* are nasal consonants; the letters *ng* together also represent a single, nasal sound. In pronouncing these sounds, the air flows through the nose, not the mouth.

Some of the most challenging consonant blends in the final position are those in which a nasal consonant (*m* or *n*) precedes a stop consonant (e.g., *nt*, *mp*). These are difficult because students use changes in mouth position as clues to the sounds in words they are attempting to spell. The subtle changes in mouth position when the nasal consonant is present or absent are hard to detect. This can be illustrated by saying the words *wet* and *went* or *rap* and *ramp* and carefully attending to the various parts of the mouth that are involved in the pronunciation. Most would agree that the mouth movements for each pair of words are nearly identical.

Some Consonants and Digraphs Represent More Than One Sound

Although most consonants and consonant digraphs represent just one sound, some represent more than one sound, or one sound and a silent pronunciation. When readers encounter these consonants or consonant digraphs, they need to have knowledge of both pronunciations, and to learn to be flexible, trying both pronunciations for the letter or letter combination until they identify a real word that makes sense in the context in which it was encountered.

- *g* and *c:* Each of these letters can represent two sounds—a "soft" sound as in *ginger* or *city*, or a "hard" sound as in *gum* or *cat*. The soft sound is most likely to occur when the letter *c* or *g* is followed by an *e* or an *i*. The hard sound is most likely to occur when the *g* or *c* is followed by the letters *a*, *o*, *u*, or another consonant.
- *s:* The letter *s* often is pronounced as /zzz/ (as in *nose, is, was, tables*).
- *wr:* When *w* is followed by *r* at the beginning of a word, the *w* is silent.
- *kn:* When *k* is followed by *n* at the beginning of a word, the *k* is silent.
- *pn:* When *p* is followed by *n* at the beginning of a word, the *p* is silent.
- *h:* The *h* is silent in some words (as in *hour* and *what*, at least in the way that most Americans pronounce these words).
- *gh:* The digraph *gh* is often silent (as in *light, weigh, though,* and *caught*) and only rarely represents the /f/ sound as in *laugh* and *tough*. More rarely still, *gh* represents the hard-*g* sound as at the beginning of the word *ghost*.
- *ch:* The *ch* combination is pronounced /k/ in words like *character, ache,* or *chord*.

Learning Challenges Posed by Vowels

Knowledge about the vowels can be helpful to teachers in understanding and responding to and/or preventing vowel errors that students may make. This knowledge will also support appropriate instructional decision making.

Teacher Terminology versus Teaching Terminology

In order to communicate clearly with teachers, this book refers to "long vowel sounds" and "short vowel sounds," as well as other labels for letter combinations and sounds (e.g., blend). Similarly, breves are used to represent the short vowel sound (*ă* as in *apple*) and macrons are used to represent the long vowel sound (*ā* as in *apron*). It is important to remember that students do not need to learn these labels or symbols. If students are already familiar with these terms, it is fine to use them, but learning these labels is not likely to help students learn to read. Therefore, instructional time should not be devoted to this objective. Rather, it is sufficient to refer to "the two sounds that the letter makes," or to /ă/ and /ā/.

Coarticulation

Within a word or syllable, the sound of the vowel can be influenced (altered) by the surrounding consonants. For example, the first vowel sound in *cattle* is quite different from the first vowel sound in the word *candle*. However, both of these vowel sounds are represented by the same letter in print.

Short Vowel Sounds Are Not Included in the Vowel Letters' Names

For most consonant letters, the name of the letter provides information about the letter's sound. For example, the name of the letter *b* is composed of the phonemes /b/ and /ē/ and the name of the letter *f* is composed of the phonemes /ĕ/ and /f/. As students are learning to read, they often use the names of letters to help them recall their sounds (Treiman, Sotak, & Bowman, 2001).

Unfortunately, for the short vowels, this link does not work. In fact, for the short vowel sounds, the sound is often in the name of a vowel letter that is *different* from the one that is conventionally used to represent that sound in print. Students who rely on the vowel sound found in the vowel letter's name often misread and/ or misspell words containing short vowel sounds. This confusion is most often evident in their spellings.

Teachers are often insensitive to the relationships between letter names and letter sounds because their knowledge of conventional letter–sound relationships is so automatic. As a result of this insensitivity, teachers may provide students with feedback that does not help them to effectively learn the conventional relationships. For example, a student who is struggling with vowels might spell the word *trick* with the letters *t-r-e-k* because the /ĭ/ sound can be discerned at the beginning of the name of the letter *e*. The teacher, however, might assume that a student who represents the short-*i* sound with the letter *e* had not effectively isolated the vowel sound in the word and might provide feedback that is based on this assumption. For example, the teacher might say, "Listen to the vowel sound in *triiiiick*—/ĭĭĭĭ/." More appropriate feedback would recognize that the student had segmented the word appropriately but had not selected the conventional letter to spell the vowel sound.

> "You've noticed that /ĭĭĭĭ/ sound, you just need to remember that we use the letter *i* to spell that sound. Remember, when you are uncertain about what letter to use for a vowel sound you can just check your key words." [These are provided in Figure 9.3.]

Figure 8.1 lists the typical substitutions/confusions that occur for students who rely on vowel letter names to help them to represent short vowel sounds. To gain some insight into how students make these errors, teachers might try the following: Say the sound of the vowel in the middle column of the chart (not the word—just the vowel sound it contains). While saying the vowel sound, begin to say the name of the letter in the right-hand column. Do not stop—glide right from the short vowel sound into saying the name of the letter. *Do this out loud.* In doing this, most people will notice that the sound of the vowel in the center column occurs at the beginning of the name of the letter in the right-hand column.

The left-hand column in the chart has the letter that is usually used to spell the short vowel sound (i.e., /ĕ/ is spelled with an *E*). If one tries to glide from the sound of the vowel in the middle column into the name of the letter in the left-hand column, the glide will not work. That's because the short sound of the vowel is not contained in the name of the vowel.

The point of this rather lengthy explanation of vowel spelling errors is to alert teachers to the reasons why readers may make certain types of vowel spelling errors so that the feedback that is provided when such errors occur is productive. In our experience, it takes most teachers some concentrated practice in order to get to the point where they readily recognize why a student spells a word in a

Letter Used in Conventional Spelling	Short Vowel Sound as Heard in . . .	Vowel Letter Name Containing That Sound
E	ĕ as in *pet*	A
I	ĭ as in *pit*	E
O	ŏ as in *pot*	I
U	ŭ as in *putt*	O

FIGURE 8.1. Sounds heard in the names of the vowels.

particular way and, as noted above, in the absence of this practice and resulting insights into the student's thinking, teachers run the risk of providing feedback that undermines the student's confidence. Thus, for example, if a student spells the word *crop* as *crip*, this error is likely due to the fact that the short-*o* sound can be heard at the beginning of the name of the letter *i*. However, most teachers, in our experience, would interpret this misspelling as being the result of problems with isolating the vowel sound in the word *crop* and might attempt to assist the student in isolating that sound. A more useful response to the student would be to notice that the vowel sound was accurately isolated but that the student did not use the conventional spelling for that sound. Thus, the teacher might say, "You figured out what the vowel sound is in the word *crop*, but we need to think more about how that sound would be spelled. Let's look at our vowel key words and think about which one of them starts with the vowel sound that you hear in the word *crop*."

Rules Are Not Reliable

Most of the "rules" for representing vowel sounds in print are quite unreliable. For example, the "silent-*e* rule" works only about 50% of the time (Clymer, 1963)—so it shouldn't be portrayed as a "rule." However, it is a useful clue or generalization related to the pronunciation of a vowel sound and, as we discuss in Chapter 9, should be explicitly taught (and practiced) if readers do not seem secure in their knowledge of the potential role of a final *e*.

Complex Ways of Representing Sounds

The printed representations of many vowel sounds are complex. It often takes more than one letter to represent the vowel sound.

- Sometimes the two letters that represent the vowel sound are separated by one or more consonants as in *snake, paste,* and *fife.*
- Sometimes the same letters represent more than one vowel sound (e.g., the *ea* part is used to represent the /ē/ in *bead,* the /ĕ/ in *bread,* and the /ā/ in *great*).
- Moreover, sometimes the same vowel sound is spelled in many different ways; all of these words have the /ā/ sound—*cake, great, weigh, play, rain, prey,* and *ballet*).
- Sometimes neither of the letters that combine to represent a vowel sound are related to the vowel sound they represent (e.g., the *oi* in *join,* *oy* in *toy,* *ei* in *vein,* and *ey* in *prey*).
- Sometimes it is hard to discern a vowel sound at all—as in some of the *r*-controlled vowels (e.g., *ar, er, ir,* and *ur*).
- Sometimes vowel digraphs commonly represent two distinct sounds (e.g., *oo* in *boot* and *look* and *ow* in *cow* and *snow*).

Teachers need to be alert to the fact that their proficiency with negotiating the complexity of written English will sometimes make it difficult for them to understand the challenges that the writing system poses for those who are less proficient.

Useful Knowledge for Reading Multisyllabic Words

Older readers in intervention are apt to be challenged by multisyllabic words. Two of the word identification strategies discussed in Chapters 5 and 6 will help them to analyze multisyllabic words: "Look for parts you know" and "Break the word into smaller parts." In this section, we discuss some of the complexities that arise in efforts to puzzle through and identify words that are composed of multiple syllables. In Chapter 9, we offer suggestions for instruction to guide readers' attempts at solving such words.

The Schwa Sound

In multisyllabic words, there is typically only one syllable that is stressed and the vowel in the stressed syllable tends to be pronounced in accord with the more predictable phonics generalizations. For example, in the word *democracy,* the MOC is stressed and the short-*o* sound is clearly articulated. However, the vowel sounds in the first and third unstressed syllables are pronounced as schwa sounds (*duh-MOC-cruh-see*). This underarticulation of the vowels in unstressed syllables can be confusing for readers who are attempting to apply the phonics generalizations that have been explicitly taught and practiced.

Common Prefixes and Derivational Suffixes

Chapter 6 provides guidance on teaching the inflectional suffixes (*-ed, -ing,* and *-es*). Identifying words with these suffixes is best addressed through use of the strategy "Break the word into smaller parts." When using this strategy, students temporarily ignore the suffix, decode the root word, and then add the suffix back on. This approach can work with other types of affixes (e.g., prefixes and suffixes) too, as described in Chapter 9.

The prefixes *un-* (meaning *not*) and *re-* (meaning *do again*) are the two most common prefixes and so are useful to teach. Other prefixes that might be considered for instruction because of their frequency include *in-, im-, dis-, en-,* and *non-*. Prefixes such as these have an easily defined and explained meaning. While these prefixes are usefully taught as decoding units, the instructional conversation should include a discussion of the impact that prefixes have on word meaning as well.

Derivational suffixes are suffixes that, when added to a root word, change the word's meaning and often its part of speech. For example, adding *less* to the word *hope* changes the verb to an adjective (*hope–hopeless*) and adding *ness* changes an adjective to a noun (*happy–happiness*). Most proficient readers are not consciously aware of how these suffixes influence changes in parts of speech (and, in our experience, many adults who are proficient readers are not even very aware of what the distinctions are between and among certain parts of speech). Therefore, for students who are experiencing difficulty with word identification, we have not made a point of focusing on changes to the part of speech but have instead provided brief explanations of the meaning changes resulting from the addition of a suffix as sometimes it is hard to define a suffix in isolation. Among the most common derivational suffixes are *er, or, tion, ment, able/ible, ness, less,* and *ful* (Fry & Kress, 2006).[1] These can be taught as decoding elements as well as units that change the meaning of the root word.

Summary

In this chapter, we attempted to make teachers more aware of some of the obstacles that readers face as they are puzzling through words written in English. Our goal was to enable teachers to better understand what readers might find challenging, so that they can more readily take the perspective of readers who are challenged by our formidable writing system and thereby better support readers as they learn to use knowledge of the sounds represented by letters and letter groups. In the next chapter, we detail an approach to instruction that we have found to be useful in helping readers to build their knowledge of decoding elements.

---

[1] A Google search using the search terms *suffix* or *suffixes* will yield lists of suffixes, their meanings, and examples of words that include those suffixes.

CHAPTER 9

Observing and Teaching Use of Decoding Elements

STUDENT GOAL

As in Chapter 8, students will learn decoding elements that will enable strategic word identification to support comprehension.

Readers in the intermediate and middle grades have generally been taught the sounds represented by the consonants, the long and short vowel sounds, and common phonograms (word families). However, some of these readers may have gaps in their knowledge such that, for some or all of these decoding elements, they do not accurately and fluently access the appropriate phonological representations. This chapter addresses assessment and instruction that will enable intermediate and middle grade readers to consolidate their knowledge of challenging consonants, the long and short vowels, and phonograms or word families. We place particular emphasis on learning to be flexible with the two sounds that each vowel represents. This chapter also addresses instruction related to vowel parts (e.g., *oi*, *ar*), the schwa sound, and prefixes and suffixes that may be unfamiliar to older readers participating in reading intervention. This chapter describes our approach to helping readers to acquire knowledge of decoding elements, and, in the case of prefixes and suffixes, meaningful elements.

Instructional Decision Making: Assessment of Readers' Decoding Knowledge

The types of difficulties that intermediate and middle grade readers experience vary considerably from student to student (Valencia, 2011). It is critical that instruction related to decoding elements be responsive to the individual student's needs, so that instructional time is not wasted in teaching skills the students have already learned or attempting to teach skills that students are not ready to learn because they do not have the foundational knowledge needed to learn the new skill(s).

The first step in planning and organizing for instruction around decoding elements is to develop a sense of what students currently know and can apply automatically. To provide an initial indication of students' knowledge of decoding elements, teachers are encouraged to use assessment tools along with notes about students' word solving during reading. The Decoding Elements Assessment and Decoding Elements Assessment Student Word Lists found on the website for this book (see the box at the end of the table of contents) were designed to help intervention teachers in our research to determine students' general level of knowledge. These documents have been revised over a period of several years based on teachers' experiences and feedback.

The assessment (and word lists) are designed to measure readers' ability to read (1) short words with long and short vowels, consonants, consonant blends, and consonant digraphs; (2) words containing vowel parts that need to be taught explicitly; and (3) longer words that can be broken into smaller parts. The assessment contains three parts, with the expectation that for many readers, only part(s) of the assessment will be needed. Of course, the teacher may choose to use another assessment that provides comparable information. Students who complete the assessment with little or no difficulty will probably not need instruction in decoding elements. Students who have difficulty with portions of the measure may need some decoding instruction.

Instructional Decision Making: Instruction to Foster Full Analysis of Words

Knowledge of the letters and letter groups used to represent sounds is necessary but not sufficient for word learning. As described in Chapter 4, words are learned only if the reader attends to all of the letters in a word (and thus the sounds they represent). Attending to the letters allows the reader to store in memory a complete representation of the word, and thus to learn words and read with greater accuracy and fluency. Beginning readers may analyze only some of the letters in words they are attempting to identify (Adams, 2011; Ehri, 2005a, 2014). If readers rely on only some letter information, they will store only partial information about the word in memory. As a result, the next time they see the word, they may have insufficient information to recall it. Such readers will often confuse words with other words that are visually similar (e.g., reading *cut* as *cat,* or *was* as *saw*).

In this book, the approach to fostering both knowledge of decoding elements and word analysis is referred to as "word building, word reading, and written spelling" (and in places shortened to Word Work). This approach has been a part of several research studies that resulted in greater reading accuracy among young children at risk for reading difficulty (Scanlon et al., 2008; Scanlon et al., 2005; Vellutino et al., 1996), as well as two studies involving older readers receiving intervention (Gelzheiser et al., 2011, 2017). We acknowledge, however, that the word-building, word-reading, and written spelling activities have always been a part of a larger intervention. The efficacy of these activities, in isolation, has not been documented, in part because of our conviction that decoding instruction is most effective if it is linked to word identification strategy instruction and opportunities to apply knowledge of newly taught decoding elements in the context of reading connected text.

Word Work encourages readers to carefully analyze both the letters and the sounds of the correspondences being learned. The goal of this analysis is to enable readers to store complete representations of the words containing given correspondences in memory. More generally, the ultimate goal is for readers to fully analyze unknown words encountered while reading, so that the representations of the words that are stored in memory are accurate, thus allowing word learning and the development of sight vocabulary, which, in turn, enables comprehension.

To develop students' ability to effectively analyze words, teachers are encouraged to model for students the process of carefully thinking about all of the sounds in a spoken word, and the letters or groups of letters that represent those sounds in the printed version of the word. This modeling can occur in the contexts of building, checking, reading, and spelling words.

A second way that teachers encourage word analysis is through the words they select for student practice. In the activity called "word building," the teacher orally presents a list of words to students, one at a time, and students analyze the sounds they hear in these words, then "build" the words using a preselected set of letter tiles. As they finish one word and start building the next one, students have to think about the part of the word that is changed. If students have built *bit,* and the next word is *bite,* they have to recognize that the beginning and ending sounds are unchanged, realize that the middle sound is different, and recall how the sound in the middle of the word *bite* could be represented in print. If students have built *bit,* and the next word is *bin,* they need to recognize what part of the word to change.

In the remainder of this section, we describe the components of Word Work in detail. We also describe how words can be selected for Word Work in a way that promotes student analysis and success.

Introducing the Process of Word Work

To begin, the teacher explains how learning the selected decoding element will help students to use a specific word-learning strategy to learn words and understand text. It should be clear to students that:

- The careful analysis they are learning to do during Word Work will help them to puzzle through the unfamiliar words they encounter while reading.
- By using their word identification strategies and carefully analyzing words, they will start to learn words as they read without having someone teach them the words.
- Learning to read a lot of words will make it easier to understand and enjoy the things they read.

KEEP IN MIND   For many learners in intervention, it takes genuine effort to learn how letters and sounds correspond in written English. Students will be more motivated to muster that effort if they see that what they are doing and learning has an authentic purpose.

Below we provide an overview of the three types of instructional activities used in the Word Work segment of an intervention session. Note that when a teacher first begins to provide instruction for a group of students, and as new and more complex aspects of the alphabetic code are introduced, the teacher would begin by modeling the kind of thinking students need to do about the selected decoding element or principle. Examples of such modeling are given later in the chapter as sample introductory lessons are provided.

Word Building

Materials

The materials needed for word building are: movable letters such as magnetic letters, letter tiles, or letters printed on card stock; a teacher list of eight to 10 preselected words; resources that illustrate key words containing the sound(s) being learned (these are described later in this chapter, along with key words that have already been explicitly taught and, hopefully, learned); and the Word Work Planning and Recording Form available on the book's website (see the box at the end of the table of contents). Figure 9.1 illustrates the letters and resources that would be used to practice the long and short vowel sounds for the letter *a*.

Student Activity

Students listen to the teacher say a word and then select the letters needed to build the word from a small set of letters provided by the teacher. They build the word by arranging the letters in the proper sequence and then check their accuracy by carefully reading the word they have built. Often, to assist themselves in analyzing the sounds in the word, students are encouraged say the word (repeatedly if need be) as they build it.

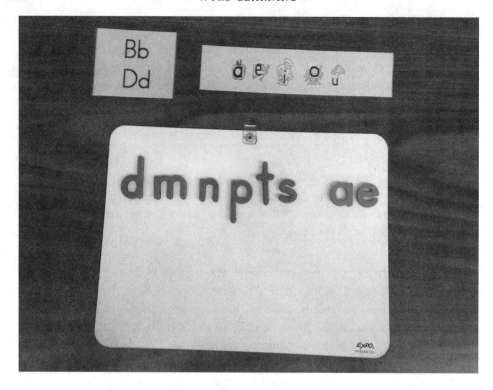

FIGURE 9.1. Letters and resources set up for a Word Work activity.

Student Thinking

In order to do this, the students must listen, think about the sounds they hear in the word, and then decide which letters represent those sounds. Students then think about the letters they have chosen, the sounds that those letters stand for, and the sequence in which those sounds occur in the word.

It's All about Student Thinking

Because teachers often have a tendency to be too helpful by doing too much of the thinking for students, in recent years we have developed the mantra "The one who does the thinking is the one who does the learning." We encourage teachers to keep this mantra in mind as they support students in these and other literacy-learning activities. While in these word-building activities teachers may be tempted to stretch out the sounds in the words to help students isolate the sounds, and while this may be appropriate at early points in instruction/practice, if students can build words only when this type of scaffold is provided, they are not becoming proficient with the process. We encourage teachers to routinely think about whether what they do supports student independence or dependence.

Supporting the Student

The teacher scaffolds this process by providing students with a small set of letters from which all the words on the day's list can be built. As students build, the teacher also provides additional support as needed, such as demonstrating how to segment the sounds in the word, reminding students to use resources, such as key words to help them remember which letter(s) represent the sounds in the spoken word, and modeling how to check words after building them.

Word Reading

Materials

The materials needed for word reading are: preselected words written on index cards, dry-erase board and marker for the teacher to write words as needed, and the Word Work Planning and Recording Form.

Student Activity

During word reading, each student reads three to four words that have been written by the teacher.

Student Thinking

In order to do this, the students must look at the letters, think about the sounds they may represent, and then blend the sounds together to form a word. This kind of analysis is the opposite of the thinking students do during word building.

Supporting the Student

Teachers may vary the level of challenge during this activity by asking individual students to read different words. Some students may benefit from the support of reading the same words they have just practiced during word building, while

---

Using Letter Tiles

The teacher may also create the words that students will read using letter tiles, as students watch (additional tiles may be needed, depending upon the words selected for reading). Doing this may help students to make the connection between the thinking done during word building and the thinking needed during word reading, and may be particularly useful at the early stages of instruction or for a student who is not making rapid progress. However, the teacher should be aware that in a small-group setting, having students read prewritten cards is a more efficient use of instructional time, and should be used when possible.

others may be ready to read new words containing the element being practiced. As needed, teachers would continue to provide necessary demonstration, modeling, and guidance while being mindful of providing students with the time they may need to puzzle through the words.

Written Spelling

Materials

The materials needed for this portion of the lesson are: student sets of dry-erase boards and markers or paper and pencils and the Word Work Planning and Recording Form.

Student Activity

During written spelling, students spell three to four words that the teacher dictates.

Student Thinking

In order to do this, students must analyze the sounds in the word, then think about which letters (or letter combinations) represent those sounds, and then write those letters in the proper sequence. The kinds of analysis required for written spelling are similar to word building with the added challenge of identifying which letters to use (without the scaffold of the small set of choices provided during word building) and write. For some students, having to form the letters (rather than use a tile) is another challenge. Having students spell words that they have been working on in other ways helps to build confidence and competence.

Supporting the Student

Teachers can vary the level of challenge during this activity by asking individual students to spell different words based on their needs and their success with the first two activities. As needed, teachers would continue to provide necessary demonstration, modeling, and guidance.

Selecting Words and Developing Lists

The words that are selected for Word Work determine, in part, what students think about and learn. The website for this book (see the box at the end of the table of contents) includes two documents that teachers can use in selecting words, Word Lists and Texts for Teaching and Practicing Long and Short Vowels, and Word Lists and Texts for Teaching and Practicing Vowel Parts. In word building, students are more likely to learn the element being taught if they have multiple opportunities to make decisions about when to use it. Here are some useful points to keep in mind when selecting words to use:

- If the teacher's goal is for students to analyze the vowel sounds in words and for students to move flexibly between the long and short vowel sounds, then the sequence of words selected will (mostly) alternate between the long and short sounds of the vowel(s).

- Select words for building that encourage students to compare the new element or principle to something they have already learned and that bears some orthographic similarity to the new part. For example, if *oi* is being taught as a new vowel part, students should alternate (mostly) between building words containing *oi* and building words containing the letter *o* or the vowel part *ou* (if *ou* is already known).

- If *oi* is being taught and students build only words containing *oi*, they will not need to attend to the *oi* part because it does not change.

- Select words for building so that the pattern of change is not entirely predictable. For example, if *oi* is part of every second word, students will realize this and will be less likely to think about the sounds and the letters in the words they are building.

- Initially, select and sequence words for building so that few changes are made and students have the chance to focus in on the new element. Later lists can increase and vary the challenge if the teacher selects words:

  o that require students to attend to several shifts at once, which increases the level of challenge. For example, to change *mat* to *make*, the student must think about how to change the vowel and the final consonant, which would be more challenging than changing *mat* to *mate*, which requires only one change.

  o with blends, which present more challenge than words with single consonants. As described in Chapter 8, some blends are more challenging than others. If the initial assessment of students' alphabetic skills suggests that they are not proficient with consonant blends, then initial Word Work activities should include only the easiest blends (i.e., *sm, fr, sl, fl, sn*). Once students are facile with the easier blends, more challenging blends can be included in Word Work. Some of the most challenging consonant blends in the initial position are *dr* and *tr*. These blends would be included in Word Work after students are facile with easier blends.

  o for students to read or spell words that haven't been practiced during the building phase, which increases the level of challenge.

  o at a different level of challenge for each student during word reading and word spelling, which differentiates instruction.

- Select sufficient words. Each word-building lesson should include building (eight to 10 words), reading (three to four words), and spelling (three to four words).

Blends Containing *r* and *l*

Blends that contain *r* and *l* can be included in blends that occur at the beginning of words. However, when the consonant *r* follows any vowel and when the letter *l* follows the vowel *a,* they influence the sound of the vowel. For this reason, it is important to avoid consonant combinations that include *r* after any vowel or *l* after the vowel *a* when the instructional focus is on consonant blends.

Instructional Decision Making:
Other Useful Instructional Practices

Resources to Support Student Independence

During Word Work and text reading, students' thinking is supported through the provision of resources designed to help them quickly and accurately recall the sound for a letter or letter group. Resources help to prevent students from "practicing" the wrong sound for a letter, and allow mental capacity to be devoted to analyzing the word, rather than searching for a sound in memory. Resources also allow the reader to access needed information without teacher assistance.

Bb/Dd Chart

If students frequently confuse the lower-case versions of the letters *b* and *d,* it is useful to provide a model that they can refer to when they read and write, and use to check their accuracy. An example of the suggested model is provided in Figure 9.2 and also included in the Words We Know and Use chart described in Chapter 7. Teachers may find the ***Bb/Dd*** resource on the website for this book (see the box at the end of the table of contents).

Most students can readily identify the upper-case versions of *B* and *D*. When they are uncertain of the identity of the visual form of the lower-case version of either of those letters, all they need to do is refer to the model. Some students may

FIGURE 9.2. *Bb/Dd* resource.

benefit from a *b*/*d* chart in the general education classroom. For students who appear to need it, an upper- and lower-case *p* can be added to the chart as well.

If students are unfamiliar with the use of a *Bb/Dd* chart, its utility should be explained when it is first introduced.

> "Sometimes lower-case *b*'s and *d*'s can be confusing. This chart will help you remember which one is which. If you are looking at a letter and you are not sure whether it is a *b* or a *d,* all you have to do is look at this chart. The letter next to the upper-case *B* [point] is a *b* and the letter next to the upper-case *D* is a *d.* You can use this chart when you are writing, too. For example, if you know you want to write a *b* and you are not sure which way it goes, just look at the chart and you'll be able to figure it out."

Once the chart has been introduced, periodic reminders to "Check the *b*/*d* chart" should be provided as necessary until students check the chart spontaneously or until students no longer confuse the lower-case letters.

Short Vowel Key Words

Many readers in intervention will benefit from using a resource that provides key words that help them to remember the sounds of the short vowels.[1] Key words are more useful to students and are easier to remember if the same key words are used in all instructional settings. In schools that have a standard set of key words in place, it is useful for intervention teachers to use those key words. If there is no standard set, the vowel key words in Figure 9.3 may be used (*apple, Ed the Elephant,*[2] *itchy, octopus,* and *umbrella*). This figure may also be downloaded from the book's website (see the box at the end of the table of contents).

Initially, students will need explicit guidance as to how the resource and/or key words can support their reading and writing efforts. The sample instructional dialogue in Figure 9.4 illustrates how this might be done. After this introduction, the resource is displayed right on a small group's work surface, where students can readily see it. As students develop more independence, these resources can

---

[1]We do not advocate providing key words for the long vowel sounds because if students know the name of the vowel letter, they also know the long vowel sound—which is just the same as the letter's name.

[2]Note that the key word used for the short-*e* sound, in many settings, is *egg*. However, the vowel sound in the word *egg*, the way many people pronounce the word, is more like a long-*a* sound. To illustrate, consider the names Craig and Greg. These names rhyme as most people in the United States pronounce them. So, we argue, the beginning sound in *egg* is not a good example of the short-*e* sound. Therefore, we encourage teachers in such settings to consider selecting a different key word or drawing a face on the picture of the key word and naming it *Ed the Egg*. Note, too, that our key word for short *e* is *Ed the Elephant* rather than *elephant* because for readers at a very early point in development, the word *elephant* would begin with the letter *l*—the name of which is also the first syllable in the word *elephant*.

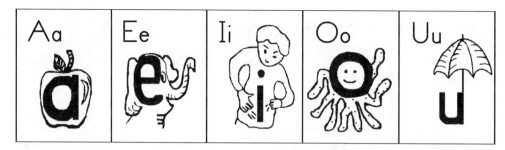

FIGURE 9.3. Key words for short vowels resource. Adapted from Scanlon, Anderson, and Sweeney (2017) with permission from The Guilford Press.

INTRODUCING KEY WORDS: A SAMPLE USING THE KEY WORD FOR e	
What the Teacher Says and Does	**Comments on the Activity**

"When you are reading along and you come to a puzzling word that has only one vowel in it and you can't remember the sound for the vowel, it might help to just look at the key word for that vowel. For example, if you were trying to figure out a word with an *e* in it, you could look at this picture that reminds you that the key word for *e* is *ĕĕĕĕd*, as in *Ed the Elephant*. That will help you remember that one sound for *e* is /ĕĕĕĕ/ [the teacher pronounces and elongates the short-*e* sound]."
 	
    The teacher might then show students the word *met*. "If I needed to figure out this word, but couldn't remember the sound for *e*, I could look at my key word, say, *Ed* /ĕĕ/, and then try that sound in the word /m/-/ĕĕ/-/t/, *met*.
 	
    "If I needed to write a word that contains the /ĕĕ/ sound but I couldn't remember which vowel letter to use, I could check the key words and think about which word has the /ĕĕ/ sound at the beginning. Then, I could figure out which vowel letter to use.
 	
    The vowel key words will be kept right here. Whenever you need to remind yourself about the sound for *e,* you can look at this picture of Ed the Elephant to help you remember."
	In order to use key words, students need to quickly and accurately identify the pictures and the sounds they represent. Teachers should make sure students know what the picture is called and can clearly pronounce the key word it represents.
	
	Showing students when and how to use the key words increases the likelihood that students will use them.
	
	Prominently displaying key words and reminding students of their utility will help students develop independence in their use of the resource. The ultimate goal, of course, is that students will know the sounds for the vowels without having to refer to the key word resource.

FIGURE 9.4. Sample teacher language for introducing the short vowel key words.

be moved off the table and onto a trifold display board where they are available if needed. If there are too many resources immediately available, they have the potential to just be confusing to students. (Note that a different board should be used for each small group so that the resource display is specific to the instruction that the students in the group have received.)

Other Vowel Parts That May Need Explicit Instruction

Once students know the long and short sounds for the vowels to the point where they rarely need to refer to the key words for them, they will be ready to learn other vowel parts. Here again, students will benefit from a resource that contains key words that illustrate the sounds made by the *r*-controlled vowels, and a few other vowel parts. Figure 9.5 contains the key words for vowel parts that may need to be explicitly taught. These key words are also available on this book's website (see the box at the end of the table of contents).

Integrated Decoding Elements and Strategy Instruction

Once students have learned a decoding element or principle, it is important that they then be shown how to apply their new knowledge while using word identification strategies to solve and learn unfamiliar words that they encounter while reading. In Chapters 5 and 6, we provided detailed guidance on what the word identification strategies are, and how to teach them.

Figure 9.6 lists the decoding elements and also the word identification strategies that would be appropriate to teach or review after the element or principle is taught during the Word Work segment of the lesson. This chart is not meant to be prescriptive—teachers are encouraged to be mindful that strategic readers are flexible, and draw upon their decoding knowledge in various ways in different contexts.

We *do not* suggest that the decoding elements be taught in the order they are presented in Figure 9.6, nor that all the elements in Figure 9.6 be taught to every reader. Indeed, a given reader may already know some or most of these decoding elements, so instruction would focus on those the reader still needs to learn.

Ample Practice

The same day that a new element is taught or practiced through Word Work, it is useful for students to read texts that offer an opportunity to apply the decoding element. In both the ISA and ISA-X research projects, teachers found the Ready Readers (first published by Modern Curriculum Press, now published by Pearson) to be very useful for this purpose. Each text includes multiple words containing the decoding element highlighted by that particular text, as well as words that contain

FIGURE 9.5. Resource containing key words for vowel parts that may need explicit instruction. From Scanlon, Anderson, and Sweeney (2017). Reprinted with permission from The Guilford Press.

some elements that were previously taught in the sequence that guides the series. Teachers can also find texts designed to provide practice with decoding elements at Reading A–Z (*www.readinga-z.com*) and at TextProject (*http://textproject.org*).

Practice with a specific decoding principle and/or decoding element continues, often over several instructional sessions, until students appear to be fairly fluent with it. We provide an example of a consolidation lesson in Appendix 9.2. Older readers in intervention often need more practice than do readers who are progressing well at earlier points in development. If after one session of word building, word reading, and written spelling, students are:

- Fast and accurate with the decoding element being taught, then the teacher can go on to the next element.
- Still quite deliberate, then the teacher can provide additional Word Work lessons in subsequent sessions to enable students to become secure in what they are learning.

Students are more likely to consolidate their knowledge of decoding elements when they have lots of opportunities to apply what they have learned as they solve words in texts. Wide reading in both texts designed to provide practice with newly taught decoding elements and traditional texts allows readers ample opportunity to apply and consolidate their knowledge of these elements.

Progress Monitoring

Teachers will find it helpful to keep track of which decoding elements students have learned. We advise teachers to create their own record form, in a fashion similar

Decoding Element/Principle	Word Identification Strategy
• Single consonants • Consonant digraphs • Short vowels • Long vowel sound/silent-e generalization • Blends	Think about the sounds of the letters in the word.
• Long vowel sound/silent-e generalization • Vowel combinations that can be decoded by trying different sounds for the vowel because they represent either the long or short sound of one of the vowels (*ai, ay, ea, ee, eu, ie, oa, oe, ue, ui*) • Vowel parts that have two sounds (*oo, ow*)	Try different sounds for some of the letters, especially the vowel(s). Be flexible!
• Consonant digraphs • Phonograms/word families • Vowel combinations that cannot be decoded by trying different sounds for the vowel because they represent a sound that is different from the long or short sound of either vowel (*au, aw, ew, oi, oo, ou, ow, oy*) • *r*-controlled vowels (*ar, er, ir, or, ur*)	Look for parts you know.
• Inflected endings (*-ing, -es, -ed*) • Prefixes such as *un-, re-, in-* • Suffixes such as *-ly, -ment, -ness* • Compound words • Words with two consonants together—especially double consonants • Consonant + *le* syllables	Break the word into smaller parts.

FIGURE 9.6. Strategies that use the decoding elements knowledge.

to the Priority Word List illustrated in Figure 7.2 (pp. 138–139). For each student the teacher would create a list of the decoding elements the student still needs to learn and record the date on which the Word Work was begun, when additional practice was required, and when Word Work was discontinued owing to apparent mastery. It's important to keep in mind that, sometimes, students learn a decoding element without Word Work—providing the key word resource and opportunities to read may be sufficient for students who have had instruction on such elements in the past—and/or students may acquire knowledge of how to decode particular elements through wide reading. Thus, while the decoding elements we discuss in this chapter all, ultimately, need to be "accessible" to students, they do not necessarily need to be explicitly taught because as students gain insights into the workings of the code, they have the potential to make progress without explicit (and potentially time-consuming) instruction. Once again, the message is that instruction should be responsive.

Instructional Decision Making: Teaching Students to Rapidly Access and Use the Two Most Common Sounds of a Vowel

It is often the case that older readers involved in reading intervention have been taught to read as though the printed representations of vowel sounds are more reliable than they are. Such students may try one pronunciation for the vowel and try to stick with it—whether it results in a word that fits the context or not.

If a student's attempt at word identification does not result in a word that fits the context, then the student needs to try alternative ways of pronouncing the word. We encourage teachers to help students to learn to be *flexible, or to try different sounds* in decoding the vowels in words when this happens. In order to use this strategy, students need to know both vowel sounds and be able to fluently shift from one sound to the other.

As described in Chapter 5, this knowledge and flexibility can allow the reader to identify short words that do not follow the spelling "rule" for long and short sounds (e.g., *have, bold*) and multisyllabic words in which the long and short sound is not predictable (e.g., *between, robin*). It also enables the reader to identify many words that have vowel digraphs, once the reader learns to try both the long and short sound for each letter (e.g., *heavy, great, beat*; *build, fruit*).

Word building, word reading, and written spelling can be used to consolidate knowledge of the vowels and to promote flexibility with the long and short sound of each vowel. Each vowel is initially practiced separately and then the vowels are practiced in combination.

A suggested order for instruction related to long and short vowel sounds is provided on the next page. This order is based on the similarities between and among the short vowel sounds (the short vowel sounds that are most different from one another are taught first) and on the frequency of usage of the vowels.

- If students already know some or all of the vowel sounds quite well, then a few of the Word Work activities suggested below may be sufficient for students to be able to move flexibly between the vowel sounds.
- If students have less knowledge of the vowel sounds, it may be necessary to do all of the Word Work activities suggested below in order to consolidate knowledge of all vowel sounds.

Here we provide a suggested order for teaching/developing fluency with the long and short vowels:

- Long- and short-*a* sounds, using long-*a* words spelled with the consonant–vowel–consonant–final *e* (C)VC*e* pattern.
- Long- and short-*i* sounds using long-*i* words spelled with the (C)VC*e* pattern.
- Review of long and short sounds for both *a* and *i*.
- Long- and short-*o* sounds with the long *o* spelled with the (C)VC*e* pattern.
- Review of long- and short-*a*, *i*, and *o* sounds.
- Long and short *e*, with the long *e* spelled with the double-*e* (C)VVC pattern, because there are very few words with the (C)VC*e* pattern for long *e*.
- Long- and short-*u* sounds, with the long *u* spelled with the (C)VC*e* pattern.[3]
- Review of long- and short-*e* and *u* sounds.

In Appendix 9.1, we provide an example of a Word Work lesson that is designed to introduce the idea of moving flexibly between the two sounds of *a*. This lesson, along with the template provided on the website for this book (see the box at the end of the table of contents) can be used to develop lessons for teaching/practicing each of the vowels and for reviewing the vowel sounds. The website also includes a copy of the Word Work Planning and Recording Form.

In the sample lessons provided in this chapter, the teacher links for students the decoding knowledge they are acquiring and consolidating with the word identification strategies that use this knowledge. As soon as students know the short sound of a vowel, they are encouraged to use the strategy "Think about the sounds of the letters in the word." As soon as students can move reliably between the long and short sounds of one vowel, they can continue to use this strategy and should be taught the word identification strategy "Try different sounds for some of the letters, especially the vowel(s). Be flexible!"

Consolidating Knowledge of the Long and Short Vowels

After the initial lesson modeled above, students will need to continue practicing building, reading, and spelling words with the long- and short-*a* vowel sound until they can move between them accurately and fluently. Less teacher support

---

[3]If students are not secure in their knowledge of the correspondences, additional cumulative review (*a*, *i*, *o*, and *e*) can be provided before introducing *u*.

and modeling is given during consolidation, as indicated in the lesson provided in Appendix 9.2. This lesson is also available on the website for this book, along with a template that teachers can use to construct their own consolidation lessons (see the box at the end of the table of contents).

Teaching Students versus Teaching Curriculum

As a general rule, it is best to continue providing consolidation lessons with the long and short sounds of a particular vowel until students are fairly secure in their ability to move between the two sounds of the vowel—referencing the key word as necessary. It is important to keep in mind that, in intervention, we should be teaching students, not teaching the curriculum regardless of what students learn.

Vowel Combinations That Can Be Decoded via Vowel Flexing

When two vowels occur next to each other in a word, they usually represent one sound. Teachers sometimes teach students, "When two vowels go walking, the first one does the talking." Unfortunately, this "rule" does not work for many words, including some of the highest-frequency words (e.g., *said, been, great*). Perhaps a better "rule" would be "When two vowels are together in a word, usually only one vowel sound is heard" or "When two vowels go walking, somebody says something."[4]

Usually when two vowels are together in a word, the sound of one of them is heard. Most often it is the long sound of the first vowel (e.g., *bean, rain, boat*). Sometimes it is the short sound of the first vowel (e.g., *head, plaid*). Occasionally, it is the long sound of the second vowel (e.g., *great, break*). And sometimes it is the short sound of the second vowel (e.g., *captain, friend*).

The list below contains the vowel parts that can usually be decoded if students know the long and short sounds for each of the vowels, and have learned the strategy "Try different sounds for some of the letters, especially the vowel(s). Be flexible!" Chapters 5 and 6 provide additional information about this strategy and strategy instruction. Because these parts can be decoded by trying different sounds for the vowels, they do not require explicit instruction beyond teaching the sounds of the individual vowels along with the word identification strategy "Try different sounds for some of the letters."

ai	*ea*	*ie*	*oa*	*ue*
ay	*ee*		*oe*	*ui*
	eu			

---

[4]This advice will be useful only if the reader knows what a vowel is. Most intermediate and middle grade readers have been taught the vowels, but instruction or review can be provided on an as-needed basis.

Instructional Decision Making: Teaching Students Useful Parts

Phonograms

After developing the decoding knowledge needed to try different sounds for the vowels, some students are ready to move right into instruction in other vowel parts. Other students benefit from some review of word families or phonograms. Review of phonograms can benefit readers in two ways. First, they learn parts that can't be fully decoded or are more difficult to decode using individual letter–sound correspondences. Second, such instruction provides students with opportunities to see that the same part shows up in many different words, and that once a part is known, it can be used to figure out unknown words using the strategy "Look for parts you know."

If students do not readily read words containing parts like these (e.g., *all, ank, ant, ight, ink, ock, old*), most of which cannot be fully decoded solely on the basis of letter–sound knowledge, these phonograms can be reviewed (and, if need be, explicitly taught).

If students require initial instruction in the use of phonograms, the reader is referred to Chapter 9 of our companion text (Scanlon et al., 2017). Most intermediate and middle grade readers have already had some instruction in phonograms (which are variously referred to as chunks, word families, and/or decoding keys by different instructional approaches/programs). For students like these, the teacher can simply select a small set of phonograms, pronounce the phonogram, and then engage students in reading words that contain the phonograms. It should be noted that for many students, if they are engaged with only one phonogram at a time in an instructional activity (e.g., building/reading/writing *light, might, night, tight, slight, bright*), the activity may not serve to build or reinforce their ability to effectively use that phonogram as a decoding element. Because it doesn't change from one word to the next, students don't really need to attend to the phonogram—what changes is the beginning phoneme(s), and as a result this is the part of the word likely to draw students' attention.

In contrast, a practice activity like the one described next may be appropriate. After teaching/reviewing a few phonograms, a brief amount of time can be allocated to making words using the phonograms. The teacher might prepare materials by cutting index cards in half. On some pieces, the teacher writes a few known phonograms and one or two phonograms that need to be learned or reinforced. On other pieces, the teacher writes known single consonants (some of which can be used to form initial blends) and digraphs. The teacher then gives students the cards, blank sheets of paper, and pencils, and asks students to see how many words they can make using the phonograms and the individual letters and digraphs. The expectation would be that students make a word using the cards, then say the word out loud to decide whether it is a real word, and then write the word on their paper if it is a real word.

Other Vowel Parts That May Need to Be Explicitly Taught

Some vowel parts (e.g., *oy, au*) and vowels followed by *r* (e.g., *or*) cannot be decoded by trying different sounds for the vowels. If observation and assessment (e.g., Section 2 of the Decoding Elements Assessment on this book's website [see the box at the end of the table of contents]) indicate that students do not already know the sounds made by these parts, students will benefit from instruction on the sounds these parts represent and from having key words to help them remember the sounds (see Figure 9.5). As was true for other decoding elements, the specific vowel parts that are taught at a given point should be determined on the basis of what the students need to learn and the reading materials that the students will read in the near future (usually on the same day).

Each of the vowel parts in this section can and should be connected to the word identification strategies. As soon as students have learned one of the parts taught in this chapter, they can be encouraged to use that part as they "Look for parts you know."

R-Controlled Vowels

Vowel pronunciations may be influenced by the letter that immediately follows. When a single vowel letter is followed by the letter *r*, the sound of the vowel is altered and it is hard to distinguish the sound of the vowel from the sound of the *r*. As a result, the short sounds of the vowels cannot be distinctly heard. These are often referred to as *r*-controlled vowels (*ar, er, ir, or,* and *ur*). The *r*-controlled vowels are generally taught as "parts" or decoding units.

> *ar   er   ir   or   ur*

It should be noted that *er, ir,* and *ur* all represent the same sound. It is important to note that there are instances (especially if the vowel sound is long) when *r* does not change the pronunciation of the preceding vowel (e.g., *fire, ear*). In these instances, students can apply the strategy "Try different sounds for some of the letters, especially the vowel(s). Be flexible!" Thus, there are no strict "rules" with regard to which strategies to try—once a strategy has been learned, we would expect students to use it flexibly and interactively with the other strategies that are available to them.

Other Vowel Parts That Have One Common Pronunciation

Sometimes two vowels together signal a sound that is different from the sound represented by either letter individually (e.g., *oy, au,* and *ei,* which is often pronounced as a long-*a* sound as in *vein*). The vowel parts that have somewhat reliable pronunciations and occur frequently enough to warrant instruction are listed below. These parts have one common pronunciation:

au   *aw*   *ew*   *oi*   *oy*   *ou*[5]

It should be noted that *au* and *aw* represent the same sound, as do *oi* and *oy*.

Teaching Vowel Parts That Have One Common Pronunciation

When these parts are introduced, it is helpful to begin by explaining to students that sometimes two vowels together represent a single sound that is different from either of the sounds the individual vowels usually represent. Similarly, when *r* follows a vowel it may change the sound that the vowel makes, so the vowel and the *r* need to be learned together as a part. As students are learning about the need to read these vowels as "parts," instruction can begin with an illustrated key word and an opportunity to practice using the key word. Figure 9.5 (p. 180) provides the illustrations of the key words that were developed for use in the ISA-X research projects, as well as the mnemonic sentences that are used for vowel parts that look similar and sound alike. The sentences can be used to help students to understand that a single sound can be spelled in more than one way. (Note that this figure can be downloaded from this book's website [see the box at the end of the table of contents].) During the ISA-X research projects, for the purpose of clarity, teachers cut apart the key word illustrations and introduced each one as it was taught. As more vowel parts were taught/learned, a large chart was assembled that included all of the parts that had been taught.

Some intermediate and middle grade readers in intervention may have been taught these sounds previously and will only need to be reminded of the sounds of the vowel parts. Other students may need an introduction and a key word to use as a resource. As needed, word building, word reading, and written spelling can be used to practice these vowel parts. Appendix 9.3 provides an example of a lesson that can be used to teach the part *ou*. This lesson can also be used as a model to develop lessons for other vowel parts, along with the template available on the website for this book (see the box at the end of the table of contents). Figure 9.7 illustrates materials set up for teaching the *ew* and *aw* parts. Note that when the parts are first introduced, the two letters are taped together to form a part, as described below.

---

[5] Most of the time, *ou* makes the sound heard in *out*. Occasionally, it makes the sound heard in *group* or the sound heard in *would*. Begin by teaching the sound as in *out* but let students know the sound can vary.

**Streamlining Instruction of Vowel Parts That Are
Alternative Spellings for the Same Sound**

Some vowel parts represent the same sound but are spelled differently. Thus, *er,*
ir, and *ur* are three different ways to spell the /er/ sound. Similarly, *aw* and *au*
have the same sound, as do *oy* and *oi,* and *oo* and *ew.* Once students can read
one of the related vowel parts, the alternative spelling can be introduced and connected to reading the known spelling. For example, once students can read the
vowel part *er,* the teacher can:

- Explain that *ir* has the same sound as *er.*
- Review the key word for *ir,* which is part of one mnemonic sentence that
  integrates the *er, ir,* and *ur* key words.
- Ask students to find and use the *ir* part to read words from the list
  included on the website (see the box at the end of the table of contents)
  for this book.
- For added challenge and practice, ask students to read (with support if
  needed) multisyllabic words containing *ir* (also listed on the website).

If this instruction is sufficient to enable students to read *ir* words with accuracy,
then it is not necessary to engage students in Word Work with *ir.*

Note that the lesson illustrated in Appendix 9.3 was written under the assumption that it might be an initial decoding lesson (for students who were already proficient with the long and short vowels). If teachers have been providing a series of
lessons on the long and short vowels, some of the language in this lesson may seem
repetitive and can be reduced.

In selecting words for Word Work, teachers should remember to select words
that:

- Initially, include the new part that is being learned and a single vowel—for
  example, *ou* and *o.* In this case, the letters *o* and *u* would be taped together
  or printed on a single card to represent the part, and *o* by itself would also
  be included in the student's set of letters.
- Later, use two parts that look and sound quite different from each other—
  for example, *aw* and *oi* or *ew* and *ou.*
- Finally, use two parts that are similar—for example, *aw* and *ew.*
- Parts with the same sound (*er, ir,* and *ur; aw* and *au; oi* and *oy*) should not
  be used in the same Word Work sessions because there is no way for a student to determine which of the alternative spellings would be included in
  the accurate spelling of a given word (unless, of course, the student already
  knew the conventional spelling of the word).

FIGURE 9.7. Letters and resources set up for a vowel parts Word Work activity.

The idea here is to gradually move students toward the point where they can make finer-grained discriminations between the sounds and spellings of the words.

A Great Way to Confuse Students and Undermine Their Confidence

Some teachers, with the best of intentions, inadvertently create confusion and a loss of confidence as a result of the words they choose for instruction around vowel parts that represent alternative spellings for the same sound. We believe this happens, in part, because teachers are so literate that they have difficulty seeing the instructional challenges they provide through the eyes of the readers with whom they are working. When there are alternative spellings of the same sound (*aw* and *au*; *oy* and *oi*; *oo* and *ew*; *er, ir,* and *ur*) it is unreasonable to ask students to determine the correct spelling in word-building and/or written spelling activities because, unless the word is already known by students, they have no way to decide which of the alternative spellings is accurate.

For this reason, alternative spellings for the same sound *should not* be used in the same Word Work activity.

Once students become fluent with using the various vowel parts discussed above in single-syllable words, teachers can show them how to look for the parts in longer words. Teachers may wish to put some of those words into sentences and encourage students to use the part they are learning to assist them in puzzling through longer words.

Teacher Terminology versus Teaching Terminology

Some of the vowel parts discussed in this chapter are vowel digraphs, in which two letters represent a single sound. Others are diphthongs—that is, a vowel sound, often represented by two letters, that starts with one vowel sound and changes to another. In our opinion, when teaching about vowel sounds, there is no need for teachers to distinguish between diphthongs and other vowel variants for students.

The following letter combinations represent the most commonly occurring two-letter diphthongs: *ow* (as in *owl*), *oi*, *ou* (as in *mouse*), and *oy*. In order to help students with their spelling, teachers may want to point out that *oy* is almost always found at the end of a word (exceptions include *oyster* and words with inflected endings such as *toys* and *enjoying*), while *oi* is usually the spelling when the sound is not the final sound in the word.

Teaching Vowel Parts That Make Two Unique Sounds and Require Flexing (*ow, oo*)

It is helpful for students to learn that some vowel parts are commonly pronounced in more than one way. The vowel parts *oo* and *ow* each commonly represent two different sounds (as in *boot* and *hook*, and *owl* and *snow*, respectively). In these instances, teachers should explain to students that just as individual vowel letters represent more than one sound, sometimes vowel parts represent more than one sound. The two sounds can be introduced using the language provided in Figure 9.8.

After being taught the two pronunciations (which should initially be taught individually), students should be encouraged to:

- Reference the key word chart as needed (see Figure 9.5) as an assist in remembering the two sounds of the vowel.
- Be flexible with the part, alternating the sounds until a word is identified that fits the context.

Instructional Decision Making

There is little research to guide teachers in helping students to learn to decode and spell words that consist of more than one syllable. Therefore, in what follows, most of the suggestions are based on practical experience rather than carefully researched procedures.

Step 1: Teacher Introduction	
Materials needed: 1. *oo* words written on cards 2. Key words for the two sounds for *oo* 3. Word identification strategy list	
What the Teacher Says and Does	**Comments on the Activity**

Names and explains: "Today, you are going to learn about the the *oo* part, which can represent two different sounds. You will get to practice the two sounds by reading words that contain the *oo* part.
    "The *oo* part can make the /oo/ [pronounce as in *hook*] sound you hear in the word *hook*. Here is a picture of a hook. Say, '*hook*.' The *oo* is <u>underlined</u> in the word *hook* [point to the word *hook*] to help you remember the /oo/ sound for the *oo*. You can use this picture of a hook to help you remember the /oo/ sound.
    "The *oo* part also makes the /oo/ [pronounce as the *oo* in *boots*] sound you hear in *boots*. Here is a picture of boots. Say, '*boots*.' The *oo* in the word *boots* [point to the word *boots*] is <u>underlined</u> to help you remember the /oo/ [pronounce as in *boots*] that the *oo* sometimes represents. You can use this picture to help you think about the /oo/ [pronounce as in *boots*] sound."
	If the teacher accurately and consistently names the activity, it is less confusing to students.

Links: "You are going to practice reading words that contain the vowel part *oo*. You will practice in a specific way that will help you to learn to try both sounds of the *oo* part. Learning both sounds for the vowel part *oo* will help you use the word-learning strategy [the teacher points to the strategy on the list] **try different sounds for some of the letters**, as you solve words you don't yet know when you are reading."	When the purpose for word building is clearly stated by the teacher, it helps students to see how their learning during this activity will help them as they read.
Models: "Watch me as I show you how to decide how to say these words." [The teacher writes *hood* on a dry-erase board.] "To figure out this word, I am going to try both sounds and see which sound makes it a real word. To help me remember the two sounds for *oo*, I can check my key words. First I am going to try the /oo/ [pronounce as in *boot*] sound: h-oo-d. That doesn't sound like a real word to me. Now I will try the /oo/ [pronounce as in *hook*] sound. *H-oo-d. Hood.* That's a real word, so I would decide that the word is *hood*. I figured it out by trying different sounds for the *oo* part."	In this portion of the lesson, the teacher does the talking and students watch and listen. The teacher should model what he or she ultimately wants students to think about and do, elaborating on the process if need be so that students understand.
The teacher continues the lesson by asking students to read words containing the *oo* part. As a follow-up activity, the teacher may choose to revisit the strategy and practice solving words with the *oo* part within sentences.	

FIGURE 9.8. Sample teacher language for introducing a part that has two sounds.

The Schwa Sound

It may be helpful to tell students that, in words with more than one syllable, one or more of the vowels sometimes represent the /uh/ (schwa) sound as in *about, America, syllable,* and *experiment* (as these words are typically pronounced in everyday conversation). Some readers will be able to recognize the word after having produced the vowel's regular sounds (i.e., pronouncing *America* with a long- or short-*a* sound), but others will not. This may be puzzling to teachers, as it will seem that the student has all the parts but has not identified the word. We encourage teachers to point out to students, in an explicit fashion, that sometimes the sounds in longer words are close but not exact. The reader may want to try the schwa sound, and to use meaning-based strategies to help settle on the word's identity.

Common Prefixes and Derivational Suffixes

Most intermediate and middle grade students will (should) encounter instruction related to prefixes and suffixes in their classroom language arts program. Therefore, common prefixes should be explicitly taught and practiced while less common suffixes that students encounter in the context of reading intervention should be briefly addressed on an as-needed basis. For students for whom the instructional priority is improvement of reading accuracy and fluency, we have not, in our past studies, made knowledge and use of prefixes and suffixes a priority. However, emerging research summaries suggest that such priorities should become part of instructional planning going forward (see Carlisle & Goodwin, 2013, for further discussion).

Listed below are some tips for helping students to learn prefixes and/or suffixes that they can treat as parts that can be temporarily ignored while they analyze the remaining part(s) of a multisyllabic word.

- Explain that a single word sometimes has more than one meaningful part (the terms *prefixes* and *suffixes* are appropriate to use if students have encountered them elsewhere).
- Explain that noticing prefixes and suffixes will help students to identify unfamiliar words.
- Illustrate the prefix or suffix in a word that students will encounter in their reading that day. Present the word so that each meaningful part is written on a separate card.
- Explain the meaning of the prefix or suffix.
- Show students how adding or removing the prefix or suffix changes the meaning of the word.
- The same prefix or suffix can be combined with other root words, and students can be engaged in attempting to identify and define the new words.
- Give students opportunities to practice using the strategies "Break the word

into smaller parts" and "Look for parts you know" in sentences that contain multisyllabic words with prefixes and/or suffixes.

- Word Work activities using root words and the affixes that have been taught can be used in mini-lessons until students are quite facile in using them. For example, if the affixes *re-, un-, -ly, -ful, -ness, -able,* and *-er* have been taught, the student might use several different root words to build and read multisyllabic words. For example:
  - *comfort, comfortable, uncomfortable*
  - *teach, teacher, reteach, teachable, unteachable*
  - *hope, hopeful, unhopeful, hopefulness*

There are some fairly common suffixes that students may find confusing because of their irregular spelling (in our experience, *ion* and *ious* often confuse readers who are attempting to use their decoding skills). For these and other suffixes with irregular spelling patterns, and for other irregular spelling patterns (such as *ture*), it is useful to simply provide the pronunciation of the word if need be and draw the student's attention to the pronunciation of the irregular spelling pattern.

Breaking Words into Parts That Are Not Meaningful

Many multisyllabic words are made up of syllables that do not have individual meanings. Readers can often find these syllables and decode the word if they attempt one or more of the following approaches (also illustrated in Figure 9.9 and available on the website for this book; see the box at the end of the table of contents). These approaches are discussed in detail in O'Connor (2014). For multisyllabic words the reader may:

- Think about how many syllables may be in the word by considering the number of vowels.
- For words with double consonants, break the word between the two consonants and decode each syllable.
- For words with two different consonants together in the middle of the word, try breaking the word between the consonants (e.g., *tablet, respond, harvest*).
- Try different pronunciations for the vowels in the syllables; be flexible—try the long and short sounds of the vowels as well as the schwa sound alternately until a word that fits the context becomes apparent.
- For words with the consonant + *le* syllable structure (e.g., *can-dle, bat-tle, stum-ble*), go back one letter from the *le* and decode that consonant and then add in the /ul/ pronunciation of *le*. Decode the first syllable and then combine it with the consonant + *le* syllable.

For other parts, we recommend the following:

• Tell/remind students that all of the vowels sometimes represent the /uh/ (schwa) sound, as in *again, above,* and *mother* (as these words are pronounced in everyday conversation).
• For words that include spelling units that are not very decodable (e.g., *tion, sion, ture*), provide the pronunciation (e.g., "That part says *shun*" or "That part says *chur*") and explain that it will be seen in lots of words and is therefore useful to try to remember.

To initially make these approaches explicit, challenging words that are encountered while reading text can be written out and then analyzed briefly in isolation. Figure 9.10 illustrates words and resources ready to use in breaking apart longer words.

Tips for Breaking Apart Words

Every syllable must have at least one vowel!	
Be **flexible** with the **sounds for a, e, i, o, u, c,** and **g**.	
Cover up **prefixes and suffixes**.	unwanted
Try breaking a word **between doubled consonants**.	stub/born
Try breaking a word between two different consonants.	en/ter/tain
Consonant + **le** syllable type.	ta-ble pud-dle

FIGURE 9.9. Tips for breaking apart words resource.

FIGURE 9.10. Words and resources set up to practice breaking apart longer words.

It is useful to illustrate that multiple approaches can be applied together in attempting to decode a multisyllabic word. It is also important to stress the need to think of words that would make sense in the context and to always confirm that the decoded word fits the context. For example, if the word *predated* was encountered while reading a history text, the teacher might write the word on a dry-erase board and demonstrate for students how they might go about figuring it out. Thus, the teacher might say:

"There are a lot of things we can try when we come to a puzzling word like this. Let's start by looking for any prefixes or suffixes or other parts we know. I see *pre-*, which we know means *before*. I also see an *-ed* ending, which means it happened in the past (it already happened). I am going to cover up those two word parts with my fingers while I look at the rest of the word. So, I've got *dat*. Hmm. This part could be *dat* or *date*, because sometimes when we take the *-ed* ending off, it is really just the *d* that needed to come off. First I'll try *dat, dat*. . . . That doesn't sound like a word I've heard before. So let's try *date*. Ah! That's a word I know! The author already used that word in this book when talking about the age when the Iroquois Confederacy was formed. Now, I need to put the other parts of the word back on. I'll start with the ending [uncovers the *-ed*]. So, now I've got *dated*. That means when it happened. If I put the *pre* back on, I have the word *predated*. *Pre* means before, so I think it means that it happened or came before something else happened. Let's keep reading and see whether 'it happened before' makes sense here."

Summary

In this chapter, we described and illustrated how Word Work and instructional resources can support students in learning and productively using specific decoding elements to enable word solving and word learning and to promote comprehension. The Word Work approach is intended to encourage students to carefully analyze the sounds they hear in spoken words, and the letters that represent those sounds. Consequently, students take on an attitude of carefully studying the words they are learning. We have also detailed how knowledge of decoding elements supports students as they strategically puzzle through unfamiliar words.

In the next major section of the book (Part III), we discuss the construction of meaning during reading, which is, of course, the central purpose of reading instruction. Furthermore, the major reason for helping students learn to effectively and efficiently solve and learn unfamiliar words is to enable them to focus most of their cognitive resources on meaning construction. This is the focus of the remainder of the book.

Sample Introductory Word Work Lesson for Long and Short *a*

DEVELOPING SHORT AND LONG VOWEL FLEXIBILITY	
INTRODUCTORY LESSON	
VOWEL—*a*	
Teacher Activities before Instruction	
What the Teacher Says and Does	**Comments on the Activity**
Assesses: In order to identify what needs to be taught, the teacher administers and reviews results of an assessment of short and long vowels with the silent-*e* generalization. The teacher also considers observations that have been made of the students while reading.	This lesson is designed for students who have some knowledge that the vowel *a* has two sounds but who still need to consolidate the sounds and to learn to move between the two sounds.
Selects words: The teacher consults the list of long-*a* and short-*a* words provided in the website document Word Lists for Teaching and Practicing Long and Short Vowels (see the box at the end of the table of contents) and chooses eight to 10 words for building, three to four words for each student to read, and three to four words for spelling.	The words selected determine the level of challenge for students. All students in the group will build words based on the same principles, but the level of challenge can be individualized by selecting different words for each student to read and/or spell.
Prepares materials: The teacher assembles the set of needed letters to use in modeling and individual student sets for word building. The teacher writes the words students will read on index cards.	Presenting students with only the letters they will need reduces the cognitive challenge of word building, and helps students to focus on learning the vowel sounds. The list of words to be read may need to be simplified if students struggle during word building.
Selects text: The teacher previews and selects texts that provide opportunities for students to apply their new/developing knowledge of the two sounds made by *a*.	The purpose of Word Work is to provide students with decoding knowledge they can apply when reading text.

Materials needed for the whole activity:
1. Words to build, read, and spell, selected from the list of long-*a* and short-*a* words in the website document Word Lists for Teaching and Practicing Long and Short Vowels (see the box at the end of the table of contents)
2. The short vowel key word for *a* (Figure 9.3) on p. 178.
3. Word identification strategy list (Figure 5.1) on p. 68.
4. Sets of movable letters needed to build the selected words (can be organized on trays)—one set per student
5. Words on index cards or a list of words for the teacher to write during word reading
6. Dry-erase boards and markers or paper and pencil for written spelling
7. Word Work Planning and Recording Form (see the website document and the box at the end of the table of contents)
8. Texts for reading after lesson that contain long-*a* and short-*a* words

Instruction Step 1: Teacher Introduction	

Materials needed:
1. Dry-erase board, with the words *mat* and *mate* written on it, and marker
2. Movable letters needed to build the words used in the teacher model
3. The short vowel key word
4. Word identification strategy list

What the Teacher Says and Does	Comments on the Activity

Names and explains: "Now we are going to spend some time **building words**. When you do these word-building activities, you have the chance to think carefully about the letters and sounds and learn more about reading and spelling. Today, you are going to learn some helpful things about the vowel *a* by reading and spelling words with *a*.
    "The vowel *a* is a letter that makes more than one sound. Sometimes *a* makes the sound you hear at the beginning of the word ăpple" [the teacher points to the key word picture].
    "We have this picture to help us remember that *a* makes the /ăăă/ sound. That's the sound you hear in the middle of the word *mat*" [points to the word *mat* written on the dry-erase board].
    "Sometimes, *a* makes the sound that is just the same as the name of the letter *a*. It makes the /āāā/ sound. A lot of times when the *a* makes the /āāā/ sound, you will see an *e* at the end of the word. The *e* at the end is silent and it is there to remind us to try the /āāā/ sound. That's the sound you hear in the middle of the word *mate* [points to the word *mate* written on the dry-erase board]."
	If the teacher accurately and consistently names the activity, it is less confusing to the learner.
	
	If the students are or have been in programs that use specific key words for the short vowels, those are the key words that should be used in intervention.
	
	If the silent-*e* has been referred to in different ways (e.g., *bossy-e, magic-e*), make that connection for students.

Links: "You are going to practice spelling and reading words that contain the vowel *a*. You will practice in a special way that will help you to decide which sound for the vowel *a* to use when you read words with *a*. Learning the sounds for *a* will help you use this word identification strategy [the teacher points to strategy on list] **think about the sounds of the letters in the word** as you solve new words in books. It will also help when you learn the strategy **try different sounds for some of the letters, especially the vowel(s)**."	When the purpose for word building is clearly stated by the teacher, it helps students to see how their learning during this activity will help them as they read.

Models: "Watch me as I show you how to decide how to build these words.
    "Let's start with the word *hat*. I say the word and think about the sounds I hear. Then I set down the letters for those sounds.
    "The first sound I hear is /h/ so I set down the letter *h*. Next I hear /ăă/, like in *aaaapple* [the teacher points to the key word], so I set down the letter *a* and, because I hear that /ăă/ sound, I will not add the letter *e* to the end. The last sound I hear is /t/ so I set down the letter *t*.
	In this portion of the lesson, the teacher does the talking and students watch.
	
	The teacher should model what he or she ultimately wants students to think about and do, elaborating on the process if need be so that the students understand.

"Now I check the word by reading it and making sure it says *hat*" [the teacher models reading the word to check by running his or her finger under the word while slowly saying the sound for each letter and then blending the word].

"Now I want to change *hat* to *hate*. *Hate* starts with /h/ so I will keep the letter *h*. Next I hear /āā/. To show that the *a* is making the /āā/ sound, I need to put the letter *e* at the end of the word. *Hate*. Next I hear /t/ so I will keep the letter *t*.

"Now I am going to check the word by reading it to make sure I have built *hate*" [the teacher checks the word by reading and articulating the sounds, then saying the entire word].

"Then I'll change *hate* to *fate, fate* to *fat,* and *fat* to *fad*" [the teacher models his or her thinking as he or she builds and checks a few more words].

Instruction Step 2: Word Building

Materials needed:
1. List of words students will be asked to build
2. The movable letters needed to build the words (one set for each student)
3. The short vowel key word
4. Word Work Planning and Recording Form

What the Teacher Says and Does	Comments on the Activity

Provides practice: "Now it is your turn. As you build each word, think about which sound for *a* you hear. If you hear /āāā/, put the letter *e* at the end of the word" [the teacher asks students to build eight to 10 words from the long-*a*, short-*a* word list].
    "Make the word *made*."
    "Change *made* to *mad*."
    "Change *mad* to *map*."
    "Change *map* to *cap*."
    "Change *cap* to *cape*."
    "Change *cape* to *tape*."
    "Change *tape* to *tap*."
    "Change *tap* to *rap*."
    "Change *rap* to *rat*."
    "Change *rat* to *rate*."
	In this portion of the lesson, students should engage in saying the sounds in the word.
	
	 The teacher should provide support as needed—stretching the sounds, isolating and articulating sounds individually, reminding students to use the key words, and so on.

Waits: The teacher waits while students build and check each word.
    "Be sure to check your word building. Read what you have made to make sure it is the word you were trying to make. Do you hear /āāā/ or do you hear /ăăă/? What do you know about spelling those sounds?"
    If needed, the teacher reminds students to look only at their own letter set and not that of other students.
	Making the student responsible for confirming the accuracy of each word helps to develop independence in problem solving.
	
	 The teacher reminds students to check both when words have been built correctly and when they have not so the reminder doesn't become a signal that something should be changed.

Collects data: The teacher uses the Word Work Planning and Recording Form to keep track of student attempts and errors to inform future instruction.	Recording what the students do as they do it helps the teacher decide what: • Feedback to provide on the spot • Level of support or challenge to provide in follow-up lessons
Provides feedback: "You stretched that word when you were trying to decide what letter(s) you needed and that helped you figure it out."	Noticing and naming what students do with success increases the likelihood that they will apply their new learning to future problem solving.

Corrects errors: The student builds the word *made* as *m-a-d*.
    "You were really thinking about which letter to pick for each sound and I saw you check it over. Good thinking. There is one thing that needs to change. The word is *made*. Think about what might need to be changed."
    If the student is unsuccessful: "OK, what are we learning about how to spell the vowel sounds? What can you change here to spell the vowel sound in *made*?"
	Providing corrective feedback as needed supports student learning.
	
	Commenting on what students did right and what needs further thought helps students build on what they know and helps to further extend their knowledge base.
	
	Giving students the opportunity to try to identify what needs modification encourages the kind of thinking they ultimately need to do without reminding.
	
	If need be, reminding students of the focus of the lesson helps to reinforce the expected learning.

Reteaches as necessary: "Remember, if the word has the sound that is the same as the name of the vowel, you'll usually need an *e* at the end of the word."	Reteach as often as necessary until students can articulate the generalization.

Instruction Step 3: Word Reading

Materials needed:
1. Words to read written on cards *or*
2. List of words to read and dry-erase board or letter tiles
3. The short vowel key word
4. Word Work Planning and Recording Form

What the Teacher Says and Does	Comments on the Activity
Explains: "Now I am going to show you some words and you'll get to read them. Remember to check for that silent-*e* because that will tell you to try the vowel sound that is just the same as the name of the letter. Also remember, if you want to try the other sound for the vowel and you are not sure about that sound, you can use the key word for that vowel to help you remember. All you have to do is think about the first sound in the key word."	The teacher again provides scaffolding on an as-needed basis by reminding students to attend to the presence or absence of the silent-*e* and by guiding them to use the key words.

Provides practice: The teacher uses the words on the long-*a* and short-*a* word list and presents students with words written on index cards or on a dry-erase board, or makes the words using letter tiles. Each student should read three to four words. 　"Look at and read this word." 　The teacher shows the words [*mad, cape, tame, cap, mat*] one at a time so the students can focus.	To be efficient, the teacher should write out some words on index cards prior to the lesson. A few words may be built by the teacher and then read by students to make the connection between word building and reading more explicit. In the initial lesson, the teacher should start with some of the words the students have just built.
Collects data: The teacher uses the Word Work Planning and Recording Form to keep track of student attempts and errors to inform future instruction.	Recording what the students do as they do it helps the teacher decide what: • Feedback to provide on the spot • Level of support or challenge to provide in follow-up lessons
Provides feedback: "You saw the *e* at the end of the word and that helped you decide which sound to use for *a*."	Noticing and naming what students do with success increases the likelihood that they will apply their new learning to future problem solving.
Corrects errors: The teacher hears the student read *mad* as *made*. 　"You paid attention to all of the letters in that word. But there is one sound that is not quite right. See whether you can figure out what needs to change." 　If the student doesn't correct the response, the teacher provides a more explicit prompt: "Think about what we are learning about. What sound do you think needs to change?" 　If need be, the teacher should provide more directive guidance: "In this word, *a* is the only vowel. There is no *e* at the end of the word. What are you learning about the sound for *a* when it is the only vowel in the word?"	Providing corrective feedback as needed and commenting on what students did right and what needs further thought helps students build on what they know and further extends their knowledge base.
Reflects: "When you read the word _____, you noticed the *e* at the end and that told you to try the /āāā/ sound."	Initially, naming what the student does and how it helped gives the student a way to start internalizing and generalizing the skill or strategy to new situations.

Instruction Step 4: Written Spelling

Materials needed:
1. List of words to spell
2. Dry-erase boards and markers *or* paper and pencils for each student
3. The short vowel key word
4. Word Work Planning and Recording Form

What the Teacher Says and Does	Comments on the Activity
Explains: "Now I am going to say some words and you will spell them. Take your time and think about each of the sounds you hear in the word. An important decision you'll need to make for each word is whether to add that silent-*e*."	As in the previous activities, the teacher scaffolds as necessary (elongating sounds, reminding students to use the key words, etc.).

Provides practice: The teacher uses a dry-erase board and marker or pencil and paper, and asks students to write three to four of the words [*sad, mad, made*] that were practiced above. "Write the word _____."	Prior to the start of the lesson, the teacher should pick out some words to spell that were built or read in the session. The list may need to be adjusted based on how readily students build or read the words.
Collects data: The teacher uses the Word Work Planning and Recording Form to record student attempts and errors to inform future instruction.	Recording what the students do as they do it helps the teacher decide what: • Feedback to provide on the spot • Level of support or challenge to provide in follow-up lessons
Provides feedback: "You stretched that word when you were trying to decide what letter(s) you needed, and that helped you figure it out." "I noticed you checking the key word for that vowel sound. That helped, didn't it?"	Noticing and naming what students do with success increases the likelihood that they will apply their new learning to future problem solving.

Corrects errors: The teacher sees that the student spelled *sad* as *s-a-d-e*.
  "You were really thinking about which letter to use for each sound and I saw you check it over. Good thinking. There is still a change to make. What do you think may not be quite right?"
  If need be, the teacher should provide more directive guidance: "We are learning about how to spell the two sounds for *a*. Which *a* sound do you hear in the word *sad*? Is that the sound that is just the same as the name of the letter? [No.] So, we don't need the silent-*e* when we spell that word."
	Providing corrective feedback as needed, commenting on what students did right, and giving them the opportunity to try to identify what needs modification encourages the kind of thinking they ultimately need to do without reminding.
	
	If need be, reminding students of the focus of the lesson helps to reinforce the expected learning.

Reflects: "When you were spelling that word, you took time to think about which sound for *a* you heard and that helped you decide how to spell it."	Initially, naming what the student does and how it helped gives the student a way to start generalizing the skill or strategy to new situations.
Links: "Today we spent time reading and spelling words with the vowel *a*. In some words, the *a* made the sound that is just the same as the name of the letter. It made the /āāā/ sound. We saw the letter *e* at the end of those words. In other words, *a* made the /ăăă/ sound, like in *aaaapple*. Those words did not have an *e* at the end. "Knowing the sounds for *a* and how to decide which sound to try will help you as you read. Remember, you can always check the key word to help you remember one of the sounds for *a*."	When the purpose for Word Work is clearly stated by the teacher, it makes it easier for students to see how the activity will help them as they read.
Instruction Step 5: Application	
Links: "Now you get to read a book. When you come to a word with the vowel *a* in it, you can use what you've just learned. "That silent-*e* is a clue that tells you which *a* sound you might try first. The clue doesn't always work—so sometimes you'll just need to try both	The purpose of Word Work is to provide students with decoding knowledge they can use when reading text.

sounds for the vowel and see which one makes a word that makes sense in the sentence you are reading."	
Teacher Activities after Instruction, to Prepare for the Next Lesson	
What the Teacher Does	**Comments on the Activity**
Reviews data and plans Word Work: The teacher reviews the data collected about students' fluency and accuracy, and decides upon next steps.	A few students may still be slow and inaccurate. Plan for extra support and additional modeling if needed during the first consolidation lesson. Many students may be accurate but still slow. Plan for less support and consider some additional challenges during the first consolidation lesson. A few students will be fluent and accurate. Plan for additional challenges during the first consolidation lesson and encourage the students to notice and name their decision making.
Plans strategy instruction: The teacher should introduce or revisit the strategy **try different sounds for some of the letters, especially the vowel(s)** after teaching about the different sounds for *a*.	The purpose of Word Work is to provide students with decoding knowledge they can use when reading text. Students who are working on accuracy during word building may require heavier support in their initial attempts to use the strategy **try different sounds for some of the letters** as they read. Additional practice during consolidation lessons along with clear links to the strategy should improve students' fluency.

Sample Consolidation Word Work Lesson

DEVELOPING SHORT AND LONG VOWEL FLEXIBILITY	
FOLLOW-UP LESSONS	
VOWEL—*a*	
Teacher Activities before Instruction	
What the Teacher Says and Does	**Comments on the Activity**
Teaches: The teacher teaches the strategy **try different sounds for some of the letters, especially the vowel(s)**.	Teaching the strategy after the acquisition lesson and connecting it to the thinking students do during Word Work establishes a clear purpose for Word Work activities.
Selects words for further instruction: The teacher reviews student responses from the first lesson and selects words from the lists available on this book's website (see the box at the end of the table of contents). The teacher chooses words that may maintain or increase the level of challenge. Adding words with digraphs or blends is one way to increase the challenge. (See Chapter 8 for additional suggestions on adjusting the level of challenge.)	Typically, all students in the group build the same words. After building, each member of the group can be given different words during the reading and spelling portions of the lesson. In early consolidation lessons, use only known digraphs and easy blends, as described in Chapter 8. In later consolidation lessons, students can be asked to practice more challenging blends as they continue to practice changes in the vowel sound.

Materials needed:
1. Word list for long-*a* and short-*a* words (see website document Word Lists for Teaching and Practicing Long and Short Vowels)
2. Short vowel key word
3. Word identification strategy list
4. Sets of letters for word building
5. Words on index cards or a list of words for the teacher to write during word reading
6. Dry-erase boards and markers or paper and pencils for written spelling
7. Word Work Planning and Recording Form

Instruction Step 1: Teacher Modeling	
What the Teacher Says	**Comments on the Activity**
Names and explains: "Today we will continue building, reading, and spelling words with different sounds for the vowel *a* so you can more easily read and spell words that include *a*."	
Links: "When you practice building and reading words, you get better at thinking about the different sounds for *a*. Then, when you are reading and you come to a new word that contains the letter *a*, you can use the strategy **think about the sounds of the letters in the word**. You can also **try different sounds for**	When the purpose for Word Work is clearly stated by the teacher, it helps students to see how their learning during this activity will help them as they read.

some of the letters, by trying the /āāā/ and the /ăăă/ sounds to see which one fits."	

Briefly reviews: "I am going to use these letter tiles to make the word *made*. When I stretch out the word [the teacher says the word slowly, elongating sounds that can be stretched without distortion and being careful to minimize the schwa sound that is articulated in the sound of *d* in isolation (/duh/)], I hear the /āāā/ sound so I will put an *e* at the end and spell the word *m-a-d-e* [the teacher names the letters while building the word]. Now I check the word by reading it to make sure I included all the right letters in the right order.
    "Now I'll use the tiles to spell the word *sad* [the teacher says the word slowly, elongating the sounds]. I spell this word *s-a-d*. I did not add *e* to this word because the sound for *a* in this word is /ăăă/. That's the same sound that we hear at the beginning of the key word for *a*. Now I read the word to check it."
    The teacher rereads the word.
	The teacher should model what he or she ultimately wants the students to think about and do, elaborating on the process if need be so that students understand.
	
	After the first follow-up lesson, reviewing the procedure with modeling may not be necessary. Instead, the teacher may ask the students, "When I am making this word, how will I know what to do?"

Instruction Step 2: Word Building	
What the Teacher Says and Does	**Comments on the Activity**

Provides practice: "Now it is your turn to build some words. As you build each word, think about which sound for *a* you hear. If you hear /āāā/, put an *e* at the end of the word.
    "Make the word *dad*."
    "Change *dad* to *fad*."
    "Change *fad* to *fade*."
    "Change *fade* to *made*."
    "Change *made* to *mane*."
    "Change *mane* to *man*."
    "Change *man* to *mat*."
    "Change *mat* to *mate*."
	The teacher should provide support as needed but also be listening for places where students are ready to do the thinking on their own and take on more challenges in their building.
	
	If students appear to need the teacher to emphasize the sound that changes from one word to the next (e.g., change māāāāt to măăăăt), the teacher should do so. However, over time, the teacher should try to reduce and eventually eliminate this scaffolding.

Waits: The teacher waits and observes while the students build and check each word. "Be sure to check your word building by carefully reading the word to make sure you have included all the letters in order."	Making the student responsible for confirming the accuracy of each word helps to develop independence in problem solving. If students are thoughtfully building words, the teacher does not need to continue to prompt for checking. If students are working quickly and waiting for the teacher to tell them whether they "got it," the teacher should continue to encourage independent checking.

Collects data: The teacher uses the Word Work Planning and Recording Form to keep track of student attempts and errors to inform future instruction.	Recording what the students do as they do it helps the teacher to decide what: • Feedback to provide on the spot • Level of support or challenge to provide in follow-up lessons
Provides feedback/prompt for reflection: "You said the word slowly and thought about which sound needed to change. "How did you know that word needed an *e* at the end?"	Noticing and naming what students do with success increases the likelihood that they will apply their new learning to future problem solving. Over time, shifting the responsibility of noticing and naming to the students helps them internalize and generalize their learning.
Corrects errors: The student writes *fade* as *f-a-m-e.* "You really listened for the sound the vowel *a* made in this word and you knew to put *e* at the end. Listen to the word again. There is something that is not quite right in the word you built."	Providing corrective feedback as needed and commenting on what students did right and what needs further thought helps them build on what they know and helps to further extend their knowledge base.

Instruction Step 3: Word Reading	
What the Teacher Says and Does	**Comments on the Activity**
Explains: "Now I am going to show you some words and you will read them. Remember to check for that silent-*e* because that will tell you to try the /āāā/ sound for the vowel *a*. Also remember, if you want to try the other sound for the vowel *a* and you are not sure about that sound, you can use the key word for that vowel to help you remember."	

Provides practice: The teacher uses the words on the long-*a* and short-*a* word list and presents students with words written on index cards or writes the words on a dry-erase board. Each student should read at least three to four words.
    "Look at and read this word [*fade, mad, mate, cap, fat*].
    "For added challenge, read this word [*snap, glad, blade*]."
	The teacher again provides scaffolding on an as-needed basis by reminding the students to attend to the presence or absence of the silent-*e* and by guiding them to use the key word.
	
	For students who need additional support, the teacher may choose to make the words to be read using letter tiles, as this may help to draw the students' attention to the individual letters that comprise the word.

Collects data: The teacher uses the Word Work Planning and Recording Form to keep track of student attempts and errors to inform future instruction.	Recording what the students do as they do it helps the teacher decide what: • Feedback to provide on the spot • Level of support or challenge to provide in follow-up lessons
Provides feedback/prompts reflection: "You saw the *e* at the end of the word and that helped you decide which sound for the vowel *a* to use. "How did you decide which sound for the vowel *a* to use?"	Noticing and naming what students do with success increases the likelihood that they will apply their new learning to future problem solving.

	Over time, shifting the responsibility of noticing and naming to the students helps them internalize and generalize their learning.
Corrects errors: The student read *made* as *mad*. "You have paid attention to all of the letters in the word except one. Think about how your pronunciation of the word needs to change."	Providing corrective feedback as needed and commenting on what they did right and what needs further thought helps students build on what they know and helps to further extend their knowledge base. Asking students to articulate the reason for changing the pronunciation will reinforce their learning.

Instruction Step 4: Written Spelling	
What the Teacher Says and Does	**Comments on the Activity**
Explains: "Now I am going to say some words and I want you to spell them. Take your time and think about each of the sounds you hear in the word."	As in the previous activities, the teacher scaffolds as necessary (elongating sounds, reminding students to use the key words, etc.).

Provides practice: The teacher asks students to use a dry-erase board and marker or pencil and paper to write three to four of the words that were practiced above.
    "Write the word _____ [*fade, mate, fat*].
    "For added challenge, write the word _____ [*snap, blade, glad*]."
	The teacher again provides scaffolding on an as-needed basis by reminding students to attend to the possible need for the vowel *e* at the end of the word.

Collects data: The teacher uses the Word Work Planning and Recording Form to keep track of student attempts and errors to inform future instruction.	Recording what the students do as they do it helps the teacher decide what: • Feedback to provide on the spot • Level of support or challenge to provide in follow-up lessons

Provides feedback/prompts reflection: "You said the word slowly so you could really think about each sound.
    "What did you do to help yourself as you spelled this word?"
    "You are really thinking about the sound of the vowel. You figured out that you did not need to add an *e*."
	Noticing and naming what students do with success increases the likelihood that they will apply their new learning to future problem solving.
	
	Over time, shifting the responsibility of noticing and naming to the students helps them internalize and generalize their learning.

Corrects errors: The student spelled *sat* as *f-a-t*. "Think more about the word *sat*. There is one letter that needs to change. Say '*sat*' again and decide what letter needs to be changed."	Providing corrective feedback as needed and commenting on what students did right and what needs further thought helps them build on what they know and helps to further extend their knowledge base. Encouraging students to do as much of the thinking as they can promotes independence.

Instruction Step 5: Application	
Links: "You've just gotten a lot of practice with different sounds for *a*. When you are reading today and you come to a word with the letter *a,* you can use what you are learning here. You can use what you've learned as you use two strategies. You can **think about the sounds of the letters in the word** and **try different sounds for some of the letters** by trying the /āāā/ and /ăăă/ sounds to see which one fits.	The purpose of Word Work is to provide students with decoding knowledge they can use strategically when reading text.

Teacher Activities after Instruction, to Prepare for the Next Lesson	
What the Teacher Does	**Comments on the Activity**
Reviews data: The teacher reviews the data that were collected about students' fluency and accuracy, and decides upon next steps.	Plan follow-up lessons as needed. If some students are still developing accuracy, in upcoming lessons the teacher should control the level of challenge, provide support where needed, and notice and name what the students do. If students are accurate but slow, the teacher should plan to provide less support, increase the level of challenge on some words, and encourage students to notice and name what they have done at a few points. If students are generally accurate and fluent, the teacher should plan to move on to the different sounds for *i* (see website for word list; see the box at the end of the table of contents).

Sample Introductory Word Work Lesson for a Vowel Part

LEARNING THE *ou* PART	
INTRODUCTORY LESSON	
Teacher Activities before Instruction	
What the Teacher Says and Does	**Comments on the Activity**
Assesses: The teacher administers/reviews the results of the Decoding Elements Assessment (on this book's website; see the box at the end of the table of contents).	Students need instruction if they are still consolidating their knowledge of the *ou* part.
Selects words: The teacher chooses a known vowel part or vowel to which *ou* will be compared. The teacher consults the *ou* list and other relevant lists on the website for this book (see the box at the end of the table of contents), and chooses eight to 10 words for building, three to four words for each student to read, and three to four words for spelling.	The words selected determine the level of challenge for students. All students in the group will build the same words, but the level of challenge can be individualized by selecting different words for each student to read and/or spell.

Prepares materials: The teacher assembles the set of needed letters for teacher modeling, and individual student sets for word building.
  [If tiles are being used, tape the *o* and *u* tiles together. If cards are being used, write *ou* on a single card.]
  The teacher writes the three to four words students will read on index cards.
	Presenting students with only the letters they will need reduces the cognitive challenge of word building, and helps students to focus on learning the vowel sounds.
	
	Presenting *o* and *u* together helps students see *ou* as a part that represents a new sound.
	
	The words to be read may need to be simplified if students struggle during word building.

Selects text: The teacher previews and selects texts that provide opportunities for students to apply their new knowledge of the *ou* part.	The purpose of Word Work is to provide students with decoding knowledge they can use when reading text.

Materials needed for the whole activity:
1. Words to build, read, and spell, selected from the list of *ou* words
2. *Ou* key word
3. Word identification strategy list
4. Sets of movable letters needed to build the selected words (can be organized on trays), one set per student. Include single letters and the *ou* part. If consonant digraphs are to be used, both letters of the digraph should be on a single card or, if using letter tiles, the two tiles should be taped together.
5. Words on index cards or a list of words for the teacher to write during word reading
6. Dry-erase boards and markers or paper and pencils for written spelling

7. Word Work Planning and Recording Form (on this book's website; see the box at the end of the table of contents)
8. Text(s) that contain *ou* words for reading after lesson

Instruction Step 1: Teacher Introduction

Materials needed:
1. Dry-erase board and marker
2. Movable letters needed to build the words used in teacher modeling
3. Short vowel key words and the key word for *ou* and other vowel key words that have been introduced
4. Word identification strategy resource

What the Teacher Says and Does	**Comments on the Activity**
Names and explains: "Now we are going to spend some time **building words**. When you do these word-building activities, you have the chance to think carefully about the letters and sounds and learn more about reading and spelling. Today, you are going to learn about the *ou* vowel part that spells the /ou/ [pronounce as in *out*] sound by reading and spelling words with the *ou* part. "When you come to a new word with two vowels, you have been practicing trying the sounds for each vowel to figure out the word. In many words, that works. But there are some vowel combinations or vowel parts that represent different sounds. Today, you are going to learn one of those vowel combinations or vowel parts, *ou*. "The *ou* part *usually* makes the /ou/ [pronounce as in *out*] sound. Here is a picture of a mouse and the word *mouse* [the teacher points to the key word picture and the written word]. The *ou* in *mouse* is underlined to help you remember that this is the key word for the sound of /ou/. You can use this picture to help you remember that *ou* usually says /ou/ [pronounce as in *out*]. Tell me the sound that you hear in the middle of *mouse*. "In this letter set, the *o* and *u* have been put together to help you remember that when *o* and *u* are together, they are a part that usually represents the /ou/ [pronounce as in *out*] sound."	If the teacher accurately and consistently names the activity, it is less confusing to students. In this example, we use *mouse* as the key word for *ou*. However, if students have been taught different key words for the vowel parts, these key words should be used. In introducing the *ou* vowel part, the teacher teaches the most common sound of the vowel combination. During follow-up instruction, the teacher can point out that *ou* sometimes represents other sounds, so students should be ready to be flexible and should think of words that would make sense. Examples of words that do not include the most common pronunciation of *ou* are: *soup, group, you, through* *dough, soul, though* *thought, bought, cough* *would, should, could*
Links: "You are going to practice spelling and reading words that contain the vowel part *ou*. You will practice in a way that will help you to learn to recognize the *ou* part in words. Learning the vowel part *ou* will help you use the word identification strategy [the teacher points to the strategy on the list] **look for parts you know** as you puzzle through words you don't already know when you are reading."	When the purpose for word building is clearly stated by the teacher, it helps students to see how their learning during this activity will help them as they read.

Models: "Watch me as I show you how to decide how to build these words.	In this portion of the lesson, the teacher does the talking and students watch and listen.
"Let's start with the word *loud*. I say the word and think about the sounds I hear. Then I set down the letters for those sounds.	
The first sound I hear in loud is /l/ so I set down the letter *l*. Next I hear /ou/, the sound that is in the middle of the word *mouse* [the teacher points to the key word as it is named], so I set down the *ou* vowel part. Then, I think about the word *loud* again and notice the /d/ at the end, so I add a *d*.	The teacher should model what he or she ultimately wants the students to think about and do, elaborating on the process if need be so that the students understand.
"Now I check the word by reading it and making sure it says *loud* [the teacher models reading the word to check by running a finger under the word while slowly saying the sound for each letter/part and then blending the parts together].	
"Now I need to change *loud* to *pout* [the teacher again models the process of thinking about the sounds and putting down letters to represent each sound].	
"Now I am going to check the word by reading it to make sure I have built *pout* [the teacher checks the word by reading, saying the sounds, and blending].	
"Then I'll change *pout* to *out, out* to *stop,* and *stop* to *stout*."	
The teacher models his or her thinking as he or she builds and checks a few more words. It would also be appropriate for the teacher to provide brief, kid-friendly definitions of *pout* and *stout*.	

Instruction Step 2: Word Building

Materials needed:
1. List of words students will be asked to build
2. The movable letters needed to build the words, including *o* and *ou* taped together to make a part (one set for each student)
3. The *ou* key word
4. Word Work Planning and Recording Form

What the Teacher Says and Does	**Comments on the Activity**
Provides practice: "Now it is your turn. As you build each word, pay special attention to which vowel sound you hear. If you hear the sound that *o* usually makes by itself—the sound that you hear at the beginning of [name the short-*o* key word that is being used]—you will just use an *o* to spell the vowel sound. If you hear /ou/ [pronounce as in *out*], use the *ou* part."	In this portion of the lesson, students should engage in saying the sounds in the word. The teacher should provide support as needed (stretching the sounds, isolating and articulating sounds individually, reminding them to use the key words, etc.).
The teacher asks students to build eight to 10 words selected from the *ou* list and the comparison list for the decoding element chosen for comparison (in this lesson, short *o*).	When students are first learning about words through word building, the teacher controls the level of challenge by asking

"Make the word *loud*." "Change *loud* to *pout*." "Change *pout* to *pot*." "Change *pot* to *spot*." "Change *spot* to *spout*." "Change *spout* to *pouch*." "Change *pouch* to *chop*." "Change *chop* to *couch*."	students to attend to one change at a time. By the time students are ready to learn about the *ou* vowel part, they can typically handle more than one shift at a time. The words listed in the model often involve more than one shift. Note that if there is reason to suspect that students may not know the meaning of some of the dictated words, the teacher should provide brief kid-friendly definitions for the words (but should not turn this segment of the lesson into a vocabulary lesson).
Waits: The teacher waits while students build and check each word. "Be sure to check your word building. The word is _____. Read what you have made to make sure it is the word you were trying to make. Do you hear /ou/ or do you hear /ŏ/? What do you know about spelling those sounds?"	Making students responsible for confirming the accuracy of each word helps to develop independence in problem solving. *Note:* Be sure to provide reminders to check both when the response is right and when it is wrong so that the reminder doesn't become a signal that something should be changed.
Collects data: The teacher uses the Word Work Planning and Recording Form to keep track of students' attempts and errors to inform future instruction.	Recording what the students do as they do it helps the teacher decide what: • Feedback to provide on the spot • Level of support or challenge to provide in follow-up lessons
Provides feedback: "You stretched that word when you were trying to decide what letter(s) you needed and that helped you figure it out."	Noticing and naming what students do with success increases the likelihood that they will apply their new learning to future problem solving.

Corrects errors: The student builds *poch* for *pouch*.
    "You were really thinking about which letter to pick for each sound and I saw you check it over. Good thinking. But there is still a change to make. Think about the word again—*pouch*. Where do you think a change may be needed?"
    If need be, the teacher would focus the student(s)' thinking: "Remember what we are learning about how to spell our new vowel part. What can you change here?"
	Providing corrective feedback as needed and commenting on what students do right and what needs further thought helps students build on what they know and helps to further extend their knowledge base.

Reteaches as necessary: "Remember, if you hear the /ou/ [pronounce as in *out*] sound in a word, it may be spelled with the *ou* vowel part. If you see the part *ou* in a word, you can try the /ou/ sound—the sound you hear in the middle of the key word *mouse*."	Reteach as often as necessary until the students can articulate the generalization.

Instruction Step 3: Word Reading	
Materials needed: 1. Words to read written on cards (both *ou* and short-*o* words) 2. List of words to read and dry-erase board and marker 3. Short vowel key words and the key word for the *ou* vowel combination 4. Word Work Planning and Recording Form	
What the Teacher Says and Does	**Comments on the Activity**
Explains: "Now I am going to show you some words and you can read them. Remember to look carefully at the letters. If the *o* is the only vowel, try the /ŏ/ sound. If the word has the *ou* vowel part, try the /ou/ [pronounce as in *out*] sound. You can use the key word for the *ou* vowel part (as in *mouse*) to help you remember its sound."	The teacher again provides scaffolding on an as-needed basis by reminding students to attend to the vowel combination (*ou*) or the presence of the single vowel *o* by guiding them to use the key words.
Provides practice: The teacher uses words selected from the *ou* and the comparison lists, and presents students with words written on index cards or writes the words on a dry-erase board. Each student should read three to four words. "Look at and read this word [e.g., *loud, spot, couch, pout*; lists may vary for different students]."	The teacher should write out some words on index cards prior to the lesson. The teacher may choose to make some words for students to read using the letter tiles, if needed to make explicit the connection between word building and word reading. In the initial lesson, the teacher should start with some of the words students have just built.
Collects data: The teacher uses the Word Work Planning and Recording Form to keep track of student attempts and errors to inform future instruction.	Recording what the students do as they do it helps the teacher decide what: • Feedback to provide on the spot • Level of support or challenge to provide in follow-up lessons
Provides feedback: "You saw the *ou* and so you tried the /ou/ [pronounced as in *out*] sound."	Noticing and naming what students do with success increases the likelihood that they will apply their new learning to future problem solving.

Corrects errors: The student read *spot* as *spout*.
    "You paid careful attention to the beginning of the word. Take another look at the rest of the word. What letters do you see? What will they sound like?"
    If needed, the teacher should provide additional scaffolding: "What sound would you expect *o* to make when it is the only vowel in a word?"
	Providing corrective feedback as needed and commenting on what students did right and what needs further thought helps them build on what they know and further extend their knowledge base.

Reflects: "When you read _____, you noticed the *ou* in the word and so you tried the /ou/ sound."	Initially, naming what the student does and how it helped prepare the student to start generalizing the skill or strategy to new situations.

Instruction Step 4: Written Spelling	
Materials needed: 1. List of words to spell (both *ou* and *o* words) 2. Dry-erase board and marker or paper and pencil for each student 3. Short vowel key word chart and the vowel combination chart developed so far 4. Word Work Planning and Recording Form	
What the Teacher Says and Does	**Comments on the Activity**
Explains: "Now I am going to say some words and you will spell them. Take your time and think about each of the sounds you hear in the word and what you know about ways to spell those sounds."	As in the previous activities, the teacher scaffolds as necessary (elongating sounds, reminding the student to use the key words, etc.).

Provides practice: The teacher distributes dry-erase boards and markers or paper and pencils, and asks students to write three to four of the words that were practiced above.
    If all students are spelling the same words, say, "Write the word _____ [*loud, chop, spot, couch*]."
    If different students are spelling different words, tell each student to write their first word and so on.
	Prior to the start of the lesson, the teacher should pick out some words to spell that were built or read in the session. The list may need to be adjusted based on how readily students built or read the words.

Collects data: The teacher uses the Word Work Planning and Recording Form to keep track of student attempts and errors to inform future instruction.	Recording what the students do as they do it helps the teacher decide what: • Feedback to provide on the spot • Level of support or challenge to provide in follow-up lessons
Provides feedback: "You stretched that word when you were trying to decide what letter(s) you needed and that helped you figure it out."	Noticing and naming what students do with success increases the likelihood that they will apply their new learning to future problem solving.

Corrects errors: The student spelled *spot* as *spout*.
    "That's very close; there is just one sound that is not spelled correctly. Try to figure out what sound that is and fix it."
    If the student is unsuccessful: "OK, what are we learning about vowel sounds today? What sound do you hear in the middle of *spot*?"
	Providing corrective feedback as needed and commenting on what they did right and what needs further thought helps students build on what they know and helps to further extend their knowledge base.
	
	Giving students the opportunity to try to identify what needs modification encourages the kind of thinking they ultimately need to do without reminding.
	
	If need be, reminding students of the focus of the lesson helps to reinforce the expected learning.

Reflects: "When you were spelling that word, you took time to think about which sound you heard in the middle and that helped you decide how to spell it."	Initially, naming what the student does and how it helped prepare the student to start generalizing the skill or strategy to new situations.

Links: "Today you spent time reading and spelling words with *ou*. You learned that the *ou* combination makes a sound that is different from the sounds of either vowel so it has to be learned as a part. Now you know that *ou* is a part and you can look for that part as you puzzle through new words when reading."	When the purpose for word building is clearly stated by the teacher, it makes it easier for students to see how the activity will help them as they read.

| **Instruction Step 5: Application** ||

Links: "Now you get to read a book. When you come to a word with the *ou* vowel part in it, you can use what you've just learned. And if you don't remember that the sound for *ou* is /ou/, you can use the key word *mouse* to help you remember."	The purpose of Word Work is to provide students with decoding knowledge they can use when reading text.

Teacher Activities after Instruction, to Prepare for the Next Lesson	
What the Teacher Does	**Comments on the Activity**
Reviews data and plans word building: The teacher reviews the data collected about students' fluency and accuracy, and decides upon next steps.	A few students may still be slow and inaccurate. Plan for heavier support and additional modeling if needed during the first consolidation lesson. Many students may be accurate but still slow. Plan for less support and consider some additional challenges during the first consolidation lesson. A few students will be fluent and accurate. Plan for additional challenges during the first consolidation lesson and encourage the students to notice and name their decision making.
Plans strategy instruction: After teaching the *ou* part, the teacher should introduce or review the strategy **look for parts you know**.	The purpose of Word Work is to provide students with decoding knowledge they can use to puzzle through unfamiliar words encountered when reading text.

PART III

Meaning Construction

In Part II, we focused on understanding the process of word learning and instructional activities designed to promote word learning. Effective word-learning skills and strategies enable readers to build sight vocabulary, and having a well-developed sight vocabulary enables readers to devote most of their cognitive resources to meaning construction and knowledge building.

In Part III, we focus on comprehension and the attitudes and beliefs, skills, and knowledge sources (other than word identification) that enable meaning construction, and on how teachers can support students' development in these aspects of literacy acquisition. We also illustrate the reciprocal relationships between comprehension and knowledge, vocabulary and language, and the ability to read fluently. Part III is organized around the following four student goals and the instruction and interactions that can help students accomplish these goals:

1. *Comprehension:* Students will use information and ideas in the materials they are reading and their background knowledge to actively construct understandings of the texts they read.
2. *Knowledge:* Students will learn science and social studies content encountered while reading and will use this knowledge to foster reading comprehension.
3. *Vocabulary and Language:* Students will learn the meanings of new words, grammatical structures, and expressions encountered in both instructional interactions and through their reading; the expansion of these language skills will, in turn, foster reading comprehension.
4. *Fluency:* Students will read grade-appropriate text accurately with appropriate speed and with phrasing and intonation that conveys the intended meaning.

As we discuss in Chapter 10, these goals are interrelated and their instruction is integrated.

Comprehension

The active and independent construction of meaning is, of course, the most important goal addressed in reading instruction. This chapter begins with an overview of comprehension and the potential barriers to comprehension encountered by students who also need to devote energy to building reading accuracy and fluency. We provide background for how teachers may address the goal of comprehension, followed by a discussion of how to promote comprehension when an instructional priority is developing students' sight vocabulary and word-solving skills.

Understanding the Reading Process: What Is Reading Comprehension?

Comprehension occurs when readers think about what is being read, and use the author's words and their own knowledge to construct an understanding of a text. Reading is thinking—readers who hold this view of reading have the intention of making meaning and exert mental effort toward this goal. They nearly always think about what the author has to say; they are also using what they know and are learning to understand and interpret the ideas presented by the author. Drawing on these multiple sources of information/knowledge allows readers to construct meaningful and coherent interpretations of text that may differ from the

interpretations of other readers because each reader constructs his or her understanding by drawing on the information provided in the text and his or her unique
background knowledge and beliefs. Engaged readers "read between the lines" and
strive to create a coherent understanding of the texts they read. As summarized by
Currie and Cain (2015), "Text does not always explicitly state all of the information needed for coherence. Therefore, readers and listeners regularly make inferences to integrate information within the text and to fill in details that are only
implicit" (p. 57).

Coherence

Comprehension researchers use the term *coherence* to refer to the idea that a
reader continues thinking about the author's words and ideas until they all fit
together to communicate a sensible message. Proficient readers typically attempt
to attain a high level of coherence, especially when they have the necessary background knowledge needed to do so. Less proficient readers may be less inclined
and/or less able to exert the effort needed to attain a coherent interpretation of
a text.

Comprehension involves the reader in thinking and processing information at
multiple levels (Perfetti, 1985). Comprehension begins with the reader processing
each word in the text and then entails integrating the text's words into idea units.
Ultimately, comprehension involves the reader integrating his or her own relevant
knowledge with the author's words, to construct his or her individual understanding of the text, often referred to as a situation model (Kintsch & Rawson, 2005).
Comprehension will suffer if the reader is limited in any or all of these areas (Buly
& Valencia, 2002; Duke, Cartwright, & Hilden, 2013; Leach, Scarborough, &
Rescorla, 2003; Perfetti, 1994).

Proficient readers often describe at least some of their reading experiences as
"getting lost in a book." Readers may describe themselves as being transported to
another place, becoming attached to the characters, or having to put a book down
because the emotion that it evokes is too intense. On being interrupted, readers
describe themselves as feeling surprised at their surroundings. At the end of a
book, they may feel they have lost friends. While this level of interaction or engagement is often associated with fast-paced fiction, readers may find informational
text about a topic of interest to be just as riveting.

It is believed that this experience of engagement occurs in part because the
readers are using their own knowledge to interpret the author's language and construct meaning. When readers get "lost in a book" they are busy constructing its
meaning. Engaged readers are constantly in an interaction or conversation with the
author and/or the characters in the book. Sometimes a teacher is tempted to ask,
"Why don't authors write books that require less knowledge and inference, so that

they are easier for students to understand?" However, the challenge of literature is the same thing that makes it interesting and enjoyable.

Readers in intervention generally have not experienced this type of engagement—at least not with text that they read themselves. The mechanics of identifying the words and their unfamiliarity with books pose barriers to engagement for some readers. Lack of engagement may have long-term consequences because if a reader has not experienced engagement with books or a passion to learn about a topic, there is not much reason to read. Engagement fosters reading that allows further engagement. One goal of intervention is to move students toward this level of engagement. Ultimately, we want students to independently (and enthusiastically) interact with text, to be able to access the author's words and ideas, and integrate them with their own existing and developing knowledge.

Levels of Comprehension

Comprehension is not an all-or-nothing affair. Each of us has had the experience of reading text for which we had some, but not full, comprehension. In setting instructional goals for readers, it is useful to remember that text can be understood on a variety of levels. Often, these levels are referred to as *literal* (in which the reader understands the information that has been stated directly in the text), *inferential* (in which the reader must use background knowledge and inference to construct understandings that the author assumes that the reader is able to infer), and *critical reading* (in which the reader may compare or evaluate texts and reflect on or evaluate the author's intentions).

Often, the level of comprehension is expected to increase with grade-level and reading expertise (see the Common Core State Standards [CCSS] for examples; National Governors Association Center for Best Practices & Council of Chief State School Officers, 2010). However, at any given point in time, an individual reader's level of comprehension can vary, depending upon the difficulty of the texts he or she is reading, his or her knowledge related to the topics in the text, and the reader's reasons for reading and the circumstances in which reading occurs. For example, a reader with ample knowledge of baseball may readily draw on that knowledge to infer characters' feelings and motives in fiction that features baseball. The same reader may have only literal comprehension of fiction featuring a less familiar topic—such as the less familiar sport of curling. Similarly, a reader may be quite successful in comparing several short, easy-to-read biographies of Thomas Jefferson, and able to infer the different authors' purposes. The same reader might not be ready to compare or evaluate longer biographies. The goal of developing readers who engage in inferential and critical comprehension does not need to be deferred until readers are able to read grade-level texts. In texts in which they are knowledgeable about the topic and that they can read accurately, instruction can help literal readers learn to make inferences, and inferential readers to read critically.

Understanding the Reading Process: Factors That Influence Comprehension

Word-Level Influences

For each word that readers identify during reading, they (unconsciously) "look up" in their stored knowledge base the meaning of the word. For words that have more than one meaning (e.g., *table*) the proficient reader (unconsciously) sorts through the meanings that are stored in memory and selects that meaning that is appropriate for the context. This processing can only occur if the reader (1) accurately identifies the words; (2) has knowledge of the meanings of the words and, in particular, knowledge of the context-appropriate meaning; and (3) is able to attend to both the larger context and the potential meanings of the word. Because word identification accuracy and vocabulary knowledge are crucial to comprehension, their development is likewise crucial. We discuss instruction to promote the growth of these skills and knowledge sources in Chapters 4–9 and 12 of this book.

The Influence of Syntax and Fluency

As the reader identifies words and their meanings, the reader starts to construct meaning units by integrating words into meaningful groups or idea units. Some of those word groups might be phrases. For example, in the italicized sentence that begins this paragraph, a reader might form into a group the words *as the reader identifies words*.

What Is Syntax?

The syntax of a language is the system of rules that govern the formation of grammatical sentences and phrases.

Other connections are also formed. For example, in the italicized sentence above, a reader might connect "their meanings" to "words" to understand the author to be referring to "the words' meanings." This process relies on inference; readers use their knowledge of syntax and what is reasonable in the general context of a text, to decide what the authors are referring to when they use the word *their*. We discuss the role of syntax further in Chapter 12.

Cognitive scientists believe that information is processed in "working memory" (Baddeley & Hitch, 1974). It is hypothesized that words can be integrated together into idea (or phrasal) groups if they are in working memory at the same time. If a reader identifies words very slowly and/or in groups that do not reflect punctuation, syntax, and meaning, they are not likely to have the words (together) in working memory that are needed to construct meaningful ideas. When readers can effortlessly identify words, they are able to hold multiple words in working memory simultaneously. This, in turn, enables readers to integrate words to form ideas and, ultimately, to link together the groups of words to enable comprehension of the larger text. Thus, comprehension will suffer if the reader does not attain a threshold level of fluency in word identification and phrasing (see Paris & Hamilton, 2009, for a discussion). It should be noted that beyond this threshold, which Paris and Hamilton suggest is the ability to read third-grade passages, increasing fluency is less predictive of comprehension, presumably because other aspects of comprehension take on greater importance. We discuss fluency in more detail in Chapter 13.

The Influence of Knowledge

The ultimate phase of meaning construction is referred to as the reader constructing a "situation model" (Kintsch & Rawson, 2005). This involves integrating information based on the author's words (and illustrations if present) and the reader's knowledge. Readers interpret the information presented by the author through the lens of the knowledge that they hold. In the next chapter, we discuss the role of knowledge development in intervention.

Readers who can identify the words in a text and who read a text fluently may appear to also understand the text. But often, this is not the case (Buly & Valencia, 2002; Leach et al., 2003). In addition to identifying the words, reading requires the reader to draw on his or her existing knowledge and to make inferences in order to construct a mental representation of what's being conveyed in the text. Consider, for example, a piece of fiction in which a character goes skiing. The author probably does not say, because he or she expects the reader to know, that skiing requires snow, a mountain, warm clothes, and ski equipment—that is, the reader is expected not just to know the definition of skiing, but also have a rich network of ideas connected to skiing.

When a character in the text breaks a ski, the knowledgeable reader wonders, "How will the character get down the mountain?" because the reader knows that, for the typical skier, skiing requires two skis. Further, the reader may anticipate that a character who is stranded in the snow may not be able to stay warm. Readers connect their knowledge of skiing to the words in the text to generate a situation model for the text. A reader who has limited knowledge of skiing may not understand the conundrum faced by the skier with a broken ski nor empathize with the physical discomforts the skier may experience due to the cold. Indeed, Currie and Cain (2015) found that, among older struggling readers, depth and breadth of knowledge (as estimated by vocabulary knowledge) predicted the ability to make the inferences required for comprehension. The extent of a reader's knowledge is a more powerful predictor of comprehension than reading accuracy (Recht & Leslie, 1988) or reading strategy knowledge (Samuelstuen & Bråten, 2005). Knowledge of familiar topics is accessed from memory by the reader with little mental effort, allowing the reader to focus attention on interpretation of the text (Cervetti & Hiebert, 2015).

Readers also use their knowledge about how books work when they interpret an author's words. Readers know that the illustrations provide helpful, and sometimes crucial, information but that the most relevant information usually comes from the written portion of the text. So if the illustration shows the character skiing down the slope, for example, the reader still reads the words and learns that the character ultimately breaks a ski and may wonder why the illustration is at odds with the author's words.

There is ample evidence that illustrations serve to enhance readers' comprehension (see Carney & Levin, 2002, for a review), especially for those readers observed to carefully cross-reference information presented in the text and the illustrations (Mason, Tornatora, & Pluchino, 2013). However, there is also evidence that, for some older readers, under some circumstances, attention to the illustrations has a detrimental effect on comprehension (Pike, Barnes, & Barron, 2010; Rose, 1986). In our experience, readers who overrely on the illustrations will find it difficult to improve their comprehension until this habit is changed. This view is shared by Beck and McKeown (2001).

Proficient readers know to balance their background knowledge with the author's words as they construct a representation of the text. A reader knows that if the author does not mention sled dogs rescuing the skier, background knowledge obtained from a movie's dramatic sled dog rescue scene is not helpful to interpretation of the text. When the reader's situation model relies too heavily on prior knowledge and experiences, it will "distort the intended text meaning" (Paris & Hamilton, 2009, p. 35; see also Beck & McKeown, 2001). Once again, in our experience, it is difficult to improve the comprehension of readers who are overly reliant on illustrations and prior knowledge until they learn to balance attention to the written text and other sources of information.

The Influence of Intention

A final useful idea explained by Perfetti, Landi, and Oakhill (2005) is that readers "set the standard" for their own comprehension—that is, readers choose (probably not consciously) how hard they are willing to think in efforts to make sense of the text. To fully comprehend a text the reader must "set a high standard" for text coherence. Readers must set for themselves the expectation that all the words and ideas in the text will make sense, and fit together to form a coherent and meaningful whole. With this expectation, readers will then act (e.g., reread or change their thinking about a text if they encounter information in the text that is inconsistent with their previous thinking about a text). The "Thinking during Reading" box on page 225 provides an illustration of how active readers process the words in a text, constructing and reconstructing an understanding of it as they read. Proficient readers rework their interpretation of text as information is encountered that does not cohere with their initial understanding of the topic or focus of the text.

Thinking during Reading

Tom looked out the window.
He knew that soon the bell would ring and he could go outside.
When the bell rang, the door opened for the pizza delivery man.
Tom ran through the man's legs and off to join the other dogs.

In our experience, many intermediate and middle grade readers in intervention have experienced books as things that do not make sense or hold much meaning. Thus, whereas the proficient readers of the text in the "Thinking during Reading" box would shift their thinking about the text as they encounter information that doesn't fit with their unfolding interpretation of it, less proficient and/or passive readers might well just continue reading without noticing that the main character in the first couple of lines of the text appears to be a different creature at the end of the text. This may happen because the less proficient reader is not attempting to construct a coherent interpretation of the text and/or it might be the result of multiple word identification challenges that keep the reader focused on word- and sentence-level information rather than the larger text. In either case, some readers may have developed the habit of "reading" the words but not constructing meaning. These readers are sometimes described as *word callers* because that is all that they do (Meisinger, Bradley, Schwanenflugel, Kuhn, & Morris, 2009).

Such readers may not even be aware that reading is thinking, and that what they are doing is not reading—especially if their previous instruction has emphasized accuracy and fluency over meaning construction. Indeed, many less able readers are unaware that comprehension is the purpose of reading (Cain, 1999). They do not know that readers need to strive to fully understand the texts they read.

Comprehension Depends on Many Factors

To summarize a bit, for students who qualify for intervention in the intermediate and middle school grades, the process of constructing meaning can break down because they are lacking in one or more of the prerequisites for and contributors to comprehension listed below. Comprehension will be limited if the reader does not:

- Readily identify the vast majority of the words in the text.
- Know the context-appropriate meanings of the words in the text.
- Read fluently (and accurately) enough to form ideas in working memory.
- Readily interpret the text's syntax.
- Have the knowledge of the world and how texts work needed to construct meaning from the words in the text.
- Have the inclination to expend the thoughtful effort that may be needed to fully understand the text, so that all the parts of the text form a coherent and meaningful whole.

Readers who *do* have the skills, abilities, and inclinations listed above are equipped to engage in the process of constructing a situation model. This theoretical representation of comprehension reveals that the purpose of all of the components of reading instruction is to foster comprehension. Whether a teacher is helping students learn to read high-frequency words or the phonological translation of a group of letters or the meaning of a vocabulary word, the ultimate goal is better comprehension.

The connections between component skills and reading comprehension may be clear to the teacher, but often are not apparent to readers in intervention. Especially for older students who are disinclined to develop their basic skills, it is useful to provide frequent reminders—as illustrated in several of our sample lessons in Part II—that developing these skills will foster understanding and enjoyment of text.

Instructional Decision Making: Setting Priorities for Comprehension Development for Students Whose Primary Need Is to Develop Sight Vocabulary and Word-Solving Skills

Readers in the intermediate and middle grades who continue to need to build reading accuracy and sight vocabulary present the teacher with a range of instructional needs, and often, teachers wonder how to best prioritize these needs. The teachers with whom we worked found the following guidelines to be helpful:

Develop Motivation

For all students, fostering readers' motivation to read is essential to developing readers' comprehension. As described in Chapter 3, this can be addressed through careful selection of the books that students read and the language that teachers use, and relatively brief instructional interactions designed to build word identification skills. In our experience, students for whom building reading accuracy is an instructional focus enjoy reading texts that are organized to also develop knowledge about science or social studies topics. These students are often not able to read their social studies and science textbooks in the classroom—but appropriate theme books read during intervention enables students to develop knowledge, content vocabulary, and a sense of mastery. Words that are repeated from text to text provide opportunities for students to add words to both their sight vocabulary and their vocabulary.

Teach to Build Sight Vocabulary

For all students who continue to need to develop their sight vocabulary and word-solving skills, instruction tailored to address what they have yet to learn should be a nearly daily feature of instruction, and will likely include high-frequency words, word identification strategies, and decoding elements, as described in Chapters 4–9. This instruction should be viewed by the teacher and described to students as a critical contributor to comprehension success.

By instruction we mean both lessons designed to enable readers to acquire new knowledge about high-frequency words, word identification strategies, and decoding elements, and ample opportunity to consolidate this new learning. Consolidation of knowledge of high-frequency words, word identification strategies, and decoding elements can occur through explicit consolidation lessons and, perhaps most importantly, as students read texts that also develop their motivation, vocabulary, and knowledge.

Develop Knowledge and Vocabulary

A reader's knowledge and vocabulary support comprehension as well as word identification. Reading is, of course, one essential way that knowledge and vocabulary are acquired. In the ISA-X research, students read texts organized according to science or social studies themes as a way to develop their knowledge and content vocabulary. This approach has been advocated in reform efforts focused on improving literacy achievement more generally (e.g., Hirsch, 2003). In the CCSS, the expectation is that teachers "infuse the English language arts block with rich, age-appropriate content knowledge and vocabulary in history/social studies, science, and the arts" (National Governors Association Center for Best Practices & Council of Chief State School Officers, 2010, p. 33).

Chapters 11 and 12 address the development of knowledge and vocabulary, respectively. Chapter 16 provides an example of a thematic unit designed to build readers' knowledge and vocabulary while also addressing other literacy goals.

Encourage a Great Deal of Reading

Reading continuous text enables students to apply and develop their knowledge of high-frequency words, decoding elements, and word identification strategies as well as their knowledge and vocabulary. Reading is a skill that develops through engagement in reading. Thus, time spent reading is a crucial part of intervention for readers who continue to need to learn this knowledge. Chapter 14 focuses on this central feature of intervention.

In intervention, at least once the teacher has gotten to know his or her students, most of the reading students do should be silent or partner reading. However, listening as students engage in oral reading provides the teacher with important opportunities to observe and guide word-solving efforts and to help students learn to read text in a way that expresses the author's intended meaning. This involves both fluency in identifying the words and prosody (phrasing and expression). In Chapter 13, we discuss the role of fluency and smooth expressive reading in both developing and demonstrating comprehension.

Use Discussion and Writing to Ensure That Reading Is about Meaning Making

Some readers don't understand why people read—by the time such readers have reached third grade or beyond, they will have spent years developing the habit of not being engaged in meaning construction while reading. To ensure that all readers understand that the purpose of reading is to construct meaning, we encourage teachers to briefly discuss the texts they are reading with students for whom increasing reading accuracy is a major focus of intervention. This discussion might be as simple as "What was something interesting you learned by reading that text?" or "Why do you think [character] did that?" For a very simple text, the discussion might occur after reading. The reading of longer texts can be interspersed with discussion. The discussion should be just long enough to convey the message that reading is about thinking, and not so long as to seriously reduce time allocated to reading. Engaging students in conversations before, during, and/or after reading will, over time, help students understand that when they engage in thinking about what the author is saying, the process of reading becomes more enjoyable and informative. More detail about discussion is provided in Chapter 14.

We also encourage teachers to be sensitive to places in texts that may be more challenging, and where meaning may break down. Sometimes a teacher can anticipate these instances (e.g., unfamiliar vocabulary, lack of picture support) and other times, students convey their confusion using changes in their voice or actions. If the problem is not something that students can address, given their current strategies and knowledge, the teacher is advised to step in so as to maintain the meaningfulness of the text. Often, having students reread a challenging page, or the teacher stepping in to read the next page, will be sufficient to maintain a flow of meaning construction by students.

Postpone Formal Comprehension Instruction and Use Noticing and Naming to Foster Comprehension

For readers whose primary instructional focus is to develop their ability to learn to identify unfamiliar words and ultimately to build sight vocabulary, our approach has been to convey to readers that all text is read for meaning, but to postpone formal comprehension strategy or genre instruction until students' accuracy is better developed. This decision is supported by research conducted by Müller, Richter, Križan, Hecht, and Ennemoser (2015). They identified second-grade readers with poor comprehension and divided them into two groups: those with and those without grade-appropriate reading accuracy and fluency. Müller et al. found that their comprehension strategy intervention was helpful if readers were accurate and fluent, and ineffective—and in some cases detrimental—if readers were not accurate and fluent. This study suggests that *reading accuracy and fluency may be a necessary attainment before readers can benefit from comprehension strategy instruction.*[1] In our work, we provided comprehension strategy instruction only for readers whose reading accuracy was near or at grade-appropriate levels.

We also note that while conducting lessons that have a clear focus on developing readers' sight vocabulary and word-solving skills, during reading and discussion teachers often have opportunities to promote student thinking, knowledge, and comprehension monitoring by occasionally noticing and naming these processes when they occur. We encourage teachers to make judicious use of these opportunities to prepare students for future instruction. Chapter 15 is intended to provide teachers with information about aspects of comprehension they might comment upon, and examples of such language. For instance, if a teacher's comments and questions relate only to the book that students are reading (e.g., "How is Tom feeling now that he has won the spelling bee?"), the reader learns little about the *processes* whereby readers construct meaning from text. In contrast, if teachers also use some language that describes *what readers do*, the processes of comprehension are more apparent to the reader. Noticing and naming readerly thinking has the potential to increase the probability that such thinking will continue to occur and perhaps become more frequent. Some examples of helpful language include:

> "You reread that sentence because it wasn't making sense to you. That's a strategy that helps readers to better understand the things they read."

> "Thinking about how the characters are feeling helps readers to predict what the characters might do next."

> "Readers set purposes so they are thinking when they read. Your goal of learning about what it is like to go to school in China will help you to be thinking as you read."

> "You're wondering if [the character] is going to make it home before dark. Asking questions like that helps readers to stay engaged."

Summary

In this chapter, we detailed many factors that contribute to a reader's ability to construct meaning from text. We also discussed how a teacher might prioritize instruction related to these factors for students who are not yet accurate readers. The next chapter addresses the topic of knowledge development, which is supported through reading and discussion of texts, and which, in turn, supports readers' comprehension as well as their ability to build sight vocabulary.

---

[1]Research on the benefits of comprehension strategy instruction has not, generally, focused on instruction for students with limited accuracy and fluency. In our work with readers who struggle with reading accuracy, we focused on helping readers become strategic word solvers. We have reasoned that a simultaneous focus on word-solving strategies *and* comprehension strategies may overwhelm readers who are not yet proficient with reading the words.

Knowledge Development

In this chapter, we describe how knowledge is developed, and how important it is to many aspects of reading. We describe the use of thematic text sets as a way to develop key conceptual knowledge related to their science and social studies curricula among readers in intervention. We then describe text sets, provide some guidance on how they can be developed, and how and why they might be useful.

Rationale: What Is Knowledge, and Why Is It Important to Comprehension?

In this book, we use the term *knowledge* to refer to information stored in an individual's long-term memory. Some stored information may be specific to a content area (e.g., honeybees are a species whose survival depends on its social organization) and some information is more general (most people avoid animals that sting). Knowledge and vocabulary are not stored in memory as isolated facts, but instead are stored "in the form of interconnected networks of information" (Kendeou & O'Brien, 2016, p. 152). These networks may be described as concepts (e.g., everything the reader knows about rivers is connected to that central concept) and/or schema (e.g., the reader's knowledge of waitresses, menus, and courses in a meal are connected in a restaurant schema). Proficient readers have schema for fiction and nonfiction that enable the reader to navigate appropriately through these texts, just as the restaurant schema allows one to function appropriately in a restaurant.

Schematic Knowledge

Schematic knowledge refers to knowledge that is structured and organized. Because individuals encounter so many, many bits of information in a typical day, it would be impossible to store and retrieve much of the information unless it were organized in some way. Schemas develop over time and are modified through experience. An individual's *schemas* affect how one perceives, notices, and interprets information (Anderson, 1984). Having relevant schemas related to the text one is reading makes it easier to understand the text and may result in modifications to the reader's existing schema(s).

When new knowledge and vocabulary are learned, they are connected to existing knowledge, further developing the network. If a reader has ample knowledge about a topic, there are many ways for the new knowledge and vocabulary to become connected, so it's relatively easy to learn more about the topic and to later access the information. If a reader has little knowledge about a topic, the network that supports storage is smaller, learning is more challenging, and the reader may struggle to apply what has been learned (see Willingham, 2009, for a fuller discussion of this topic).

Many readers in intervention lack background knowledge and vocabulary. This may be due, at least in part, to their limited engagement in reading, especially the reading of nonfiction texts, which is one important avenue for the development of knowledge. Students who have had unsatisfactory experiences with reading may avoid reading and thus have less opportunity to learn from reading. Further, their lack of background knowledge makes it more difficult for them to understand what they read, so even when they do read they are likely to learn less from what they read. Thus, they fall even further behind in their knowledge base relative to their peers (Cunningham & Stanovich, 1998). For these reasons, we believe that opportunities to read to develop content-area knowledge are especially important for readers in intervention.

Teachers should be aware that readers' knowledge will also influence their reading accuracy and word learning. Readers with greater knowledge have a richer context to draw upon as they use code- and meaning-based strategies to identify unfamiliar words, and a more supportive network to which the unfamiliar word's identity can be attached. Readers with greater knowledge learn the meaning of new vocabulary words more readily, as discussed in the next chapter. Knowing a word's meaning is required before a reader can confirm a word's identity, so knowledge further supports word identification and learning.

As we discuss in Chapter 13, more knowledgeable readers are also more fluent readers. This is because knowledge enhances the ability to identify words and enables the reader to read with phrasing and expression that conveys the (understood) meaning of the text (Schwanenflugel & Kuhn, 2016).

In summary, knowledge supports readers' word identification, word learning, vocabulary development, fluency, and comprehension. Developing readers' knowledge is essential but is often neglected in intervention settings.

Understanding the Reading Process: Factors That Influence Knowledge Development

Two ways that readers can acquire new information is to be taught by a knowledgeable other or to read informational text. Certain reader practices support learning from informational texts. Readers learn if they attend to new information. That new information may be contained in the author's words and/or the illustrations or other graphic features in the text. To help them remember, readers may mark the new information in the text and/or write notes about the information they encounter.

It is easier to learn new facts and ideas if the reader also learns critical concepts to which new facts and ideas can be attached (Adams, 2009; Cervetti, Jaynes, & Hiebert, 2009). Teachers or informational text can accelerate the learning of conceptual knowledge (which in turn supports the learning of facts and information) by using several ideas drawn from theory about concept learning.

First, it is helpful to *focus knowledge development around a few "big ideas"* to which other information can be attached (McRae & Guthrie, 2009). For example, while reading about colonial America, one teacher focused students' thinking on what the colonists had to do to *survive*. This idea that the colonists struggled to survive was summarized by the teacher as "You've got to survive." This central idea provided a "place" for students to connect and understand many specific facts (colonists grew sheep for wool, sheared their coats, spun the thread, wove cloth, and sewed clothing). Although one student theorized that surely at that time in England a girl could go to the store and buy a pair of shorts, this framework helped readers to begin to develop the knowledge that colonial life included many physical challenges.

It is helpful to the learner if the teacher or informational text *labels* a concept or conceptual knowledge (by providing the vocabulary word *colony* or stating that "Survival was not easy for the colonists"). The label tells the learner that there is something to be learned. The informational text or the teacher can also draw attention to the *distinctive features* of the idea or concept by comparing positive examples (winters were cold and the colonists' houses were drafty) and negative examples (colonists could keep warm because they had lots of wood available for heat). A familiar example that is similar to the idea that survival was challenging (having to put up a tent and start a fire while camping) can also help to develop knowledge. A text or a teacher who engages students in *thinking actively* about the conceptual knowledge (e.g., asking students to consider why the colonists had small houses) also promotes conceptual learning.

Knowledge about an idea such as the colonists' struggle for survival may not be learned in one lesson or one book—rather, it may well be learned through *multiple experiences* with information related to the idea, and abstracted by the learner from those experiences. The understanding is developed as the student learns about how the colonists worked to make their own shelter and clothing, how they grew their own food, and how everyday things like shoes and farming implements were made by hand.

Pockets of Knowledge versus Knowledge Development

The process of knowledge development is different from the common practice of providing readers with knowledge needed to understand a specific text. In this approach, teachers may "activate background knowledge" through student sharing prior to reading (Pressley et al., 1992), or teach text-specific knowledge, a practice often referred to as teacher "front-loading" (Fisher & Frey, 2012). In either case, relevant knowledge is told to those who lack it. This one-time exposure to specific facts or "pockets of knowledge" (Cervetti et al., 2009, p. 84) generally results in poor retention because the learner lacks knowledge structures that would enable the integration and retention of the facts. Activating background knowledge, or front-loading, may allow a student to navigate a specific text but does little to develop the critical concepts and knowledge that would support understanding of a range of texts.

One way to develop critical concepts is to engage students in the reading of sets of content-rich informational texts that allow English language arts and content learning to be integrated (Cervetti & Hiebert, 2015). In the ISA-X research projects, students read *thematically organized text sets,* where the themes were science or social studies topics also being taught in the general education classroom. In each theme, students read several books on a single topic, which provided students with repeated exposure to certain "key" science and social studies concepts and vocabulary words in different contexts. Students also encountered the same concepts in the general education classroom. Repeated exposure to the vocabulary and ideas in a text set allows students to learn vocabulary and develop concepts and schema (Adams, 2009). Attainment of this learning has the potential to ultimately influence the comprehension of a range of texts.

Instructional Decision Making: Thematic Text Sets

In our work with intermediate and middle grade readers, we realized that a lack of content knowledge was a barrier to comprehension and limited students' ability to read grade-appropriate text. We designed the ISA-X intervention to be organized around the reading of thematically related texts. The purpose of the text sets was to allow reading instruction to simultaneously accomplish two goals: (1) to promote reading proficiency and (2) to develop readers' knowledge of science or social studies topics. An example of a text set is included in Chapter 16.

We use the term *thematic text set* to refer to a carefully sequenced group of trade books about a science or social studies topic. The text sets include both nonfiction and fiction texts. They are generally organized so that students begin by reading a series of easy nonfiction texts on the topic, and then more challenging nonfiction. The set often concludes with fiction texts; students use the knowledge they have acquired from the informational texts to interpret the fiction texts.

In reading and discussing these texts, teachers and students were encouraged to see books as the "content experts" (rather than the teacher). The goal was for students to develop knowledge about important topics by reading, and to learn that reading was an enjoyable and effective way to develop knowledge and that doing so was within the readers' grasp. Figure 11.1 illustrates how one reading group recorded the knowledge they were learning. Ultimately, the goal was for

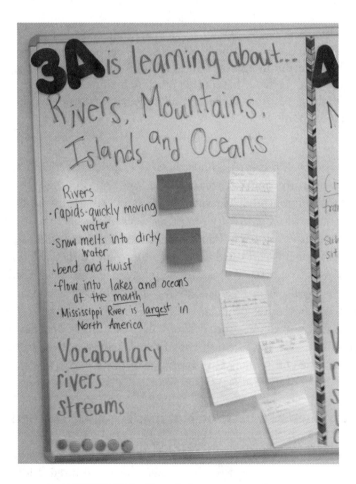

FIGURE 11.1. Knowledge summary chart.

students to read to acquire sufficient knowledge so that, at the end of the theme, they could read text that was closer to being grade appropriate.

We used the following principles to organize the thematic text sets.

Coherence with Content Instruction

Theme topics were drawn directly from our state's curriculum standards in science and social studies; topics were among those included in the science and social studies curriculum that students were learning in the general education classroom. We also selected topics for which books of a range of difficulty levels and genre were available. We relied heavily on a website for librarians, Titlewave.com (*www.titlewave.com*), when identifying how many books would be available on a topic. The site lists all books in print on a topic and orders them by reading level.

Knowledge Development

Multiple nonfiction texts about one topic were reviewed and selected based on our judgment of their appeal, clarity, and contribution to a sequence intended to develop knowledge. The intent was to provide multiple exposures to new concepts and ideas to build knowledge through the reading of many related informational texts or biographies.

Illustrations

Illustrations and other graphics are a source of information that is readily accessible to readers, although they may need to be guided to access and interpret it. For example, if students read a series of nonfiction books about rivers, they encounter a range of illustrations that show how rivers develop, what they are useful for, and the wildlife that depends on a river. Strategic readers rely on the illustrations provided in texts, because the illustrations provide knowledge that will support their conceptual learning as well as word identification and construction of meaning.

Narrative

Willingham (2009) makes the interesting argument that learners are more likely to remember facts and ideas if they are linked to the conflict and its resolution in an engaging *narrative*. Thus, our text sets included narrative fiction as well as nonfiction.

Different works of narrative focus the reader's attention on different aspects of particular concepts, and are thus useful for developing elaborated understandings. In selecting fiction for a thematic unit, we considered what the narrative focused the reader's attention on, and thus what aspects of the concept will be learned by reading the narrative. In *Jack and Rick* (McPhail, 2001), the river is a barrier but the characters build a bridge to overcome the barrier; *River* (Atwell, 1999) focuses on how people use rivers for transport, as a source of energy for factories, and for enjoyment.

Addressing Multiple Instructional Goals

Readers in intervention cannot afford to squander instructional time. In order to do more with limited instructional time, we planned the reading of thematically related texts to address important language arts goals as well as develop content knowledge.

Develop a Sense That Reading Has Value

As they progressed through the text set, readers developed their knowledge base through reading. The text set began with simple texts to introduce the topic, so there was no need for "teacher front-loading." Teachers were encouraged *not* to teach content so that knowledge grew from reading, rather than teacher instruction. As students experienced learning from books, they came to understand that reading is a way to develop important and useful knowledge. The teachers with whom we worked also conveyed this directly to students by saying:

> "You will have the chance to learn about [topic] when you read these books."
>
> "We learned a lot about [topic] by reading this book!"

Develop Self-Efficacy

As described in Chapter 3, as students acquired knowledge independent of teacher instruction, this had the effect of increasing readers' self-efficacy. Readers saw themselves as individuals who could read to learn interesting information. Readers were able to bring "wow facts" and anecdotes they had read to the general education classroom to share during science or social studies instruction.

Maximize Reading Time

As described in Chapter 14, more time spent reading is recommended to increase the reading proficiency of older struggling readers (Fisher & Ivey, 2006). The use of themes increased time spent reading because the reading of related texts replaced teacher front-loading as a way to develop student knowledge in preparation for reading to further develop knowledge.

Maximize Student Thinking and Engagement

When students read closely related texts, the knowledge they develop allows them to be more *engaged* in what they read. As knowledgeable readers, students had more to say during discussion. They noticed discrepancies between previously read books and new information encountered in current books. Teachers promoted this engagement with feedback about readers' engagement:

> "Have you noticed? After we read a bit about a topic, you guys have some really interesting questions, and those questions make us want to read more. Let's keep reading to learn the answers to these great questions."
>
> "You have so much to say now that we have read about this topic."
>
> "Reading is turning you into someone with a lot of interesting ideas and information to share."

Read Some More Challenging Text

A consistent diet of instructional-level text will limit readers' development (Shanahan, 2014; this idea is discussed in more detail in Chapter 14). We organized text sets so that students moved from reading easier to reading more challenging texts within a topic. Gelzheiser (2005) found that students who read a balance of instructional and challenging texts within a theme made greater reading gains. Gelzheiser hypothesized that, in part, these gains occurred because a thematically structured mix of genre and difficulty levels enabled students to develop background knowledge that would support the reading of texts that would be too challenging without that knowledge.

Develop Genre Knowledge

Some themes had a language arts goal of developing knowledge about genre. These units had a focal genre for which students read multiple texts in the genre—for example, folktales (in the Native American and Colonial Life units) and biography (in units on exploration, early settlement, and the American Revolution). Thus, for example, after learning about the culture of the Iroquois and Algonquin tribes, students read a series of Iroquois and Algonquin folktales.

A Typical Thematic Text Set

In the ISA-X research projects, a typical theme would begin with a very simple introduction by the teacher, naming/defining the new topic and explaining its significance. Rather than beginning the theme with the teacher providing students with information about key concepts and vocabulary, we began with students reading several very accessible nonfiction texts with the goal of building basic knowledge about the topic. This reading typically occurred in a shared, small-group format, so that the teacher was able to monitor students' learning at this initial stage, and assist with the pronunciation of words that were not in the students' spoken vocabulary (given that it is not possible to confirm that a word has been accurately identified if the word is not in one's spoken vocabulary).

Often, the introductory texts had only one line of text and a helpful photograph or illustration on each page; some texts might be written at a level deemed to be below students' instructional level. As students learned facts, these might be marked with "sticky notes" and recorded by either the teacher or the students, then posted on a larger summary of what the group was learning. As students developed knowledge about the theme topic, they read more independently of the teacher, in pairs or alone.

After reading, students discussed all or parts of more challenging nonfiction texts to deepen and consolidate their knowledge base. With additional knowledge, they asked more sophisticated questions and were able to engage in critical comparisons of texts. Each of these nonfiction texts also served as an opportunity for students to practice the word identification strategies they were learning, as well as to encounter high-frequency words and decoding elements.

Students might then read a challenging culminating work of fiction for which the knowledge they had acquired was useful. Thus, rather than depending upon the teacher to provide background knowledge, reading the thematic texts prepared readers with knowledge they could draw upon as they made predictions, interpreted the illustrations, and thought about the characters' motivations. Their knowledge might continue to develop as they read new facts about the topic included in historical or realistic fiction. In other units, rather than read one culminating text, students might read a series of shorter works in the focal genre, with the objective of becoming acquainted with the genre.

Developing the Text Sets

Lists of thematically related texts are provided in Gelzheiser, Hallgren-Flynn, Connors, and Scanlon (2014). This article also provides suggestions and resources that teachers can access to develop their own sets of thematically related texts.

For most themes, a first step was to select a *culminating fiction text*. Typically, this text was longer and more grade appropriate in difficulty than other texts in the unit. The culminating text was analyzed to determine the background knowledge that would be helpful in understanding the text. Nonfiction texts were then selected to develop as much as possible of the needed knowledge. Once students had read these texts and developed some useful knowledge related to the concepts and vocabulary needed for the culminating text, their cognitive resources could be directed to making inferences, addressing word identification and syntax challenges, and sustaining understanding in the longer text. As Adams (2009) describes, "as students learn the core vocabulary, basic concepts, and overarching schemata of the domain . . . gradually and seamlessly they will find themselves ready for texts of increasingly greater depth and complexity" (p. 184).

For some themes, there were easier versions of the culminating text available. In this case, we had students read several versions of the same fictional story, with the goal of preparing them to read the more challenging text. For example, *The*

Legend of Sleepy Hollow was read multiple times: first in a "controlled vocabulary" format (retold by Standiford, 1992); then again as a graphic novel (retold by Hoena, 2008); and finally, in a chapter book format (adapted by Mattern, 2007). This sequence provided scaffolding to readers so that they had ample knowledge (in this case, about the characters and events of the folktale) to read increasingly challenging text with independence. Students were happy to engage in this process, noting how each author had a different approach to building suspense and ultimately leaving the identity of the Headless Horseman unknown.

In choosing nonfiction, our view was that *there could never be too many nonfiction texts*. If there were too many easy texts on a topic, some could be offered to students for independent reading. If there were several comparable texts, different pairs of students could read different texts, and present what they learned to the group. If a group of nonfiction books on the "same" topic is assembled, it quickly becomes apparent that they differ in substantial and interesting ways.

Summary

In this chapter, we discussed the value of engaging readers in reading multiple texts on the same or related topics, with the texts being organized from less to more challenging. In intervention, we found it useful to have readers begin with reading easy informational texts to build knowledge and vocabulary related to the topic. They progressed to more grade-appropriate informational and fictional texts, which they were able to read with greater accuracy and comprehension as a result of their experience with the easier texts. In our view, organizing students' reading experiences in this way has multiple advantages, including helping students to build content knowledge, vocabulary, sight vocabulary, and a sense of efficacy for reading and learning. In the next chapter, we delve deeper into ways to support the learning of the meanings of unfamiliar words and some of the other language challenges that texts may pose.

CHAPTER 12

Vocabulary and Language

> ## STUDENT GOAL
>
> Students will learn the meanings of new words, grammatical structures, and expressions encountered in both instructional interactions and through their reading; the expansion of these language skills will, in turn, foster reading comprehension.

In this chapter, we discuss the relationship between reading comprehension and language skill with a particular emphasis on knowledge of word meanings—that is, vocabulary. We also discuss why many of the students who are receiving reading intervention in the intermediate and middle school grades often have more limited vocabularies and language skills than their same-grade peers. With regard to vocabulary, we address the development of two types of vocabulary: (1) sophisticated general vocabulary words that are used across a variety of contexts and content areas, and (2) content vocabulary words that are encountered in science and social studies texts. In the context of intervention, we do not place major emphasis on formal instruction of either type of vocabulary. Rather, we make the case that vocabulary and other language skills are expanded through meaning-focused interactions with and about texts in which understanding of the word meanings and other language structures are learned and refined as students grapple with the content in thematically organized texts. In this chapter, we provide suggestions for helping students understand and use the more sophisticated language encountered in the books they read and respond to.

Rationale: What Is Vocabulary, and Why Is It Important?

We use the term *vocabulary* to refer to students' knowledge of words' meanings. Research indicates that readers with stronger vocabularies comprehend texts more effectively (e.g., Cunningham & Stanovich, 1998; Quinn, Wagner, Petscher, & Lopez, 2015). Research also shows that comprehension of texts leads to the development of new and more explicit knowledge, including new vocabulary knowledge (Duff, Tomblin, & Catts, 2015). Indeed, the relationships between comprehension and vocabulary grow stronger as students move through the elementary grades (Catts, Hogan, & Adolf, 2005; Vellutino, Tunmer, Jaccard, & Chen, 2007). Because of what has been learned about the relationships between vocabulary and reading comprehension, recently there have been calls for including a focus on vocabulary development as a regular part of intervention (Loftus & Coyne, 2013).

For the purpose of instruction, some experts have described different types, or tiers, of vocabulary words (Beck, McKeown, & Kucan, 2013). Tier One words are words students are likely to learn and use in everyday conversation—for example, *sad*—without explicit instruction. Tier Two words are generally useful words that are more sophisticated, and may be encountered more often in books than in conversation—for example, *glum* or *sorrowful*. Learning meanings of such words can allow the reader to discern the author's meaning and shades of meaning. For example, a character who is *glum* is different from a character who is *sorrowful*. Tier Three words are also sophisticated, but are used in more narrow contexts—for example, science or social studies terms like *photosynthesis* or *equator*. Learning Tier Three vocabulary promotes the learning of important content. In this chapter, we discuss the development of both Tier Two and Tier Three words, as both play a role in fostering reading comprehension.

Vocabulary versus Sight Vocabulary

On occasion, we encounter teachers who are not clear about the distinction between the seemingly similar terms *vocabulary* and *sight vocabulary*. The word *vocabulary* is used to refer to knowledge of word meanings. *Sight vocabulary* refers to the body of words that a reader can identify automatically and in all contexts when they are seen in print (they can identify them *on sight*). For readers who are still learning to puzzle through unfamiliar printed words, the body of words for which they know the meanings is larger than their sight vocabularies. For proficient readers, the number of words they can identify on sight and the number of words for which they know the meaning is quite similar.

In this chapter, our focus is on *knowledge of word meanings*.

It is helpful to remember that knowledge of word meanings can occur on several levels. Consider the sentence "Samuel tucked his shirt into his *breeches*." Because the context is supportive, readers may be able to *infer* that the word *breeches* means some kind of pants, even though they may not be able to *produce* the word in their spoken language or define the word. Using context will likely result in *partial* knowledge of the meaning of breeches—that is, the context may not be sufficiently detailed to allow readers to know what distinguishes breeches from pants, jeans, and shorts.

For most words, knowledge of the meaning of a word increases as the learner encounters the word in different contexts. Thorough learning of the meaning of a word generally does not occur in a day; it occurs over time and across contexts. In fact, Bloom (2000) argues that children learn the meanings of "one hundredth of each of one thousand different words a day" (p. 25). Vocabulary knowledge can continue to develop throughout a lifetime. Even a simple word like *dog* gains additional meaning as the learner encounters new breeds or learns about dog behavior through firsthand experience, television, and books.

Vocabulary Network(s)

As we discussed in the previous chapter on knowledge development, psychologists believe that the reader's mind organizes knowledge of the meanings of words into a complex network of interconnections (Kendeou & O'Brien, 2016). When readers learn the meaning of the new vocabulary word *breeches*, they connect the meaning of the new word to the meaning of other words they already know, like *pants, shorts,* and *jeans.*

The network theory has two important implications. One implication is that a reader with a smaller vocabulary, and thus a smaller network of existing word meanings, will have fewer places to connect the meaning of newly learned words. This reader will find it more challenging to learn new vocabulary, while the reader with a broader vocabulary will have more connections readily available to support vocabulary learning.

Recent research suggests that the vocabulary network supports vocabulary learning in a fascinating way. This research suggests that adding knowledge to any word in the network results in knowledge that spreads throughout the network (see Adams, 2009, for a discussion). Thus, learning the word *breeches* adds to readers' understanding of *pants, shorts,* and *jeans*—and any other words in this network. This research also suggests that time invested in promoting vocabulary development enables the learning of the meanings of newly encountered words and the refinement of knowledge of related words.

Understanding the Reading Process:
Factors That Influence Vocabulary Learning

Time Spent Reading

Research suggests that, at least for older students and adults, most of their learning of new words occurs in the context of reading (Nagy, Herman, & Anderson, 1985; Sternberg, 1987), and not through direct instruction. This is because time for vocabulary instruction is limited, while books offer unlimited exposure to many words that do not come up in everyday conversation (Cunningham & Stanovich, 1998). Consider this description of Pumpkin Island before a storm:

> The ledges behind Pumpkin Island are covered with gulls, all sitting solemnly faced in the same direction. There is no giggling and cackling as your wake splashes the ledge today. (McCloskey, 1957, p. 38)

In conversation, one might say, "There are quiet birds sitting on the rocks. The birds get wet when the boat goes by." In contrast, the author's written description includes some more sophisticated words that are specific to the particular context (*ledges, gulls, wake*), as well as sophisticated words that could be used in everyday conversation (*solemnly, faced, cackling, splashes*).

Because of the many opportunities that reading offers for vocabulary development, at least for those who focus on meaning construction as they read, it is not surprising that Cain and Oakhill (2011) found that readers who had weak reading comprehension skills showed less growth in vocabulary between the ages of 8 and 16 than did readers with stronger comprehension skills. At the same time, a reader who lacks knowledge of the meaning of many context-specific and more generally useful sophisticated words would find it challenging to understand passages like the description of Pumpkin Island above.

Experience and Vocabulary Knowledge

Some students begin school already behind their peers in vocabulary knowledge. Children who grow up in poverty are more likely to begin school with more limited vocabulary knowledge than students who come from more economically advantaged backgrounds (Hoff, 2006). Often, children growing up in poverty have fewer opportunities to learn language through conversation, and are not exposed to the rich vocabulary in books through frequent read-alouds (Neuman & Celano, 2012).

As noted above, knowing fewer word meanings is problematic because new word meanings are learned through connections to existing knowledge. Students with limited vocabularies learn new words more slowly than their peers, because their existing vocabulary knowledge is more limited. Slower vocabulary growth among students who begin with limited vocabulary has been documented in the primary grades (e.g., Kempe, Eriksson-Gustavsson, & Samuelsson, 2011) and beyond. Thus, vocabulary growth is somewhat of a "the rich get richer, the poor get poorer" phenomenon (Cunningham & Stanovich, 1998).

In addition to perhaps starting their education with a more limited vocabulary, there are a number of reasons why vocabulary growth may stagnate as readers with limited reading skills move through the grades. These include the following.

Less Challenging Texts

In many instances, the reading materials used in intervention settings make use of "controlled vocabulary" texts that are intended to make it easier for students to read (decode) the words. To accomplish this, these texts have simpler vocabulary and therefore offer fewer opportunities to learn the meanings of new words.

Limited Reading Experience

As noted in Chapter 3 on motivation, students who continue to need reading intervention in the intermediate grades and beyond often avoid reading because it is unrewarding and frustrating. Unfortunately by reading less, they encounter fewer opportunities to learn the meanings of new words or to refine their understanding of the words they know.

Lack of Fluency

When they do read, many readers in intervention settings need to devote substantial cognitive resources to the process of figuring out the identities of the words in the text. Thus they have have fewer resources to allocate to attending to—and perhaps attempting to infer the meanings of—newly encountered words. It is engagement with the *meaning* of text that helps to increase the reader's vocabulary. Plus, because of their lack of fluency with word identification, these readers may read fewer words in a given period of time than will their more proficient peers.

Limited Vocabulary

Learning the meanings of new words involves a process of connecting the new words with already known words. If readers already have a limited vocabulary, they may not know the words that are used to explain the newly encountered word. For example, in an informational book about China, the word *tradition* is defined in the glossary as "a custom, belief or practice that people in a particular culture pass on to one another" (Riehecky, 2008, p. 46). A student with a limited vocabulary may well not know the meaning of several words used in this definition—for example, *custom* or *culture*.

Limited Word Consciousness

When students are not exposed to the rich vocabulary of books and find vocabulary learning to be difficult, they may not be curious about words or aware of potential words to be learned. After encountering a student who knew what a *turnstile* was at the amusement park but not what it was called, we realized that some students "live in a largely unnamed world," surrounded by objects, emotions, and events for which they do not have precise labels or descriptions.

Instructional Decision Making:
Observation of Students' Knowledge of Word Meanings

It is easy to overestimate students' knowledge of word meanings, partly because often, students do not signal when they don't know a word's meaning. However, being sensitive to students' vocabulary knowledge is important because if teachers allow students to read without addressing the meaning of unknown words that are critical to understanding the passage, this may convey to students that it is acceptable to read without comprehension. For students who are in need of intervention, one of the most important messages that teachers can convey is that the words in text have a purpose and should make sense.

Obviously, it is easiest for a teacher to know whether students have insufficient knowledge of a word's meanings if the students themselves communicate this. For this reason, students should be encouraged to stop and seek the meanings of words they encounter in print if they are uncertain about what's happening in a text because they don't understand one or more of the words. Sometimes, this will mean asking the teacher; other times it might involve using the context in which a word is embedded or a glossary if available. Teachers can create an environment in which students regularly stop and seek word meanings if they (1) explain to students how seeking word meanings will support their learning, and (2) make it clear that readers regularly need to seek word meanings, especially in content-area texts.

Students may feel as though revealing a lack of vocabulary knowledge is an indication of a shortcoming; teachers need to make it clear that revealing a lack of vocabulary knowledge is a strength that will, in the long run, help them grow their vocabularies and enable them to more readily understand and enjoy the things they read. Teachers can convey the value of asking for word meanings through the feedback they provide to students who seek vocabulary knowledge. Statements like those below are useful in creating an environment in which students ask about word meanings:

"That's what learners do—they ask about words!"

"You are thinking like a reader! When you realized that you didn't know the meaning of that word, you did something to find out about it."

"Asking about the meaning of that word helped you to understand this passage."

It is also helpful if teachers become sensitive to signs that students may not be familiar with the meanings of some words in the text. Continuing to puzzle over the identity of a word even though the student appears to have adequately decoded it is frequently a signal that the student does not know the meaning of the word and, therefore, cannot confirm that the word has been accurately decoded. For example, one fourth grader in our research was not able to identify the word *skiing*, even when she could produce the /sk/ blend, and the *-ing* ending. Further, the text included a clear photograph of several skiers. A conversation revealed that (to the teacher's surprise) this student, and another in the group, had never encountered skis, and so could not identify *skiing* (of course it didn't help that the first *i* in the word is pronounced as a long-*e*!).

Reading with less fluency may also signal that a student does not have sufficient knowledge of a word's meaning to be confident of the interpretation of the portion of the text in which the word is encountered. For example, if a reader does not know the meaning of all the words in a sentence, he or she may use less appropriate phrasing, because, in the absence of knowledge of word meaning(s), the context does not support reading with expression.

We have also encountered students who disengaged from reading and put their head down on the table, or refused to read, when their comprehension was impacted by a lack of understanding of the word meanings. Until students have learned that it is helpful to ask for clarification of word meanings and that it is something that is celebrated rather than frowned upon, teachers should be aware that readers may demonstrate in a range of ways that they do not understand the author's words.

Instructional Decision Making: Preparation to Support Vocabulary Development

In 1986, Stahl and Fairbanks conducted an analysis of approaches to vocabulary instruction that were found to be effective and identified three principles that could guide teachers' instruction. These principles have stood the test of time (Kieffer & Stahl, 2015). As summarized by Rimbey, McKeown, Beck, and Sandora (2016), the principles are "(a) providing students with more than one or two repeated exposures, (b) providing students with both definitional and contextual information, and (c) actively engaging students with words in deep and meaningful ways" (p. 69). These principles are readily applied in the context of an intervention approach that employs thematically organized texts, which provide opportunities to repeatedly encounter content vocabulary (Tier Three words) in a variety of contexts. The principles can also be applied with regard to the sophisticated and more generally useful words (Tier Two words) that are more likely to be encountered in written materials and in discussions about those materials than in everyday spoken language.

In order to take maximum advantage of the materials that the students will read and discuss, for purposes of vocabulary and language development, teachers need to try to anticipate:

- Which words students may not know the meanings of.
- Which of these words have meanings that can be inferred based on context.
- For which words "kid-friendly" definitions and/or explanations need to be prepared in advance of the session in which the words will first be encountered.

Obviously, it would not be possible to devote instructional time to all of the words for which the students might not know the meanings. Therefore, teachers are encouraged to pay special attention to words that are central to understanding and discussing the texts being read.

Tier Two Words

When teachers plan to provide definitions of Tier Two words, they should be prepared in advance, because it is often difficult to think of clear examples or kid-friendly definitions on the spot. It may be helpful to use a children's dictionary for ideas about how to state the word's meaning. For example, *courage* is defined as "the ability to face fear or danger; bravery," in one children's dictionary (*https:// kids.wordsmyth.net/we*). Beck et al. (2013) encourage teachers to develop their own definitions of words they plan to explicitly teach. For Tier Two words, they suggest that teachers:

- Explain the meanings of new words using words and concepts that the students already understand—for example, students know what it means to do something that they are afraid to try.
- Use kid-friendly language in defining the word—for example, "If someone is courageous, he or she is not afraid to try to do something that may be dangerous or really hard to do."

Tier Three Words

For several reasons, Tier Three words are often more challenging to learn than the generally useful Tier Two words discussed in the previous section. First, students may not have the concepts for the terms to be learned, so that they need to learn both the concept and what it is called. Second, the concepts themselves may be abstract—for example, "colony" in social studies. Learning the word *colony* is more challenging than learning the word *courage* because students lack the abstract concept for colony, while they certainly have a conceptual grasp of attempting to do something that may require courage.

Further, authors may assume that readers have a relatively complete understanding of the network of meanings in which a given vocabulary word fits. However, for some content vocabulary items students are likely to have only partial knowledge. For example, many of the students who participated in our research projects lived near and were familiar with only one river, the Hudson. Their concept of "river" was something brown, and large and deep enough to require bridges and allow shipping. These students had no idea why rivers were represented using blue lines on a map; they were unaware you could swim in a river, and even seventh graders who lived right along the river did not know they could follow the river to New York City (150 miles away). After listening to students share what they knew about rivers, teachers could then plan instruction that addressed gaps in students' understanding. For example, to understand the importance of the Hudson River during the American Revolution (the British wanted to capture the river to divide and conquer the colonies), readers need to understand that rivers serve as boundaries that are difficult to cross, they are sources of food and water, and they are used to transport people and goods. For these reasons, important cities are often located on rivers. Readers must know this network of meanings related to rivers in order to understand that if the British held the Hudson River, the Patriots would be unable to transport the grain that was grown in western New York downstream to the citizens and troops in New York City.

In the previous chapter, we described how teachers can foster the learning of critical concepts; these same principles apply when developing concepts for Tier Three vocabulary. For example, when beginning to teach what is likely to be a completely new concept such as "colony," initially, the teacher can label the concept and draw attention to the distinctive features of the concept by comparing positive examples (New York and Massachusetts were colonies) and negative examples (the wilderness to the west and England were not colonies). Illustrations provide readily accessible information about the colonies; readers benefit from studying and discussing these. An example that is similar to the concept (e.g., children have to obey their parents, the colonists had to obey the king) can also help to develop the concept. Engaging students in thinking actively about the concept—for example, asking students to discuss why the colonists wanted to be free of England—is also recommended to promote concept learning.

Concepts such as colony or the network of meanings in which the concept of a river fits will not be learned in a single lesson; readers will require many experiences with the networks of meanings to fully understand the concepts. As described in the previous chapter, one way to provide these experiences is by using thematically organized text sets. If students read multiple nonfiction and fiction texts that describe what a colony is or the role of rivers in history, and also encounter the words in the general education classroom, they are on their way to more fully learning concepts and vocabulary words.

Instructional Decision Making:
Providing Word Meanings and Encouraging Word Learning

When and how teachers choose to provide word meanings and pronunciations should take into consideration the centrality of the word to comprehension of the text and the contextual support for inferring word meanings. Below we suggest three ways in which word meanings might be addressed.

1. Teach the written representation and provide the pronunciation and meaning of the word in advance of the students' reading. This option would be most appropriate for words that are centrally important to understanding the text. Or

if students will be reading independently or with a partner, the teacher might elect to show, pronounce, and briefly define words that he or she anticipates will serve as barriers to making progress with the text, even if the words are not central to understanding the text.

2. Confirm or provide the word's pronunciation when the word is encountered in context, and guide the students in inferring the word's meaning. This approach would be most appropriate when the context in which the word occurs is sufficiently supportive to enable such inferencing. We provide suggestions for helping students to learn how to infer word meanings in the section "Teaching Students to Hypothesize about a Word's Meaning" below.

3. Confirm or provide the word's pronunciation when the word is encountered in context and provide a brief, kid-friendly definition or synonym for the word.

In each of these situations, it is important to have the students look carefully at the word and repeat the pronunciation of the word after the teacher has pronounced it as this will assist students in storing both a visual (orthographic) and phonological representation of the word in memory.

As noted above, students should also be encouraged to ask about the meanings of words that are unfamiliar to them, and for those words, teachers can briefly provide a synonym or rephrase the sentence to convey the word's meaning. With this bit of information from the teacher, these words can be among the thousand words that the student learns a little about each day.

Ambiguous Words

Some words that students encounter in text have multiple meanings—for example, *figure, trial,* or *hide*. Students may know one, but not all of the meanings of such words. Proficient readers automatically access the correct meaning of such words. However, less proficient readers will often access the wrong meaning, largely because it is the only meaning they know. As a result, their understanding of the passage may be limited. Teachers should be alert for occasions when a reader is confused by such ambiguity and provide the context-specific meaning of the word.

Developing Students' Word Consciousness

While vocabulary instruction is one important way that readers will learn new words, most vocabulary learning occurs without instruction, through encounters with words in context. This incidental vocabulary learning is more likely to occur when students become "word conscious,"—that is, attentive to word meanings and interested in learning the meanings of new words. Teachers can foster word consciousness by:

- Modeling interest in and enthusiasm for words.
- Using sophisticated words in their own speech.
- Responding with enthusiasm when students use interesting words in spoken and written language.

Reading, of course, provides a powerful context for vocabulary learning. As noted above, children's literature is full of words whose meanings are unknown to the readers who are in need of intervention. Reading provides an authentic purpose for learning vocabulary, and a context that supports vocabulary learning.

Teachers are encouraged to be mindful of the words whose meanings are discussed. Teachers can look for opportunities to use and encourage the use of those words as the texts are discussed and written about and in their conversations more generally.

Academic Word List

The Academic Word List (AWL; Coxhead, 2000, 2011) was developed primarily for the purpose of supporting the vocabulary development of high school and college English learners in order to prepare them for successful college careers. The list consists of words that are used widely across multiple content areas in academically oriented texts. There are 570 word families on the list; a word family here is the root word and its various forms resulting from the addition of affixes—for example, *approach, approachable, approached, approaches, approaching, unapproachable*. The list is further broken down into 10 sublists, with the first sublist of 60 words containing the most frequently occurring of the word families. Words on this list include words such as *analyze, assume, benefit, distribute, create, indicate, proceed,* and *respond*. These and many other words on the list can certainly be meaningfully worked into both instructional and informal interactions with students for the purpose of expanding their vocabularies. Over time, drawing on higher-numbered lists as the students move through the elementary grades and beyond can serve to support the college and career readiness goals of the CCSS (National Governors Association Center for Best Practices & Council of Chief State School Officers, 2010). (Even some of the words on the highest-numbered sublist can be used in conversation—for example, *assemble, collapse, enormous, persist*). The suggestion here is that if teachers use more sophisticated vocabulary in routine interactions and instruction with students, the students are likely to acquire more sophisticated vocabulary and thus be more likely to accomplish the college and career readiness goals set by the CCSS. (Note that the Coxhead AWL is readily available on the Internet at various sites that can be found via a Google search.)

Intentional Opportunities for Use

We encourage teachers to *intentionally use new vocabulary words that were encountered when students are discussing and/or writing about the texts they have read* both on the day they are first encountered and subsequently. For example, at the end of the session, the teacher might plan a *written response* that encourages students to use one or more of the words that were discussed, as follows:

> "Which of the new words that we came across today describes a character that we read about today? Use this word to write about why you would or would not like to meet this character."

> "We've been coming across a lot of interesting words in our reading. Remember to use some of them when you write about the facts you've found. For example, if you were going to write about the population of China, you might say that it is *enormous* rather than *big* or *huge*."

For each instructional group, it is useful to keep a list of the vocabulary words that have been explicitly taught or have come up in reading and discussion so that the teacher has a handy reminder of the words that might be worked into conversation. The list might be posted so it serves as a reminder for the students as well. The most valuable practice will involve students using the words in the

---

Why *Not* to Ask Children about the Meaning of a Word

In our observations of teachers conducting read-alouds, we have been surprised by how often they start by asking the children to provide the meaning for a word that they intend to teach the meaning of. For example, in preparing to read a book about octopi, they might ask, "Does anyone know what an octopus is?" The problem with starting out with a question like this is that, often, children will not know what the word is—which the teacher has apparently anticipated. However, many times in situations such as this, a child will offer a definition that is wide of the mark, thereby providing incorrect information to the other children in the group. Interestingly, often in these situations, the teacher will not come right out and indicate that the definition is incorrect. Instead, a teacher might say, "Could be. Does anyone else have some ideas?" We view this type of instructional interaction as problematic because it allows the other children in the group to believe that what the first child offered is at least partially correct. As a result, the children who originally had no information about the concept now have faulty information, which may lead to confusion going forward. Our advice to teachers is that if you think many of the children in the group will not know the meaning, provide the definition/explanation right from the start of the conversation—for example, "Today in our new book we are going to be learning about hibernation. Hibernation is. . . . "

context of authentic communication. Teachers should try to remember to use taught vocabulary words in their discussions and, on occasion, notice and name the students' use of the words that have been taught/learned.

Teaching Students to Hypothesize about a Word's Meaning

Graves (2006) offers some suggestions that can help students develop an approximate idea of a word's meaning using context. A first step is to point out to students that context may provide hints or clues about a word's meaning. If readers do some thinking, they may be able to generate a hypothesis about what a word means. A better understanding of the word's meaning may emerge if the reader is persistent and continues to look for clues about the word's meaning in other contexts. Graves suggests that readers:

- Monitor whether what they are reading makes sense.
- Slow down when they don't know the meaning of a word.
- Reread that sentence and the previous sentence, looking for clues to word meaning.
- Substitute the hypothesized word meaning and read to see whether it makes sense.

It is best to begin teaching students about this process in places where the context provides fairly explicit support for the meaning of unfamiliar vocabulary. Examples of this would be a context that provides a simple definition, uses a synonym or antonym, or where the meaning can be inferred from the illustrations and/or mood and tone of the text. For example, this sentence includes a supportive context for the meaning of the word *population:* "China has the biggest *population*

Children's Books

In our work with preservice teachers, we sometimes encountered individuals who have not yet realized that many books classified as "children's books" are not intended to be read *by* children but are instead intended to be read *to* children. The ultimate goal of reading instruction is, of course, that ultimately, students should be able to read any book that is intended to be read to children. However, many children's books assume that the reader will have fairly sophisticated reading skills and should not be offered as reading material for students with limited oral reading skills. In classroom contexts, though, such books can and should be used to promote vocabulary development as teachers read these books aloud to students and discuss the content and some of the novel vocabulary that may be encountered.

of any country in the world. More than one billion people live there" (Riehecky, 2008, p. 10). Less explicit contexts can be examined when the students are familiar with the strategy.

We encourage teachers to make clear to students that context will not always be useful in inferring word meanings. For example, in the sentence about breeches mentioned earlier, it is relatively easy to infer what breeches are. In contrast, in the sentence, "Samuel found the *breeches* on the ground," all that can be inferred is that breeches are some type of physical object. Further, contexts can sometimes be downright misleading, as when irony is used—for example, when someone claims that an act was *courageous* when in fact it was *cowardly*. This variability in contextual support for inferring word meanings provides yet another reason to engage readers in as much reading as possible so that, over time, they can add incrementally to their knowledge of word meanings.

Promoting Knowledge and Self-Efficacy

Students are more likely to make connections and build knowledge if they see a purpose for acquiring knowledge. One way to foster knowledge development among readers in intervention is to help them see the connections between what they do in intervention and what they do in the classroom. One reason that the ISA-X intervention used science and social studies themes that were aligned with the students' general education program was to foster this sense of connection and to build confidence in the learners. Many of the readers we instructed stated that through reading thematically related texts on science and social studies topics, they became more knowledgeable about the topics than their classmates who were not involved in intervention. When readers in intervention develop a level of expertise, it has the potential to help them to redefine themselves as capable learners.

Instructional Decision Making: Addressing Other Language Challenges

Figures of Speech

A figure of speech is a phrase in which the words do not convey their literal meaning. A student may accurately read that a character had "butterflies in his stomach," or that bears "live on their fat" during hibernation, and know the meaning of all the individual words, yet remain confused. It is helpful to acknowledge to students that *figures of speech can sometimes cause confusion* and to then provide an explanation of the meaning. It is also helpful to note that the author's purpose is often to make the book more interesting to the reader, by using such colorful or imaginative expressions. A teacher might say:

"That does sound a little strange, doesn't it? A lot of times authors write things differently from how people would say them if they were just talking to each other. This makes the book more interesting to read."

If the figure of speech is a relatively common one, teachers may want to treat it like a new vocabulary term, have students repeat it, and provide opportunities to practice using it while discussing or writing.

Literary Syntax

When teaching young children about the purposes of print, teachers sometimes say that "print is talk written down." However, when it comes to the syntax of sentences in books, this is far from true. The syntax in books may be quite different from what students have encountered in speech. To wit, no one says, "Once upon a time . . ." during conversation; instead, they say, "A long time ago. . . ." For readers in intervention, who generally read less than their peers (and who may have less exposure to literary language in their home experiences), a lack of familiarity with the syntax of books may impede both word solving and comprehension.

Teachers and proficient readers are so familiar with "book syntax" that they may not recognize the challenge it poses to readers in intervention. Even controlled vocabulary texts may present syntactic challenges, as in the following example:

"Niagara" comes from a Seneca Indian word. It means "thunder of the waters." And the waters do thunder. (Bauer, 2006, pp. 12–13)

A student may read the words in this text correctly, but feel unable to confirm that the reading is accurate because the unfamiliar syntax of the last sentence is confusing. Thus, it may be fruitful to periodically *acknowledge to students that books have distinctive syntax* that can sometimes cause confusion and to rephrase the sentence for them, and then ask the students to read the original sentence again. Having students reread sentences with unusual syntax that have been rephrased for them by the teacher can help students to build familiarity with book language.

As students gain more exposure to book syntax, they will become better able to interpret it. Here again, *wide reading and discussion of text* is an important strategy in helping students become proficient readers. Listening while others read is an opportunity to attend to literary syntax. Listening makes fewer demands on the reader than reading—therefore, more cognitive resources are available for pondering the syntax and interpreting the information. Sensitizing students to the goal of meaning making in reading and the interesting ways in which sentence formation can influence interpretation of text has the potential to increase their awareness of the broad variety of ways in which sentences in books are written.

Summary

In this chapter, we discussed why knowledge of word meanings is crucially important to one's ability to comprehend text and to engage effectively in conversations and learning more generally. Readers who have a history of limited reading experience and/or limited engagement in meaning construction while reading are apt to have limited knowledge of word meanings. Therefore, it is important that attention to vocabulary development be an integral part of reading intervention (and, ideally, across the instructional day). Readers can expand their knowledge of generally useful Tier Two words and content-related Tier Three words through their reading of progressively more challenging and topically organized science- and social studies–related texts. Teachers can assist students in growing their knowledge of word meanings by using newly encountered words and encourage them to use these words in their discussions and writing about texts. Teachers can also encourage word consciousness and enthusiasm for learning word meanings by noticing when students use newly encountered words and by helping students realize that when they are unsure of the meaning of a word it is appropriate to either ask about it or seek its meaning in other ways. Similarly, students should be encouraged to seek clarification when they encounter complex syntax or unfamiliar figures of speech that interfere with their ability to construct meaning. In the next chapter, we discuss the relationship between fluency and comprehension.

CHAPTER 13

Fluency and Comprehension

> **STUDENT GOAL**
>
> Students will read grade-appropriate text accurately with appropriate speed and with phrasing and intonation that convey the intended meaning.

In this chapter, we discuss the relationship between oral reading fluency and the ability to comprehend written text. We discuss the components of fluency, factors that influence fluency, how fluency is assessed, and the ways in which instruction can support the development of oral reading fluency. Before we begin, it is important to note that fluency development was not an explicit focus of the ISA-X intervention. We took the position that fluency was an outgrowth of developing automaticity with word identification and reading with a focus on meaning construction and of engaging in wide reading of text in supported and independent contexts. We include a chapter on fluency in this book because, in many settings, fluency is a major focus of progress monitoring and, therefore, important for teachers to fully understand. Fluency is used as an assessment of progress because there is a substantial body of research that indicates that measures of fluency are moderately related to measures of reading comprehension, which are more time-consuming to administer.

Rationale: What Is Fluency, and Why Is It Important?

A fluent reader is able to accurately and quickly identify the words in the text—while doing so, the fluent reader groups the words into meaningful phrases that serve to convey the author's intended meaning, and uses the correct intonation to communicate that meaning. The later components are often referred to as *prosody*

256

Intervention Effects on Fluency

It is important to note that the relationship between fluency and comprehension becomes weaker as students move from the primary to the intermediate and middle school grades among students in general (i.e., not just students who receive intervention). It is also important to note that most intervention studies with intermediate and middle school readers yield limited to no improvements in fluency, including one of our own studies (Gelzheiser et al., 2011), although improvements in comprehension are often attained (Flynn, Zheng, & Swanson, 2012). Unfortunately, most studies of intervention with intermediate and middle grade readers, including our own, are relatively brief. We hypothesize that it is this brevity that at least partially accounts for the limited effects on fluency. Indeed, even in studies that were focused on the development of fluency (which ours were not), O'Connor and her colleagues found that gains in fluency were not evident until after 7 weeks of intervention (O'Connor, White, & Swanson, 2007; O'Connor, Swanson, & Geraghty, 2010; O'Connor et al., 2013).

(Kuhn & Levy, 2015). Thus, fluency involves accuracy, automaticity, prosody, and comprehension, at least at the sentence level. Readers who read accurately and quickly but with inappropriate prosody (e.g., word-by-word or in multiword groups that do not reflect the author's meaning) do not comprehend text as well as those who read with appropriate prosody (Schwanenflugel & Kuhn, 2016).

Fluency in Independent versus Grade-Level Texts

Students in the intermediate and middle school grades who are not yet reading grade-level texts with sufficient accuracy will be, by definition, unable to read grade-level text with grade-appropriate fluency unless they are reading well-practiced texts. They may, however, manage to read easier texts fluently—texts that are at or near their independent reading level. In more challenging texts, students lack fluency because a substantial portion of their cognitive resources is devoted to the process of puzzling through the words. They may literally read one word at a time.

Prosody is possible if word identification is so automatic that the reader's eyes are actually focused a word or two beyond the word he or she is articulating during oral reading (Inhoff, Solomon, Radach, & Seymour, 2011). This span between where the reader's eyes are focused and what he or she is saying helps the reader to determine the intonation to apply to the word that is being articulated because, by having the eyes ahead of the voice, the reader knows what's coming next. This eye–voice span is possible only when word identification is automatic.

Proper intonation is also determined by the larger context in which a given sentence occurs. Consider the sentence *This is my computer.* The sentence could be read as a simple statement. Alternatively, it could be read in a way that stresses ownership: *This is **my** computer.* It could also be read in a way that stresses the ownership of a particular computer relative to a larger group of computers: ***This** is my computer.* In the latter two instances, the stress placed on the words *my* and *this* subtly changes the meaning of the sentence. Thus, the prosodic aspect of fluency is inextricably linked to comprehension of text in that it both conveys comprehension and facilitates it. For instance, in the example above, readers would know which words required emphasis only if they had an adequate understanding of the larger text.

Fluency is important for a number of reasons. First, readers who can read fluently are more likely to enjoy reading and therefore engage in more reading. Second, fluent readers do not have to devote cognitive energy to identifying the words in the text and can, therefore, devote that energy to making sense out the material being read. This, in turn, helps them to build the language skills and knowledge base upon which comprehension depends. Third, fluent readers are able to read more in a given period of time than their less fluent peers and, as a result, have the potential to read and learn more. Thus, the development of fluent readers is certainly an appropriate goal to pursue. However, it is very important that in pursuit of developing fluent readers, teachers convey the reason that fluency is valued— because being fluent enables readers to enjoy and learn from their reading.

In Chapters 4–9, we discussed instruction intended to help readers develop their sight vocabularies as well as their knowledge of decoding elements. As stated there, the purpose of developing that knowledge is to enable readers to read the words in connected text effortlessly so that their cognitive resources can be devoted to constructing the meaning of the text. The development of automaticity in word identification is an important contributor to reading fluency. However, the skills and strategies discussed in those chapters will lead to automatic word identification only if they are applied in the context of substantial amounts of reading of continuous text.

Understanding the Reading Process: Factors That Influence Fluency

There is accumulating research (e.g., Barth, Tolar, Fletcher, & Francis, 2014) that demonstrates that the speed with which a reader (especially one who struggles with word identification) reads a given text is influenced by multiple factors related to the characteristics of the text, including:

- Difficulty level of the text in terms of the reader's ability to automatically identify the words and/or to access the context-specific meanings of the words or idioms. For example, *can*, *bridge*, *bank*, and *table* are common words with multiple meanings.

- The length, complexity, and familiarity of the sentence structures, as illustrated by the two passages that follow. Although the first is shorter, its syntax is more complex and may be more challenging to read.
  - Sam, the youngest boy in the group, tried hard to act like he wasn't afraid to jump over the stream.
  - Sam was the youngest boy in the group. He was afraid to jump over the stream. He tried not to let the other boys know he was afraid.
- The familiarity of the topic—readers who play baseball will likely read the sentence below more fluently than those who have barely heard of the game.
  - When it was the pitcher's turn at bat, the outfielders moved closer to the plate.
- The genre and text structure elements—for example, readers who have never read folktales will likely be slowed a bit when they realize that the animals talk.
- Whether the information presented in the text is consistent with the reader's existing knowledge—even the most proficient readers are likely to stall when they encounter information that is at odds with what they think they know.

Yet another factor that can influence oral reading fluency is the approach to word solving that students adopt. For example, for students who are learning to be strategic word solvers it is not at all unusual to see them slow down and be quite thoughtful as they puzzle through words. This process makes them more accurate but slower readers than their peers who are willing to skip unknown words and/or ignore mispronunciations and keep moving through a text. Students who are willing to skip words and/or ignore mispronunciations clearly have a different understanding of what reading is all about (e.g., reading quickly with little attention to meaning construction), as compared with those who are willing to slow down and puzzle over words so that they can construct meaning. We suspect that the slower group is or, in the long term, will become the stronger comprehenders. Thus, the relationship between measures of rate and accuracy (such as the number of words read correctly per minute [WCPM]) and reading comprehension will also be influenced by the instruction students receive.

Instructional Decision Making: Listen, Observe, Assess

Assessment of reading fluency has become common practice in schools. Such assessment involves the teacher in listening to individual students orally read texts that are at specific levels of difficulty (generally at the student's grade placement) and noting the student's performance. In many settings, the indicators of fluency are limited to reading accuracy and reading rate. However, as we discuss later in the chapter, in our opinion, and in the opinion of researchers concerned with the relationship between fluency and comprehension, it is important to capture information about the student's prosody as well.

Measures of Accuracy and Rate

Common approaches to evaluating fluency typically involve the calculation of WCPM. This has become a popular tool for progress monitoring because the tool takes relatively little time to administer. The research indicates that students who obtain higher scores on a measure of WCPM tend to score higher on measures of reading comprehension (Schwanenflugel & Kuhn, 2016).

To measure WCPM, the teacher gives a child an unfamiliar (typically) on-grade-level text to read and, using a timing device to track time to 1 minute, listens to the child read the text while marking miscues/errors and omissions on a printed copy of the text. The teacher marks the point in the text where the minute ends and then allows the child to read to a logical stopping point (rather than stopping the child midsentence). To compute WCPM, the teacher would count the total number of words up to the 1-minute mark and then subtract the number of words on which a miscue or omission occurred. The result is the child's WCPM. Figure 13.1 provides norms for WCPM for grades 3–8. These norms are drawn from widely referenced norms for grades 1–8 compiled on a broadly representative national sample by Hasbrouck and Tindal (2006). Norms are provided for three different times in the school year. Thus, evaluation of a student's standing relative to expectations should be based on the norms for the time of year closest to the time of the assessment. According to Hasbrouck and Tindal, scores that fall within 10 words either above or below the 50th percentile for a grade level at a given point in time would be considered to be in the expected or average range.[1]

While WCPM is certainly a predictor of performance on measures of reading comprehension, it is far from infallible. For example, the Dynamic Indicators of Basic Early Literacy Skills (DIBELS; Good & Kaminski, 2002) is one of the most widely used tools for assessment of reading rate in grades 1–3 and is widely used for identifying students in need of intervention. However, Schilling, Carlisle, Scott, and Zeng (2007) found that DIBELS oral reading fluency scores misidentified 37% of third graders as being at low risk for reading comprehension difficulties—that is, their reading rate was fast enough that they were predicted to comprehend on grade level but they didn't. Further, Francis et al. (2008) found that students reading purportedly comparable DIBELS passages showed substantial differences in fluency performances, suggesting that the passages were of varying difficulty. Given the emphasis on measures of accuracy and rate that has emerged over the last decade or two, it is possible that, at least in some settings, students are learning that what's valued is reading the words as fast as they can, not understanding the text as best they can. This is a disturbing possibility.

---

[1]Details related to collection of the data upon which these norms are based can be found at *www.brtprojects.org/wp-content/uploads/2016/05/TechRpt33_FluencyNorms.pdf.*

Grade	Percentile	Fall WCPM	Winter WCPM	Spring WCPM
3	50	71	92	107
	25	44	62	78
	10	21	36	48
4	50	94	112	123
	25	68	87	98
	10	45	61	72
5	50	110	127	139
	25	85	99	109
	10	61	74	83
6	50	127	140	150
	25	98	111	122
	10	68	82	93
7	50	128	136	150
	25	102	109	123
	10	79	88	98
8	50	133	146	151
	25	106	115	124
	10	77	84	97

FIGURE 13.1. Oral reading fluency norms, grades 3–8.

Measures of Prosody

Schwanenflugel and Kuhn (2016) argue that measures of WCPM are not sufficient and that indices of prosody should be included in fluency assessments. Their summary of the research related to using measures of fluency to predict reading comprehension performance indicates that adding a measure of prosody to fluency evaluations improves the prediction of reading comprehension outcomes by as much as 20%. They argue that including measures of prosody is especially important because there is evidence that "children who read at acceptable rates but with poor expression comprehend less well" (Schwanenflugel & Kuhn, 2016, p. 109). Therefore, for teachers who choose, or who are required, to formally assess oral reading fluency, we urge them to assess both WCPM *and* prosody. Further, in contexts where teachers are required to assess all students' fluency in on-grade-level passages, we encourage them to also assess their students who are reading below grade level on passages that are in the range of their instructional/independent reading levels (passages on which the student can accurately identify approximately 95% of the words or more) in order to get a sense of fluency in contexts when the text is not too challenging. This will provide an indication of whether students are attempting to construct meaning as they read.

Assessment Isn't Always Needed

Teachers who routinely listen to individual students read, making note of their word identification strategies (as we suggest in Chapter 6), and who engage their students in conversations around texts (as discussed in Chapter 14), will have little need for a measure of prosody. These interactions around text during instruction will provide the teacher with ample information as to whether students perceive reading as being about meaning making.

Several qualitative scales for evaluating prosody during oral reading have been developed. For example, the scale published by Rasinski (2004) guides teachers to consider four dimensions of fluency:

1. *Expression and volume*—the intonation and loudness of the reader's voice.
2. *Phrasing*—whether slight pauses while reading reflect meaningful segments in the text.
3. *Smoothness*—the evenness of the phrasing and expression.
4. *Pace*—the speed/rate of reading.

Teachers are to rate performance on each dimension using a 4-point scale. In contrast, the Oral Reading Fluency Scale used in the National Assessment of Educational Progress (2002) utilizes a single 4-point scale to evaluate prosody (see Figure 13.2). The scale essentially asks teachers to consider the multiple elements included in Rasinski's (2004) assessment of prosody. The latter scale strikes us as easier and more efficient for teachers to employ while still drawing teachers' attention to some of the most important elements of prosody and thereby helping teachers to identify the aspects of fluency that may require instructional guidance.

Fluent	Level 4	Reads primarily in larger, meaningful phrase groups. Although some regressions, repetitions, and deviations from text may be present, these do not appear to detract from the overall structure of the story. Preservation of the author's syntax is consistent. Some or most of the story is read with expressive interpretation.
	Level 3	Reads primarily in three- or four-word phrase groups. Some small groupings may be present. However, the majority of phrasing seems appropriate and preserves the syntax of the author. Little or no expressive interpretation is present.
Nonfluent	Level 2	Reads primarily in two-word phrases with some three- or four-word groupings. Some word-by-word reading may be present. Word groupings may seem awkward and unrelated to larger context of sentence or passage.
	Level 1	Reads primarily word-by-word. Occasional two-word or three-word phrases may occur—but these are infrequent and/or they do not preserve meaningful syntax.

FIGURE 13.2. National Assessment of Education Progress Oral Reading Fluency Scale. From National Assessment of Educational Progress (2002).

Although, as noted, we did not focus explicitly on fluency development in the ISA-X research studies, virtually all of the instruction involved in the intervention supports the development of fluency given that the development of oral reading fluency depends on:

- Having and using the ability to effectively puzzle through unfamiliar words encountered in context (the self-teaching mechanism we discussed in Chapter 5).
- Being able to automatically identify the most frequently occurring words (as discussed in Chapter 7).
- Knowing the meanings of most of the words encountered in given text (as discussed in Chapter 12).
- Being familiar with the syntax and grammar of both spoken and written language (also discussed briefly in Chapter 12), as such knowledge will influence the prosodic components of fluency.
- Understanding that written language is supposed to make sense (which was discussed in some detail in Chapter 10 and has been an underlying theme throughout this book).

Instructional Decision Making: Teaching to Foster Prosody and Fluency

Whether teachers formally track prosody or are simply mindful of the components of prosody when listening to students read, it is important to try to find opportunities for those who are dysfluent when reading texts that they can read with a high degree of accuracy to develop fluency. In our work with highly dysfluent students in clinical settings, we have found it useful to begin to address fluency by engaging students in reading and rereading easy texts (texts they can read with at least 95% accuracy). We adopt this tactic both because it is easier for students to attain fluency in these types of materials and because, for students who have had little or no experience with reading fluently, sounding fluent while reading can be highly motivating.

In the research on instructional approaches to developing fluency, the use of more challenging texts (e.g., texts in which the reader can identify 85–90% of the words) has also been found to be successful. But often in these instances, readers are provided with a model of fluent reading of the text before they attempt to read it.

Select Appropriate Tasks

There are multiple and widely accepted ways to support the development of reading fluency. All of them, of course, involve reading connected/continuous text. The approaches basically entail a combination of modeling and practice with reading texts that present varying degrees of challenge—depending on the type of

Fluency and English Learners

For students who are learning English as a second/additional language, the relationship between reading fluency (as measured by WCPM) and reading comprehension is still apparent but it is weaker than it is for native speakers of English (Crosson & Lesaux, 2010) and, not surprisingly, the strength of the relationship is dependent on the English learner's (ELs') proficiency with the English language. Thus, for ELs with strong English language skills an assessment of oral reading fluency is likely to be a better indicator of their ability to comprehend text than it is for students with weaker English language skills. It is important to note that Quirk and Beem (2012) found that for many students who are ELs, there was a substantial gap between their status on a measure of reading fluency and their status on a measure of reading comprehension. Measures of WCPM are likely to overestimate their text comprehension ability—that is, for example, students who appear to be reading at or above grade level on a fluency measure will likely perform more poorly on a measure of comprehension than would similarly fluent native-English speakers. Thus, it would seem that measures of fluency need to be interpreted with caution when considering the status of English language learners. Based on these findings, Schwanenflugel and Kuhn (2016) argue that the existing national norms for fluency are not valid for ELs.

support the reader will receive during reading. In what follows, we describe some commonly used approaches.

Reasons for Fluent Reading

Throughout this book, we have made a point of encouraging teachers to provide students with a rationale for the instruction and practice activities in which they engage students. With regard to fluency instruction and practice it is important to explain to students that making the effort to read text so that it sounds like spoken language (smooth and expressive) will help them to better understand the author's message. This, in turn, will make reading more interesting and enjoyable.

Modeling

Communicate the Characteristics of Fluent Reading

Other than difficulty with accurate and automatic word identification (which we discuss at length in previous chapters), two of the most frequent fluency-related characteristics of readers in intervention is that they ignore punctuation and that they read word-by-word or in multiword "chunks" that do not correspond to the meaningful phrases in the sentences. For readers who ignore punctuation, teachers can periodically demonstrate how noticing and using sentence-ending punctuation affects the intonation applied to the final word in a sentence and how the shift in intonation changes the meaning of the sentence.

The tall boy ran as fast as he could.
The tall boy ran as fast as he could?
The tall boy ran as fast as he could!

Similarly, for students who do not read in meaningful phrases, the teacher might periodically demonstrate the difference between reading text word-by-word versus in multiword (meaningful) phrases that make it easier to pay attention to the author's meaning.

The / tall / boy / ran / around / the / table / and / out / the / door / as / fast / as / he / could.
The tall / boy ran / around the / table and / out the / door as / fast as / he could.
The tall boy / ran around the table / and out the door / as fast as he could.

Teachers have found it useful, on occasion, to have students listen to the teacher read and evaluate the teacher's fluency as he or she reads word-by-word, or in multiword strings with pauses that are not aligned with the phrasal boundaries of the passage, or when paying no attention to punctuation. The point of engaging in this type of activity is to draw students' attention to the characteristics of appropriately expressive reading. Students generally think it is pretty funny when they get to evaluate whether their teacher is sounding like a smooth and expressive reader. This experience helps them to learn to attend to what appropriate prosody entails and ultimately to reflect on their own reading. Once they have had some practice "evaluating" the teacher's reading, they can be encouraged to evaluate their own reading and, when doing so, students can be encouraged to reread sentences that are not initially read with appropriate prosody.

KEEP IN MIND Being able to read with appropriate prosody requires that the reader know what comes next in the sentence. When readers cannot quickly identify all of the words in a sentence, the phrasing and intonation they apply to the sentence is apt to be off. Encouraging students to reread sentences that are not initially read in a smooth and expressive manner is a useful way to promote fluency. For example, the teacher might say, "Now that you've figured out all of the words, you can go back and read the whole sentence so you can really think about what the author is saying."

Read Texts to Readers in Advance of Their Reading

Many studies focused on promoting fluency among students who experience reading difficulty involve the teacher reading texts (or passages within texts) to readers before they attempt to read them. The teacher modeling of fluent reading is intended to enable readers to read more fluently when they then read the text. Following the reading by the teacher, there would be a brief discussion of the meaning of the text, to communicate to students that the purpose of fluency practice is to enable them to *comprehend* more effectively. If there is no discussion of the meaning of the text, teachers run the risk of conveying the wrong message about the purpose of reading in general. Based on the discussion, the students or the students and the teacher together set a comprehension-focused purpose for the students' reading of the text.

Practice

There was a time when it was believed that if students read texts repeatedly, this would build fluency with the repeatedly read texts and with new texts as well (National Reading Panel, 2000). However, more recent reviews of the literature suggest that it is the volume of reading that students do that is critical to fluency development whether that volume is due to repeated readings or to wide reading (Kuhn & Stahl, 2003). In our opinion, especially for readers at an early point in their development of oral reading skills (i.e., those reading at the end of first-grade level and below), there is value in engaging them in some repeated reading, as this allows them to stabilize the identity of words they may have had to puzzle through on their first reading of a text. However, as we discuss in Chapter 14, as students develop their reading skills, we encourage wide reading owing to the advantages of other aspects of literacy development such as adding words to their sight vocabularies, extending knowledge of word meanings, and increasing world knowledge. O'Connor et al. (2007) found that reading the same passage repeatedly or reading novel text resulted in comparable gains in fluency, but that students preferred reading novel text.

Below we describe fluency practice approaches that have been found to be successful in promoting reading fluency and reading comprehension among students who struggle with the development of fluency. Typically, when repeated reading is used, students either read the same text until they reach a specified criterion in terms of WCPM or they are simply asked to read the text a specified number of times (usually three to five times).

Reading While Listening

This technique involves students in simultaneously reading a text and listening to the text being read (either on a recording or by a teacher or other more proficient reader). When this activity is conducted in a small-group context it is typically referred to as *choral reading*. Given that readers could appear to be engaged in this act but in fact simply be engaged in repeating the words they hear, it is important that readers be held accountable for engaging in fluency practice. This can be accomplished by asking them to individually read randomly selected portions of the text.

Unassisted Repeated Reading

This technique involves the readers in simply reading a text multiple times and attempting to read more accurately and fluently on each successive reading. Reading/memorizing amusing poetry or jokes can provide motivation for engaging in such practice.

Assisted Repeated Reading

This technique involves the teacher or another proficient reader listening to the student read and noting miscues or other inaccuracies (e.g., omissions, problems with phrasing). The student's attention is drawn to the problem, guidance is provided on how to correct the problem, and the student rereads segments of the text where the problems occurred. Then the student rereads the entire text again.

Motivating Dysfluent Readers to Practice Fluent Reading

Often, older readers who struggle will initially resist engaging in multiple readings of easy texts because they consider both the texts and the activity to be babyish. However, students often find appeal in the activity when they have the opportunity to produce recordings of their readings that will be made available in listening centers in classrooms serving younger students. Thus, students would need to practice reading a given text multiple times until their reading of it sounds smooth and expressive—at which point the recording would be made.

This, of course, is not an activity that would be appropriate in the intervention setting aside from the initial introduction of the purpose and approach. In the intervention setting, students should be engaged in reading texts that provide some challenge with regard to word identification, as such texts provide the teacher with the opportunity to guide the development of effective word identification strategies and to promote independence in the application of those strategies.

Supported Reading of Novel Text

The portions of intervention sessions when the students and the teacher read texts together presents one of the main instructional contexts in which teachers have the opportunity to guide the application of developing word identification strategies and to encourage the development of the self-teaching mechanism. This is also the time when the teacher has the greatest opportunity to notice and attend to the students' oral reading accuracy, rate, and prosody. In this context, assuming that the teacher has selected appropriately challenging texts for students to read, the students will encounter words that they need to puzzle through. Once such words have been accurately identified, to promote fluency and to encourage word learning, students should reread the sentence in which the puzzling word was encountered. And, if need be, they should be encouraged to reread with appropriate rate and prosody.

Other Opportunities to Develop Fluency

Fluency development can be addressed during times when students read independently of the teacher. As we describe in the next chapter, reading aloud to a partner and reading independently are opportunities for the reader to further develop accuracy and fluency. Reading to a partner can foster fluency because it provides a genuine reason to read with expression and to convey the author's meaning. Reading independently provides students opportunities to develop their sight vocabulary and in that way fosters fluency. Independent reading can and should occur during and outside of intervention. The more that students read, both during and outside of the intervention session, the more accurate and fluent a reader they will become. Ways to encourage independent reading are included in the next chapter.

Summary

In this chapter, we have demonstrated that the ability to read text fluently (with appropriate accuracy, pace, and prosody) is both the result of comprehension (at least at the sentence level) and an enabler of comprehension because most of the reader's cognitive resources can be devoted to meaning construction. The primary way to increase readers' fluency is to ensure that they engage in a great deal of meaning-focused reading of text, some of which is quite easy for them to read given their current oral reading skills and some of which provides some (but not too much) challenge. The latter type of text provides more opportunity for building the reader's sight vocabulary, and as sight vocabulary grows, the reader's ability to fluently read and comprehend progressively more challenging texts expands. Engagement in both repeated reading and wide reading have been found to contribute to the development of fluency. The consensus of opinion with regard to improving reading fluency is that it is the volume (amount) of reading that a reader does that matters most. The more fluent readers are in reading a given text, the more prepared they will be to fully participate in discussion and responding to the text. The next chapter addresses reading, discussion, and written response to texts read.

CHAPTER 14

Reading, Discussion, and Written Response

In the previous chapters, we described the instructional goals for students in intervention that are related to both word learning and meaning construction. In this chapter, we discuss how the following three teaching activities can be used to help students accomplish those goals: (1) silent, partner, and oral reading and rereading; (2) discussion; and (3) written response. We begin by reviewing the roles that reading plays in intervention, and also briefly discuss selecting texts of appropriate difficulty. We then explain the discussion practices used in the intervention, and the evidence that discussion is important in meaning construction. We similarly explain our approach to written response and discuss how it contributes to students' growth as readers. Last, we describe ways that reading, discussion, and written response can be used to promote students' independence as readers.

Rationale: What Is Reading, and Why Is It Important?

In this book, we use the term *reading* to refer to students identifying words and constructing meaning from continuous text. Reading may occur silently or orally; students may read alone, with a partner, or in a group context. When students read a text for the first time, we say they are reading *novel text*; students may also *reread* texts that have been read previously. When a student is following along while another student is reading, this may not constitute reading, depending upon how engaged the student is.

Reading is important because students learn to read by reading. The more reading they do, the more quickly they will become proficient. Hiebert and Martin

269

(2009) drew this conclusion after reviewing numerous studies that measured reading time in different ways, including observations of individual students, analysis of the time that teachers allocated for reading during lessons, and surveys that included reading outside of school. In our research, time allocated to reading and discussion was the best predictor of student gains in reading comprehension (Gelzheiser et al., 2017).

Why might reading time be so important? When they are reading, students have the opportunity to address all of their intervention goals simultaneously. Reading has the potential to motivate more reading, as students experience the pleasure of reading. As students read, they learn word meanings and acquire knowledge that enables them to read more challenging texts. Reading provides the reader with the opportunity to engage in and practice the kind of thinking that readers do, such as asking questions, setting purposes, and making predictions. Reading allows students the opportunity to learn how fiction and nonfiction are structured, and to use that knowledge strategically to support comprehension.

Reading also provides readers with opportunities to practice the decoding elements and high-frequency words they are learning, and to apply the word identification strategies that enable students to learn to identify unfamiliar words encountered while reading (Share, 1995). As readers build their sight vocabularies through reading they are able to comprehend progressively more challenging texts as they need to devote less attention to word solving and as a result can devote more attention to meaning construction. For the reasons just detailed, we planned the ISA-X to include ample reading time.

Goals for Reading Time

In the most recent ISA-X research project, we encouraged teachers to allocate 25–30 minutes of every 40-minute intervention session to reading and discussion of text, with much of that time being devoted to reading, rather than extensive teacher or student talk. When individual students take turns reading orally in group contexts, the time for each student to read is reduced. In these groups, we further recommended that each student spend a minimum of 5 minutes reading orally and/or silently. Of course, this is a low minimum. If a learner practiced only 5 minutes a day, it would take a very long time to learn to play tennis or to drive a car, and reading is arguably more complex than either of these activities.

Understanding the Reading Process:
Factors That Influence Reading Time

Providing time for reading is a simple, versatile, and powerful tool for improving students' achievement. Surprisingly, it is greatly underutilized! Decades of observations done in general education, special education, and remedial reading settings have consistently found that students spend remarkably little time reading during the school day (Allington, 2009a). Typical amounts include 9 minutes of independent reading per day (Hiebert & Martin, 2009) or 0–17 minutes per intervention lesson (Swanson, Wexler, & Vaughn, 2009, p. 213). A recent study found that middle school students with learning disabilities spent only 0.2% of their intervention time in independent reading (Ciullo et al., 2016).

If reading time is so powerful, why do teachers provide so little time to do it? For the teachers in our research projects, three factors seemed to reduce the time that teachers allocated to reading: (1) competing instructional priorities, (2) format selected for student reading, and (3) lack of awareness of how much time students actually spent reading.

Other Instructional Priorities

During intervention, teachers have to balance time allocated to reading with time allocated to direct instruction and skill practice. If the teacher talk is not succinct, if discussion is not focused on relevant topics only, or if practice activities are not well organized, there is not sufficient time left for the students to read. To increase the time that their students spent reading, the teachers in our research found it helpful to:

- Keep mini-lessons brief.
- Keep discussion focused on the text rather than allowing diversions.

One Student's Perspective

A teacher we know reported the following comment from a student: "Ms. M, I know you wanna tell us stuff this morning, but can we finish reading this chapter? Like, without you? We know about all the strategies, and we use them, and if we forgot how they help us it's pretty much right there. So, can we just try? I want to read the rest of the protests by the Patriots today. I bet King George gets more angrier than he did with the Tea Party."

Reading Format

The format that teachers select for student reading will directly affect student reading time. If 10 minutes of an intervention session is available for reading, each student will read for 10 minutes if each reads silently. Each student will read for 5 minutes if assigned to a partner and the two alternate reading orally. Each student will read for only 2 minutes as a member of a group of five students who are taking turns reading orally. According to Allington and McGill-Franzen (2010), oral reading is the dominant form of reading in remedial and special education settings, even though there is no evidence that supports this practice. To increase the time that their students spent reading, teachers with whom we worked found it helpful to:

- Engage readers in partner (sometimes called buddy) reading regularly.
- Use silent reading and rereading as appropriate for students' instructional goals.

Yet there are times when silent or partner reading does not provide students with sufficient support, and oral reading in a group is warranted. At the end of this chapter, we describe how silent, partner, and individual oral reading can be used responsively and judiciously.

Teacher Awareness

In our research, we found that teacher awareness also influenced reading time. Teachers were surprised when we shared with them our data on how much time they devoted to students reading and to other instructional activities. We suspect that teachers' lack of awareness results from their cognitive engagement. When a teacher is teaching a lesson or managing a skill activity, time may pass quickly, from the teacher's perspective. When all the students in the group are reading silently and the teacher is observing, from the teacher's perspective, time passes much more slowly. In our experience, teachers perceive lessons to be shorter than they actually are, and student reading to be longer than it actually is.

Teachers can determine how much time students are reading, and how much time is allocated to other instructional activities, if they periodically record intervention sessions, listen to these recordings, and then note when student reading begins and ends. This awareness can then be used to set a goal for reading time—for example, that at least half of every intervention session is spent reading and discussing text—ideally with more reading time than discussion time. It may also reveal that some students spend far more time reading than do others, a pattern that some of our intervention teachers found they needed to address. More data can be collected by the teacher to determine whether this goal is being met.

Promoting Reading Outside of Intervention and School

Even with concerted effort to maximize time spent reading during intervention, there is a limit to how much time during intervention can be devoted to reading, especially in a group setting. Reading growth will be accelerated if students read at times beyond the intervention setting and the school day. One may argue that an intervention teacher's role encompasses more than the 30–40 minutes of direct contact. Part of a teacher's role is to encourage students to experience self-efficacy as readers, and become engaged and interested in the themes they are reading about in intervention. If this occurs, students may continue to read outside of the intervention setting if they are offered texts related to the theme/topic to read. Teachers can promote outside reading by getting to know the students as individuals, finding out what their interests are, and trying to locate materials that will feed those interests. Song lyrics, joke books, science and sports magazines, and series books that follow characters across adventures can all offer hooks that may get a reader to start developing a lifelong reading habit.

One authentic and manageable way that teachers can demonstrate an interest in their students' outside reading interests is by allowing a minute or two at the beginning or end of a session to talk about what individuals have been reading beyond school. This sends the clear message to students that they are perceived as readers and that their reading choices are respected.

Instructional Decision Making:
Selecting Texts for Reading That Are of Appropriate Difficulty

Reading experts agree that students need to read text that is at an appropriate level of difficulty. However, they don't agree on what constitutes appropriate difficulty. In this section, we briefly review what is known about optimal difficulty level, and share our best judgment of how to proceed when the guidance from experts is not consistent.

Why Is Instructional Level Important?

Pressley and Allington (2014) argue that students should read primarily in texts in which their reading is highly accurate. In text in which readers can readily identify almost all of the words, they may use context to support word identification, make inferences that support the construction of meaning, and hypothesize the meaning of new vocabulary. In more challenging text, as the proportion of unfamiliar words grows larger, it is more challenging for the reader to identify the words, construct meaning, and infer the meaning of unfamiliar words. Reading frustration-level text does not allow the reader to learn new knowledge or enjoy a good story.

However, to grow as readers, students must, of course, encounter texts where they do not already know all of the words. More challenging texts provide students with opportunities to add word meanings and refine their knowledge of the meanings of partially known words, and to add words to their sight vocabularies—assuming, of course, that these students have been taught and are able to use the word identification strategies, high-frequency words, and decoding elements discussed in Chapters 4–9. "Just-right text" is important because it provides readers enough opportunities to learn and sufficient support to succeed.

Text Challenge and Reading Time

One of the many reasons to try to ensure that students engage in reading texts that are not too challenging is that, while research indicates that time spent reading is a good predictor of growth in reading skills, the relationship between time spent reading and reading growth probably has more to do with the amount of text that a reader reads. If a text is challenging, readers will read less text in a given period of time than they would if they were reading easier text.

Selecting an Instructional Level

Some reading experts (see Allington, 2009a, for a discussion) have emphasized the importance of students succeeding as they read; our stance is to agree that students are more likely to continue to engage in reading if they understand and enjoy the things they read. Allington (2009b) suggests that instructional level be defined as 95% accuracy or greater.

Other reading experts (see Shanahan, 2014, for a discussion) have emphasized the need for instructional-level text to provide ample opportunities to learn. They suggest that instructional-level text may be as challenging as 80% accuracy, if appropriate teacher support is provided. There is research evidence to support the idea that greater growth occurs when readers are supported in reading more challenging text (Kuhn & Schwanenflugel, 2009; O'Connor et al., 2010; Stahl & Heubach, 2005).

Further complicating this debate is the fact that the functional instructional level of a text is dependent upon the reader's background knowledge (Kendeou & O'Brien, 2016; Recht & Leslie, 1988). For example, Recht and Leslie measured readers' knowledge of baseball and then asked more and less proficient readers to read a passage about baseball. Readers' baseball knowledge (rather than their reading ability) was highly related to their comprehension of the passage. Thus, two readers with identical skills may have different abilities to read the same book if they differ in their knowledge of the topics and ideas in the text. Because readers vary in their knowledge, it may not be logical to assign a single difficulty level score to a text.

Our own research suggests that readers make the most progress if they read texts that vary in difficulty level (Gelzheiser, 2005). If teachers consider students' instructional level to be a range, rather than a single level, readers will read some texts in which they are successful and motivated to read more, and other texts in which they have more opportunity to learn to identify words, construct meaning, and develop vocabulary knowledge. In our experience, it is not necessary or even helpful to restrict readers to text of a single difficulty level. This argument for varying text difficulty is also made by Fisher and Frey (2015).

Using Thematically Related Texts to Support the Expansion of Instructional Level

As we described in Chapter 11, one way to develop readers' knowledge is to engage them in the reading of texts organized around social studies or science themes. In our research, students began by reading easier texts to develop knowledge about a topic; as they developed knowledge they were then able to read more challenging texts about the topic.[1] With increasing knowledge, students were able to manage a range of difficulty levels for texts related to a theme.

Rationale: What Is Discussion, and Why Is It Important?

In this book, we use the term *collaborative, conversational discussion* to describe reading groups' interactions in which individuals spontaneously share with one another what they are thinking as they construct meaning during reading. While discussing, readers point out clues and evidence from the author, share relevant knowledge, and connect what they are noticing to questions, purposes, or predictions they have generated. Readers respond to one another in a discussion format, and build understanding together. During such discussions, the teacher may contribute, but ultimately, readers are not talking *to* the teacher in a collaborative discussion. The teacher may provide a stimulus for the discussion and may step in if conversation is not productive. But the teacher's goal is for the text, rather than the teacher, to be center stage during discussion.

Discussion is also an opportunity for teachers to learn about students' thinking and comprehension of what they have read. In order to teach responsively, a teacher uses discussion as an opportunity to thoughtfully and deliberately *listen* to students' thinking. Listening during discussion can allow the teacher to gauge student understanding and to adjust instruction accordingly.

There are many reasons for including collaborative discussion in a language arts program. The first reason is that research shows that discussion enhances readers' comprehension (Kucan & Palincsar, 2013), especially the comprehension of low-achieving students (Murphy, Wilkinson, Soter, Hennessey, & Alexander, 2009). Several theories have been offered for why this might be the case:

---

[1] We used text difficulty scores as one way to organize books from easier to more difficult but also depended on teachers' judgment with regard to which texts their students were ready to handle.

- Discussion provides readers with opportunities to learn from other readers or the teacher (Goatley, Brock, & Raphael, 1995). Specifically, students may learn to use the language or problem-solving approaches that the teacher has modeled during discussion (Almasi & Garas-York, 2009; Maloch, 2002).
- The act of explaining text meaning to others during discussion may increase the speaker's understanding (Van den Branden, 2000).
- Discussion may help readers to identify gaps in their own understanding by exposing them to others' more coherent understanding of a text (Van den Branden, 2000), which might then encourage readers to set higher goals for their own personal comprehension.
- The process of creating understanding on the group's "shared workspace" can influence how readers construct understanding on their "personal workspace" (Malloy & Gambrell, 2011).

Discussion and English Learners

Discussion has especially positive effects on the reading comprehension of students who are learning English as a new language (Murphy et al., 2009).

Another reason to include discussion in intervention is that it is often included in literacy standards. For example, the CCSS (National Governors Association Center for Best Practices & Council of Chief State School Officers, 2010) suggest that students who are college and career ready are able to engage in productive, evidence-based conversations with peers and adults. The standards suggest that content-focused conversation prepares students for success in adulthood. Even though conversation is a critical part of the CCSS, it has received less attention than other aspects of the standards (Snow & O'Connor, 2016).

Collaborative discussion can also be used to support other literacy goals. Discussion with peers and adults affords students the opportunity to develop and receive feedback about their expressive language (Goatley et al., 1995; Lightner & Wilkinson, 2016). Conversation may serve as a bridge to written expression, as it provides readers with limited writing skills with a less demanding means to share their thoughts about what they have read. If they first expressed their ideas in a conversation, we observed that many students were then more willing and better able to write about their thinking.

Conversation with peers is a way for readers to build their motivation to read and to learn from reading (Almasi, McKeown, & Beck, 1996). After engaging in peer-to-peer conversation, Almasi et al.'s fourth-grade students were quite articulate about their desire to read more.

Discussion supports the goals of developing readers' knowledge and vocabulary because it gives students the opportunity to ask about ideas and word meanings, and share the things they found interesting or novel in a text. Discussing and using an author's words and ideas can enable all readers to better learn the vocabulary and knowledge available in the text.

As we describe in the next chapter, discussion is also an opportunity for the teacher to notice and name the comprehension-fostering thinking that readers are doing, and in that way, to promote comprehension. While we do not advocate formal comprehension strategy instruction for readers who have yet to develop grade-appropriate reading accuracy, this informal approach during discussion can prepare students for such instruction if they appear to need it once they have attained grade-appropriate proficiency on the accuracy dimension.

Understanding the Reading Process: Factors That Influence Discussion

Productive Discussion Is about a Few Key Points

In our work with readers in intervention, we were influenced by the work of Beck and McKeown and their colleagues (Beck, McKeown, Hamilton, & Kucan, 1997; McKeown, Beck, & Blake, 2009). They suggest that discussion is most productive if it engages readers in sharing and explaining how they understand the text, in their own language. To do this, the teacher selects a few critical points in the text. As we described in Chapter 11, while reading informational text the teacher would select places in the text that help to develop the central conceptual knowledge. In reading about bees, for example, if the central idea is that bees survive by working as a social group, then the teacher might want to ensure that readers discuss the roles played by different workers in the hive. In fiction, the teacher might select times when the author presents an important insight about a character, when a turning point occurs, or when the teacher anticipates that students might be confused. During reading, the teacher stops at these points (or uses sticky notes with similar prompts when students are reading with a partner or independently). The teacher encourages discussion/thinking with an *open-ended invitation for students to describe and explain the text content:*

"Let's talk about what just happened here."

"[Character] has been through a lot. Let's talk about him for a minute."

"Let's talk about what we've been learning so far."

"How does this connect to what we read earlier?"

Depending upon students' responses, the teacher may ask *follow-up questions* that encourage greater explanation of the text:

"Why do you think [event] happened?"

"Say more about that."

Productive Discussion Allows for Student Questions and Interpretation

One way that readers engage in thinking about text is to ask questions and then look for answers as they read. Readers ask questions about such things as something they want to learn, a word they don't know the meaning of, a place in the text that is confusing, the author's or character's motivations and/or reasoning, and so on. In the next chapter, we discuss how teachers can promote such questioning through the comments they make during discussion. Here we point out that student questions to the group that seek to promote understanding are to be expected and encouraged during discussion.

Because it will promote discussion, motivation for reading, and student independence, we encourage teachers to direct the group to use the text as a way to collaboratively answer one another's questions. If the teacher answers the question, there is no need to read or for students to contribute ideas.

Similarly, we encourage teachers to avoid confirming that what students have said matches the teacher's interpretation since this may convey to students that there is one correct interpretation of the text—the teacher's interpretation. If the discussion becomes focused on the students generating thinking that matches that of the teacher, readers may refrain from sharing their thinking (Almasi et al., 1996; Good, Slavings, Harel, & Emerson, 1987).

Once students start to contribute regularly to discussion in an appropriate manner, it is productive to gradually release responsibility for discussion to students. Some of the teachers with whom we have worked encouraged discussion among students and independent of the teacher through dramatic means. Teachers have told students that they are "going behind the curtain" or "becoming invisible." This is helpful to both the students and the teacher as a way to define new roles. Others have sent a subset of students off to discuss what they have read, while the teacher reads with the remaining individual or small group.

Of course, the level of independent discussion that a group can attain will vary from text to text, and the teacher's level of support needs to adjust as well. Teachers may want to return to a more directive role when the group is beginning to read about a new topic, a more challenging text, or a new genre. Even a more challenging idea within a clear text may warrant additional, temporary teacher involvement.

Productive Discussion Addresses the Author's Words

In their work guiding primary grade students to discuss texts being read aloud, Beck and McKeown (2001) found that some students shared their thinking only about the illustrations or their prior knowledge, rather than what the author had written. Further, teachers were often unaware that this pattern was occurring. Similarly, some of the readers in our research commented mostly on the illustrations or their background knowledge as they read—and had little to say about the written text. These readers were not learning to better understand the text because they were not thinking about what the author was saying, even though they were accurately reading the author's words. Thus, they needed to be guided to attend to the author's words as well as the illustrations and their background knowledge.

If readers tend to overrely on the illustrations or their background knowledge, the teacher can clarify for them that discussion uses multiple sources of information with the goal of understanding the text. Teachers can do this by providing a rationale for attending to the author's words, sharing their thinking as they do so, and then providing supported opportunities for readers to engage in this type of thinking.

One way to do this is to find a portion of a book in which the illustrations are ambiguous, but the words provide clarification. Teachers can use such examples to illustrate how they used the author's words to help themselves to understand. For example, the last illustration in *Off to Sea* (adapted by Nichols, 2006) shows Jim standing in front of a group of men. It's only by reading the author's words that the reader will learn that Jim is volunteering to watch the pirates and report back to the men, who then welcome him to their team.

Similarly, the teacher can provide models of background knowledge and experiences that promote understanding of the author's words. If a student frequently shares personal experiences that do not advance understanding of the text, the two kinds of observations can be compared. In *Race on the River* (Nickel, 2011) Mikey is at the river with his older brother A.J., and A.J. can do everything better than Mikey.

> STUDENT: This reminds me of a time I swung on a swing at the river. Me and my dad were fishing and we had fun, swinging on a tire swing.
>
> TEACHER: The author told us that A.J. can do everything better than Mikey. When I'm with someone who does everything better than me, it makes me feel jealous. Thinking about how characters might feel can help us think about what they might do next.

Productive Discussion Addresses the Big Picture

In addition to discussing critical points in the text, teachers found it useful to use discussion to encourage students to think about the text as a whole. They did this by asking questions like those below when the group reached the end of the chapter or text.

"Why do you think the author chose this book/chapter title?"

"Why did the author write this book? What does he or she expect readers to experience and/or learn?"

Rationale: What Is Written Response, and Why Is It Important?

In this book, we use the term *written response* to mean thoughts that a reader has about what has been read, or about the reading process, that are recorded in writing by the student or the teacher (see Figure 14.1). Written response includes bulleted lists and phrases, paragraphs, and longer summary works. Written response may occur while reading (notes), at the end of a text or intervention session, and/or at the end of a set of related texts. The purposes of written responses may be to foster motivation for reading, to promote knowledge development, and/or to foster reading comprehension. Indeed, in a summary of studies examining the relationships between reading and writing, Graham and Hebert (2011) concluded that "writing about material read improves students' comprehension" (p. 710).

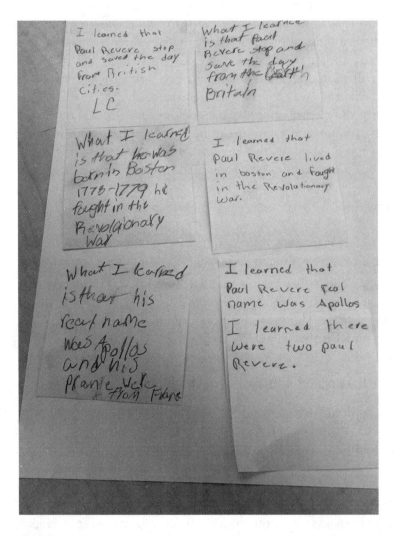

FIGURE 14.1. Written response to promote knowledge development.

Another Way for Students to Share Their Thinking

One of us (DMS) recently observed a teacher working with a group of fourth graders who needed reading and writing support (the teacher was not part of the ISA-X or the ISA, nor was she familiar with either intervention approach). Her students were engaged in partner reading and then one student shared his or her thoughts about what was read while his or her partner wrote them down. The students then reversed roles. The teacher explained that the purpose was to simplify the processing as one student could focus on constructing the message while the other student could focus on the mechanics of capturing the message in writing. This approach has the potential to encourage the students to dig deeper in their thinking about text and to build both comprehension and comfort with the mechanics (spelling, punctuation, etc.) of writing.

Each day, the teachers in our research projects were encouraged to engage students in developing a written response to the reading.[2]

Writing can be motivating because it allows each reader to represent a unique and permanent perspective about the text. Reflecting on what has been read and then writing about it can help readers to understand how much they are learning by reading, or enjoying reading. Reflecting on and writing about themselves as readers can also promote motivation for reading.

Writing can be used flexibly to *address different literacy goals*. For informational text, the writer may find it promotes learning and comprehension to simply list the interesting or new facts being learned while reading or after reading. In more complex fiction, the reader may find it useful to create a character list or list of key events. As we discussed in Chapter 12, writing can be structured to encourage students to use and learn vocabulary terms that were encountered earlier in the session and/or in previous sessions. Discussion and writing at the end of a text is an opportunity to extend students' thinking about a text, as the student looks back and thinks about the text as a whole. Similarly, if students have read a group of texts about the same topic, a brief culminating piece of writing offers the reader the opportunity to integrate the knowledge that has been learned across texts—for example, listing all the ways that bees work together to survive.

The *topic* for writing can be text or topic specific, or teachers can use more generic prompts. It is also useful to invite students to suggest a topic that they would like to write about.

Individual students will vary in their preference for *oral versus written response*. Some students in intervention find the act of putting words on a page

---

[2]In the most recent research project, intervention sessions were 40 minutes long. If intervention sessions are briefer than that, teachers may find that it is more productive to engage students in writing every other day.

to be challenging. As noted above, for students like these, we've found it helpful to encourage them to share their thinking orally, and then write. Often, these students will add to their written response if given the opportunity to read it to the teacher or a peer. In some cases, it may be appropriate for the reluctant writer to dictate a response to the teacher.

Other students are quiet during discussion but have more to say in their written responses. Writing offers these students the opportunity to collect their thoughts before they share.

Authentic written response is shared with an *audience*. If students are reading informational text, the facts student have learned and identified in writing can be attached to a poster that features the central concept or idea. If students are continuing to read a longer book, reading what was written about a book on the previous day is one way of activating knowledge. Or students may share their writing by reading it to the teacher or one or more peers in the group after they finish writing.

In written response, the goal is to develop students' comprehension and motivation, rather than *spelling, penmanship,* and *punctuation.* (This is not to suggest that these aspects of literacy development are not important but rather that, on the continuum of concerns for students in intervention, spelling and punctuation are of lower priority than the ability to read and interpret text.) Students can be encouraged to refer to their "Words We Know and Use" chart (see Figure 7.6 on p. 155) for the spellings of the high-frequency words they have been learning, and to refer back to the text to help them spell challenging and content words. However, students should be discouraged from spending too much time checking the spelling of every word—that isn't the point. Writing pieces can also be used by teachers as a source of information about the student's knowledge of the decoding elements, as elements that are not spelled conventionally may not be decodable for the students either. This insight may lead to subsequent lessons on the decoding elements.

Using Resources to Promote Conventional Spellings

Many students don't think to use resources, such as the text they just read or the "Words We Know and Use" chart (see p. 155), to enable them to spell some of the words in their written responses. Inattention to producing conventional spellings, when there is a handy resource to reference, is a habit that we try to interrupt because producing unconventional spellings and then reading and rereading the texts that are produced can interfere with the reader's ability to automatically recognize the conventionally spelled version of the word when it is encountered in other contexts. We have found it useful to encourage students to use these resources by making it sound like a bit of a privilege: "You *get to* use conventional spelling by checking your resources."

Instructional Decision Making:
Responsive Use of Reading, Discussion, and Writing

When the Teacher Is First Getting to Know a Group of Students

The first couple of sessions that a teacher has with a new group of students may be organized differently, so that the teacher learns about the readers' characteristics, and the students and the teacher begin to develop a collaborative relationship.

Reading

Listening to *individual students reading orally in an instructional group* may be appropriate in the first sessions that a teacher has with a group. Listening to each student in the group read gives the teacher the opportunity to observe each reader's strengths and set goals for instruction.

Discussion

If teachers make a point of *inviting comments and asking open-ended questions* that do not have one correct answer, this may encourage students to share their thinking, and enable the teacher to understand the extent and type of thinking that students are doing. Similarly, in a teacher's initial contacts with a group, it can be very informative to ask questions that do not direct the students to attend to any particular feature in the text. This will enable the teacher to identify what students are choosing to attend to—for example, the illustrations or the author's words—which may provide ideas for how intervention should proceed. Examples of questions, comments, and follow-up questions that do not have a correct answer that we have found useful include:

"What are you thinking?"

"What are you noticing?"

"Now that we have read some more of the story, what are your thoughts?"

"Hmm. . . ."

"Say more about that."

Writing

Many students in intervention are reluctant writers. As teachers are first developing a relationship with students, they may want to provide students with short writing tasks that do not have a single correct answer, so that students are not anxious about the content of their response. Some writing prompts we have used in intervention include:

"What we read about today makes me wonder about . . ."

"I learned something interesting today. . . ."

"One thing in this book that is like my life is. . . ."

"I plan to tell my [friend, parent, teacher] about. . . ."

When Students Are Acquiring
a New Word Identification Strategy

Introducing a new strategy takes time—students will fully understand the strategy only if they have the opportunity to practice reading text. We suggest the following structure to provide the opportunity to read with teacher support.

Reading

When students are first acquiring a new word identification strategy or first learning about interactive strategy use, the teacher's close observation and assistance will help to ensure that students try the new strategy, and execute it fully. To provide students support as they learn and practice strategies, having *individual students read orally in an instructional group* is often appropriate. As students' competence grows, this level of support is reduced, and students transition to practicing their strategies in partner or independent reading. For students who have very limited reading accuracy, teacher assistance may need to be provided on a more regular basis.

When a group is reading together, reading turns should be *unpredictable,* from the students' perspective, to encourage students to follow what other students are reading or saying. We suggest that the teacher (not students within the group) call upon individual students to read orally, and vary the order of students as well as the content and amount of reading. If students within the group have different ability levels, the teacher can ask students who are the most likely to be successful to read the more challenging passages. Students should be reminded to *follow along* while others read orally, and provided a reason for doing so: "When you look at the words while another student reads, it helps you learn to read words you don't already know, and that will help you to be able to read words more quickly in the future." Looking at the words and following along has the potential to provide reading practice that supports word learning, assuming that the student is able to follow along at the same rate as the oral reader. If students have significant word-learning needs, it is appropriate to encourage them to follow along using a finger or card to point to the text as another student is reading orally.

Students should also be expected to remain engaged in thinking about the text while another student is reading orally—that is, to "choose to keep learning." Because it is easy for students to "tune out" when another student is reading, it's also important to carefully *judge the length of each student's reading turn.* Even the most diligent student can get tired of listening. On the other hand, reading only one sentence does little to build a reader's stamina.

Discussion and Writing

During the initial stages of word identification strategy learning, discussion will include comments from the teacher about the utility of the strategy—for example, "Breaking the word into smaller parts allowed you to read a very long word!" In order to allow plenty of time for reading and strategy practice, less time may be spent discussing or writing about the content of the text in the acquisition stage. In lessons that focus on consolidating strategies, there should be somewhat less discussion of the strategies and more opportunity for discussion of the content of the reading and writing.

When Students Are Beginning to Read about a New Topic, or Beginning a More Challenging Book

If students are beginning to read a set of books about a new topic, or beginning a book that poses challenges because of its length and/or content density, we suggest the following support from the teacher.

Reading

When students are starting a text set on a new topic, or beginning a book that is longer than what they typically read, they will often benefit from the teacher's close observation and assistance. When what students are reading poses more challenge, *individual students reading orally in an instructional group* may be appropriate. As students' knowledge grows, this level of support can be reduced, and students should transition to partner or silent reading to allow each student more time to read.

Rereading

Asking students to reread a previously read text offers several benefits. Rereading allows students to reencounter unfamiliar words, and through practice, to move toward including these words in the body of words that they recognize automatically. Rereading may simply allow the reader to enjoy a text for a second time. Readers may gain more information or insight during rereading, so some texts are reread for greater clarity of understanding. A regularly scheduled rereading time offers students the opportunity to *choose* to read a book from a basket of previously read texts. Alternatively, if students are in the process of reading a lengthier text, rereading can focus on the section that was read in the previous session so as to refresh the student's thinking about the text.

Students will be most engaged while rereading if the teacher structures rereading to convey the message that *rereading is purposeful* and about constructing meaning. Interruptions should be minimized, and students should be encouraged to reread meaningful portions of text (e.g., a whole short book or a whole chapter). Either the teacher or the student should specify a purpose for rereading. Some examples include:

> "I'm rereading this text because it is [funny/exciting/interesting]."
>
> "I'm rereading this text so I can remember more of the facts so I can become an expert about the Statue of Liberty."

When rereading has a purpose, *closure* can also convey to students that reading is meaningful. Some examples include:

> "What did you enjoy about/learn from the text that you reread today?"
>
> "Did rereading that part of the book give you any more ideas about the question you asked yesterday?"

Discussion

When students are reading text about which they have less knowledge, it can be helpful if the teacher provides clear expectations for discussion. Some examples follow:

> "Let's read the first section and then stop and share what we have noticed about the characters and setting so far."
>
> "Let's read the first two pages and share what we have learned."

Writing

If students are first reading about a new topic, they will have limited knowledge. In this initial stage, it is appropriate for students to share orally what they have learned by reading, and for *the teacher to record the group's responses on a chart*. Similarly, if students have just started a longer book, the teacher can record information that students identify about the characters and setting.

Students can use the information on the chart to summarize what they know so far, or to generate questions or expectations for upcoming text(s). As readers develop knowledge, they can be expected to write and add their own contributions to the charts. The chart shows readers that building knowledge and thinking about text is a process that unfolds over time, and illustrates to readers that the more they read and write, the more they can understand and learn.

When Students Are First Consolidating a New Strategy or Are in the Middle of a Topic or Longer Book

Most intervention sessions will involve consolidation. This format, or the one that follows, can be used in these instances.

Partner Reading and Writing

Intervention time is limited and teachers have limited time to spend with individual students. Therefore, to give students additional reading practice they can be set to reading in pairs. Generally, we recommend that the students in the pair be as similar to each other as possible with regard to oral reading and word-solving skills so that the texts that they read are appropriately challenging for both members of the pair and, therefore, time spent reading is as productive as possible.

Partner reading usually involves two students alternating reading aloud to each other and supporting each other's thinking. Reading orally to a partner is an opportunity for students to practice the strategies and the ways of thinking that they are learning with *less support from the teacher, but with some support available from a peer.* For that reason, partner reading is done when students have already had teacher instruction and support for strategy use, and need some support as they practice the strategies they are learning. Similarly, it is appropriate when students have some knowledge about a topic or have started a longer book and are reading to learn more.

To ensure that students are learning but are not overwhelmed, partner reading generally uses *texts that pose some, but not too much, challenge.* These would include texts that a student can read with a high degree of accuracy and texts for which students have sufficient background knowledge. If the text is more challenging, the amount of partner reading should be shorter; longer segments of easier texts may be read with a partner.

As noted previously, partner reading allows substantially more reading for each individual than occurs when students take turns reading orally in a group. Partner oral reading should be a routine part of instruction for students who still need to develop their sight vocabulary and word-solving skills because many such students may have developed the habit of skipping or simply mumbling through words that they do not readily recognize. The amount of reading time individual students engage in can be increased if the intervention session also includes some silent reading of previously read text.

If all students are reading with a partner, the teacher may move from pair to pair in order to *observe* students as they practice word identification strategies, or to *listen* to students' thinking and meaning construction during the reading process. Alternatively, while others are engaged in partner reading, the teacher may choose to interact with an individual student. This time may be used to listen to one student read, and observe the student's word identification strategies, use of decoding elements, thinking, and/or fluency. Or a *lesson* targeted to just one student can be provided at this time.

Maximizing Student Thinking during Partner Reading

Before students begin reading with a partner, the teacher will likely meet with them as a group to share a structure for partner reading. At this time, the teacher may provide the group with a purpose or question to guide reading, or the group may generate this. The teacher can suggest that partners stop to place sticky notes or to write comments when they encounter information relevant to their question or purpose. This information will be shared with the group after completing the reading. Alternatively, the teacher may point out that he or she has left sticky notes within each reader's text that indicate when the oral reading partner should change roles with the silent reading partner. The teacher's notes may contain questions that the partners should ponder and respond to.

When students are reading aloud to a partner, they are more likely than during silent reading to attempt unfamiliar words. This increases the probability that the unknown word will be accurately identified and eventually added to the reader's sight vocabulary. Further, a reader's partner may be able to provide assistance in the form of a suggested strategy that will lead to accurate word identification. In partner reading situations, students should be encouraged to wait until the reader indicates that he or she would like suggestions for word identification strategies to try when the reader is puzzled by a word. While it is acceptable for the peer to ultimately provide the pronunciation of an unknown word, it is helpful if both members of the partnership think about the word identification strategies that might be helpful to try.

In addition to taking turns reading the text to each other, partners should also be encouraged to react to and discuss the text. We want students to always approach reading as a meaning-making enterprise.

When teachers notice that a pair is not reading productively, it will be useful to review expectations for partner reading prior to the next partner reading session. Students are often more focused if they are reminded of the *purpose of partner reading: to become more independent as readers,* through reading and more independent thinking and practicing with word identification strategies.

Discussion after Reading

After all the partners have completed their reading, the group can meet to share and discuss what they have learned and been thinking. Students can refer to the ideas they have recorded on sticky notes. This serves as a concrete reminder that conversation starts with information from the text and readers need to return to the text to support their discussions. After the discussion, facts or thoughts on sticky notes can be added to a poster for the topic or chapter book further illustrating what students are learning and thinking while reading.

When Partner Reading Is Successful

Reading and Writing

Once teachers understand their students' skills and strategies and have observed them to be strategic readers with only the support of a peer, students should engage in some *silent reading daily*. Silent reading of novel text is done when students have already had teacher instruction and support for strategy use, and are ready to practice these without teacher or peer support. Depending upon students' skill level, at first, silent reading may be limited to rereading of previously read text.

Recent research suggests that engaging students in silent reading that is supported and monitored as described below is effective in promoting reading gains (Rasinski, Samuels, Hiebert, Petscher, & Feller, 2011; Reutzel, Jones, Fawson, & Smith, 2008). An obvious advantage of silent reading is that it has the potential to *maximize time spent reading* by engaging all students in independent reading. During silent reading, all students have the opportunity to engage in their own puzzling over words and thinking about the ideas in text. Learning to effectively engage in silent reading prepares the students to do the predominant type of reading they will do throughout their lives.

Because it offers no teacher monitoring or assistance, silent reading is generally done using *texts that pose some, but not too much, challenge*. These would initially include previously read texts that are being reread. Novel texts that students read silently should be those that the student can read with a high degree of accuracy and for which students have sufficient background knowledge.

Before students begin reading silently, the teacher will likely meet with them as a group to provide some guidance. At this time, the teacher may provide the group with a purpose or question to guide their reading, or the group may generate this. Rather than telling students to read a certain number of pages, it is more engaging if students read until they acquire information relevant to their purpose or question. The teacher can suggest that students stop to place sticky notes or to write comments when they encounter ideas or information relevant to the question or purpose. This information will be shared with the group after completing the reading. Alternatively, the teacher may point out that he or she has left sticky notes within each reader's text that indicate questions they should ponder and respond to. Such questions should be open-ended questions rather than questions that are directly answered in the text.

Learning How to Read Silently

For students who have significant reading accuracy difficulties, we recommend that during the first 30 or so intervention sessions, silent reading be limited to rereading previously read text, with silent reading of novel text introduced as follows.

As students are first reading novel text silently, it can be helpful to *begin* the book with a brief bit of teacher-led oral reading, and then move into a relatively short but meaningful segment of silent reading, followed by discussion. As students become more independent, the challenge and/or length of the silent reading segment can be increased. When students have experienced success with silent reading, the teacher is encouraged to have students read longer selections, and/or begin a book with silent reading.

Silent reading can be introduced by explaining to students that the goal is for them to take strategies they have been learning while reading independently and use them for the rest of their lives. Silent reading practice will prepare students for more independent silent reading. During silent reading, *students should be expected to use the strategies that they have been learning.* Eventually, the strategies that students are learning should become so habitual for them that there is no longer a need to discuss them.

Teachers are sometimes uncomfortable in a situation where they have a small group of students and the students are all reading silently. In this circumstance, it can be helpful for the teacher to remember that the *goal of intervention is to develop confident, active, independent readers* who learn to do what they are expected to do in school (and out)—construct meaning with texts read silently.

While students are reading silently the teacher may choose to *observe* and make note of students' engagement and problem solving as they read. Watching where students direct their visual focus while reading or noting their use of finger-pointing or self-talk can be very informative. Alternatively, the teacher can listen to individual students read in a side-by-side situation and take the opportunity to provide individualized guidance for strategy use and/or meaning construction. Yet another alternative for the teacher would be to provide a mini-lesson targeted to just one student during this time.

Discussion

During or after silent reading, teachers and students can discuss the text they have just read. In this way, teachers have the opportunity to help students to build confidence in their ability to construct meaning as they read.

One way to develop independent readers and thinkers is for the teacher to ask the readers to explain how they reached conclusions they share. Teachers have found it useful to replace "That's right" with a response that is more informative to students:

"How did you figure that out?"

"What makes you think that?"

"Why do you think . . . ?"

"That does seems like an important clue from the author."

"I remember that also!"

Using prompts such as those listed below makes it easier to redirect students when what they have said does not appear to be correct:

"Can you show me where you found that clue in the book?"

"I don't remember that—can you show me where the author said that?"

"Say more about that." (Sometimes the students' thinking that seems incorrect actually makes sense but the teacher simply hadn't thought of it that way.)

Discussion can also be an opportunity for teachers to encourage students to articulate the progress they have made as readers. Students can reflect on the strategies that they just used independently. The teacher can provide students with feedback regarding how using the strategies helped the reader to understand the text.

Written Response

A useful way for teachers to monitor the understanding of individual students after silent reading is through written response. Writing prompts can be open-ended: "What are some things that caught your attention in this chapter?" If the teacher decides to ask a more specific question, it is usually helpful to the reader to receive that question before reading.

Culminating Written Response

Some teachers prefer to keep day-to-day writing simple—for example, just bullet points collected during or after reading. Then, when the group has completed a set of books on a topic or a longer book, a period of time is devoted to writing a longer and more complex response. After reading a set of books on the Statue of Liberty, one teacher had her students write a letter to a parent or guardian explaining why they wanted their family to visit the statue. This was an authentic reason for students to revisit the books and a way for students to share what they had learned with a family member.

Summary

In this chapter, we once again emphasized the importance of ensuring that readers engage in as much meaning-focused reading as possible—because readers learn to read by reading. Small-group oral reading, partner reading, and independent silent reading all have a role to play in intervention contexts but it is important to keep in mind that the ultimate goal of reading instruction is to produce readers who independently and effectively solve words and construct meaning while doing so. Encouraging students to discuss and write about the things they are reading and learning from text, initially in small-group oral reading contexts and ultimately in silent reading contexts, will move them toward the goal of independence. Helping them to learn to set their own purposes for reading, generate their own questions, and/or make predictions about how text will unfold will move readers toward independence, especially if they also learn to read with an eye toward determining whether their purposes were met, their questions were answered, and/or their predictions matched the author's thinking. We take up these comprehension-fostering processes in the next chapter.

CHAPTER 15

Promoting
Comprehension-Fostering Processes

The readers who are the focus of this book benefit from intervention focused on developing their ability to learn to identify unfamiliar words and to build their sight vocabulary. As we described in Chapter 10, formal comprehension strategy instruction would be postponed for these readers until their accuracy goals have been met, and it is entirely possible that such instruction would not be needed if the readers are (or have become) routinely and actively engaged in meaning construction as they are reading. In this chapter, we describe how engaging in posing questions, setting purposes, and making predictions can help readers to stay engaged in the process of constructing meaning while reading. We describe these engaged reader processes, and then give examples of guidance that teachers can provide to help readers to apply these processes as they read and discuss texts. We describe how nonfiction and fiction are structured and why knowledge about their structure can help readers to comprehend what is being read. We also give examples of the type of guidance that teachers can provide to help readers acquire and use knowledge of text structures as they read and discuss texts.

Throughout, we remind teachers to keep the students' instructional priorities in mind. While all readers should always be thinking about the meaning of what they read, for those readers who have yet to attain proficiency with word solving and word identification, it is essential that instructional planning and delivery develop these aspects of the reading process. The advice we provide in this chapter is intended to support teachers' efforts to enhance students' thinking while not making instruction of comprehension skills and strategies the major focus of intervention lessons.

Rationale: What Are Engaged Reader Processes, and in What Ways Are They Important?

Reading is thinking. Researchers have described what proficient readers do as they engage in reading (e.g., Duke et al., 2011). Readers set purposes, process deeply, and behave strategically as they read—that is, readers generally have a goal when they begin to read a text, and routinely evaluate progress toward that goal. Readers interact with text, thinking about what might happen next, drawing inferences, asking questions, and making adjustments in their reading or thinking as needed. Strategic readers have different purposes and approaches for different kinds of texts.

Some readers in intervention do not engage in this kind of thinking as they read, as discussed in Chapter 10. One way to convey to readers the idea that the goal of reading is constructing meaning is to encourage readers to engage in goal-directed reading for understanding. In our research, we sought to accomplish this by having readers ask questions and read for the answers (i.e., read for the purpose of learning the answer to the question), or set a purpose for reading (i.e., set a comprehension objective and read to meet it), or make a prediction and read for the answer (i.e., read for the purpose of ascertaining whether what was predicted actually happened). Each of these cognitive processes helps the reader to set a goal of comprehension, rather than allowing the reader to see the purpose of reading as saying the words correctly. *It should be noted that questions, purposes, and predictions are grammatically different manifestations of the same mental process of setting a comprehension goal and reading to meet that goal*—that is, a reader might say:

> "What happened to Pocahontas?" (question)
>
> "I'm reading to learn about what happened to Pocahontas." (purpose)
>
> "I think Pocahontas is going to go to England." (prediction)

Purpose setting, questioning, and predicting are a subset of processes that are often referred to as comprehension strategies. Numerous researchers have developed and studied interventions that are designed to increase readers' comprehension by promoting their use of comprehension strategies. Some studies have examined the effect of teaching just one strategy; others have taught students multiple strategies. Reviewers synthesizing this research have concluded that *explicit comprehension strategy instruction has positive effects* on older struggling readers' comprehension (e.g., Gersten, Fuchs, Williams, & Baker, 2001; Kim, Linan-Thomson, & Misquitta, 2012; Solis et al., 2012; Wanzek & Kent, 2012). However, the reviewers also noted that, in most studies, the effects of strategy instruction were often evaluated using the researcher's own assessment, and not the kinds of standardized tests a school might use. When standardized comprehension measures were used, effects were smaller or nonexistent (Solis et al., 2012). A further limitation is that, in the majority of studies, students were taught by research staff, not practicing teachers (Kim et al., 2012; Wanzek & Kent, 2012). Thus, we currently have only limited research evidence to demonstrate that comprehension strategy instruction provided to readers in intervention by practicing teachers will result in improved performance on standardized comprehension tests. As we noted in Chapter 11, research evidence suggests that knowledge development is more effective than strategy instruction in fostering comprehension.

Another useful investigation was conducted by McKeown et al. (2009). They compared the effects of two approaches to comprehension instruction: strategies instruction versus discussion focused on the content of the text. Their measures showed an advantage for the content intervention over strategy instruction, and suggest the value of allocating instructional time to discussing the meaning of the text being read.

Given these mixed findings, if students are routinely engaged in thinking about the meaning of the text while they read, we encourage teachers to focus discussion on the content of what is being read, as described in Chapter 14. For students who do not routinely engage in the process of constructing meaning, the remainder of this chapter provides some guidance as to how to promote such thinking.

As we have already indicated, instruction intended to promote engagement in meaning construction does not occur as formal comprehension strategy lessons (which would involve naming, modeling, and providing guided practice with each of the strategies). Instead, instruction intended to draw students' attention to meaning construction occurs in the context of meaning-focused discussions of texts being read.

Understanding the Reading Process: How Do Engaged Readers Think during Reading?

Questions

Teachers and students may be used to a pattern in which the teacher is the questioner and students seldom, if ever, ask questions. However, engaged readers stop to ask their own questions as they read, then read for answers. The reader's goal for understanding takes the form of a question to which the reader would like to learn the answer through reading.

Questions are the most natural and versatile of the engaged reader processes. Questions are appropriate for all genres, and are common in students' everyday conversations. Questions pose little risk for the reader (a question cannot be wrong) and do not necessarily require knowledge on the part of the reader (although a knowledgeable reader may ask a more interesting question and/or questions that wouldn't occur to a less knowledgeable reader). Sometimes authors are intentionally vague to keep the reader asking and reading, asking and reading.

Purpose Statements

By purpose setting, we mean that the reader has a meaning-related reason for engaging in reading. A purpose may be narrow or broad:

"I want to learn what they eat in China."

"I want to learn how everyday life in China compares with life in America."

Like questioning, purpose setting can be done in either fiction or nonfiction. However, a reader will have different purposes for reading nonfiction as compared with fiction. Readers often set a purpose of learning something from informational text. With fiction, a purpose that readers often have is enjoyment and entertainment. Once readers have met the main character(s) and learned of the conflict(s) they face, readers often read with the purpose of learning how the conflict(s) are resolved.

Predictions

Predictions are what the reader thinks the author will have happen in the story (not what the reader would like to see happen). They are most appropriate in narrative text (fiction or biography). Predictions are based on the reader's background knowledge and clues from the author's words and/or the text's illustrations. Because most informational text is not organized in a chronological fashion, readers have few opportunities to predict what will happen next in informational texts.

Questions, Purposes, and Predictions Are Revisited

Once readers have asked a question, set a purpose, or made a prediction, they then read to *collect evidence* that addresses their thinking. In this way, they are reading with the goal of understanding. Readers monitor their thinking as they read to determine whether their questions, purposes, and/or predictions have been addressed and/or whether there is need for modification in their thinking. Because authors love to surprise readers, it is expected that readers will need to revise their thinking about the text. Books that unfold as expected could be boring books—memorable, interesting, and exciting books are the ones that require us to revise our thinking as the text unfolds.

Questions, Purposes, and Predictions
Draw on the Author's Words and Ideas

Teachers are encouraged to help students understand that a useful question or purpose is one that the reader has reason to believe the author might address, and a useful prediction uses clues the author has provided and predicts something that the reader believes the author might make happen. Such questions, purposes, and/or predictions are useful because they encourage the reader to focus on understanding the text being read.

Questions, Purposes, and Predictions Draw on the Reader's Knowledge

What students already know about a topic or genre is useful to them as readers. When engaged in meaning construction, many of a reader's questions and predictions stem from knowing something about a topic (animals need food) but wanting more specific information (What do bees eat?). Similarly, a reader will ask different questions in fiction versus nonfiction.

Because they draw on prior knowledge, teachers should expect more reasoned questions, purposes, and predictions from students when they have more knowledge about the topic. If a reading group is beginning to read about a new topic, students may have little to say, and feel uncomfortable, if they are asked to generate questions or purposes when they know little about a book and/or subject matter. Teachers using a thematic approach will likely notice an improvement in the quality of students' questions and purposes as they read more books in the unit and develop knowledge.

Instructional Decision Making: Using Noticing and Naming to Shape Students' Questions, Purposes, and/or Predictions

Improving the Frequency of Student Participation

While reading and discussing a text, the simplest way to improve participation is a carefully timed expectant pause by the teacher, perhaps amplified with "Hmm. . . ." This minimal prompt signals to students that a question, comment, or prediction is in order. For many readers, this is sufficient to encourage their participation.

If teachers openly notice and name students' questioning, purpose setting, and/or predicting, students are more likely to continue to engage in those behaviors. Feedback that refers to "what readers do" will help students to see that they are learning a generally useful way of engaging with text that can be used often.

"That's an interesting question, let's see whether/how the author addresses it."

"That's what readers do; they have a purpose for reading."

"I'm going to write down that question so we can all think about it."

Encouraging Students Who Are Reluctant to Predict

In our experience, it is not unusual to encounter an older reader who will *refuse to make a prediction*. Often, this is a consequence of previous instruction in which teachers referred to predictions as right or wrong, depending upon whether the outcome that the student predicted occurred in the text. To avoid the appearance of being wrong, some students simply stop making predictions.

It is useful to discuss with such students the fact that *authors like to surprise readers*. If a reader could always predict what was going to happen next, books might be boring. In exciting books, the reader's predictions are often somewhat or very different from the way that events turn out. Readers make predictions because it is fun to anticipate and, often, to be surprised.

It's helpful to some readers to understand that what the author tells them about a *character's feelings and goals* will often help them to predict how the character will respond. If the author is less than explicit about how a character is feeling, readers can use their own background knowledge, thinking about how they would feel in situations that resemble what is presented in the text to infer how a character might feel. The dialogue below illustrates how such a conversation might occur during reading.

TEACHER: How do you think [character] is feeling now that he hears the bears?

STUDENT: Afraid.

TEACHER: So what do you think [character] will do?

STUDENT: Climb a tree.

TEACHER: So you thought about how the character was feeling, and used that to predict what the character might do next. Thinking about characters' feelings can help you understand what you are reading and can help you predict what will come next in the book/text.

TEACHER IN A LATER TEXT: Your prediction was based on what you knew about how the character was feeling.

Another technique that may be helpful with reluctant predictors is to ask them to generate *several predictions*. The teacher can ask, "What are some different things that might happen?" If the reader has generated multiple hypotheses, they can't all match the author's thinking, so the pressure to do that is reduced.

Encouraging Students to Revisit and Revise

If students regularly do not revisit their questions, purposes, and/or predictions, it can be helpful if the teacher writes them where the group can see them. *Recording* serves two purposes: (1) it makes the questions, purposes, and/or predictions seem important; and (2) it serves as a reminder to revisit them. Other times, students will benefit from the teacher informally modeling the process of *collecting evidence*, using a question or purpose that the teacher has set (not one of the students' questions). Or the teacher can notice when a student has done this. The sequence would look something like this:

> "Carlos's question was 'What do bees eat?' He just noticed that it says bees collect nectar and bring it back to the hive, and wondered if they eat the nectar. Carlos is looking for evidence related to his question, and that is helping him to keep thinking while he's reading."

Active thinkers revise questions, purposes, and predictions on a regular basis. As they move through a text, they may learn things that lead them to revise their thinking. Teachers should be ready to share their thinking as they revise their own thinking, and notice when students to do the same.

- *Student:* "Oh, Andre has been discovered. Now I don't think he will make it to America." *Teacher:* "So you are changing your prediction, huh?"
- *Teacher during reading:* "The author just told us how the Statue of Liberty was made. So I've met my first purpose. Now I'm wondering how they got such a big statue to America. I'm going to set that as my next purpose." Or, "That's my next question."
- *Teacher after reading:* "You changed your thinking about _____ several times while reading that book. Readers are thinkers; they change their thinking when the author tells them things that they didn't expect."

Encouraging Informed Questions, Purposes, and Predictions

We have found it useful to have students read the first few pages of a text before encouraging them to pose a question, set a purpose, or make a prediction. Meaning-focused readers have a fairly general purpose as they start a book/text, and the first couple of pages/paragraphs of a text help readers to refine their questions/purposes/predictions. Students, especially those who are unaccustomed to reading for meaning making, will benefit from having some knowledge of the text to give them a basis upon which to develop their purpose statements, questions, or predictions. With the support of this knowledge and the more reasoned engagement in meaning making, greater comprehension is likely to ensue.

Rationale: What Is Text Structure Knowledge, and Why Is It Important?

Often, authors of literature and nonfiction texts follow certain conventions of structure and organization as they write. A reader who is aware of, and attends to, these conventional structures will find it easier to follow the author's message, understand, and recall what has been read (Goldman & Rakestraw, 2000; Meyer, 1987). Although some books for children are not well structured (Armbruster, 1984), generally, experts agree that having and using knowledge of the unique features and organization of stories and informational texts can be helpful to the reader (Gersten et al., 2001; Hebert, Bohaty, Nelson, & Brown, 2016; Williams, 2015).

For stories, for example, having a schema for how they are organized enables readers, each time they read a new story, to look for the story elements, and use their story schema to store what they have read in memory in an orderly way (Mandler & Johnson, 1977). That schema allows the reader to chunk information and reduces cognitive demands on the reader. Having and using a story schema helps to ensure that important elements in the story are attended to and recalled. Indeed, if a proficient reader is misled about the genre and reads with the wrong set of expectations, comprehension suffers (Zwaan, 1994).

Story Schemas

Readers who have well-developed story schemas will expect the following elements to be included in a story:

- Setting
- Characters
- Problem/conflict
- Attempt(s) to solve the problem/conflict
- Resolution
- Conclusion

Readers may read consciously to identify those elements or they may do so implicitly.

Many readers have a great deal of tacit knowledge about the conventional structures used in fiction and nonfiction texts. Beginning readers have much less knowledge of the conventions of fiction and nonfiction (Englert & Thomas, 1987; Mandler & Johnson, 1977)—they seem to approach all text with the same set of expectations. Further, there is some evidence that readers in intervention are less likely than grade-level peers to *use* their text structure knowledge to direct their attention and foster comprehension (Short & Ryan, 1984).

Our experience with intermediate and middle grade readers with limited reading skills suggests that many of them have learned *what* the features of informational text are, but often they don't understand *how* these features can be used to help them more readily access and interpret the author's message. Thus, at the beginning of intervention, the readers with whom we worked often skipped over useful features such as chapter titles, headings, and captions. They had yet to learn how these features support comprehension—for example, that titles and headings are big hints to the reader as to what the upcoming text will be about. This information can be conveyed to students in a brief conversation during reading and discussion, allowing explicit instruction to be focused on word-learning goals.

Understanding the Reading Process: How Do Readers Understand Nonfiction?

Nonfiction may be defined as text presented as factual by the author, with the purpose of providing the reader with accurate information about a topic (informational text) or person (biography) or other subject (e.g., a "how-to" book). According to Duke and Bennett-Armistead (2003), "the primary purpose of informational text is to convey information about the natural or social world, typically from someone presumed to know that information to someone presumed not to, with particular linguistic features such as headings and technical vocabulary to help accomplish that purpose" (p. 16).

It can be confusing to students to simplify this definition to "nonfiction is true," since nonfiction texts may include things that are not true. For example, because scientists continue to improve their knowledge, some informational texts name Pluto as a planet while others state that it is not a planet. Similarly, different biography and history texts written about an era when there are few reliable sources (e.g., the early settlement of Jamestown) often present conflicting "facts."

The purpose for reading nonfiction is to learn and enjoy (new) ideas and factual information. Readers read nonfiction with the expectation that they will learn something more than they already know about a topic. Traditionally, children have had less opportunity to read or listen to nonfiction, as compared to fiction (Duke, 2000; Jeong, Gaffney, & Choi, 2010). However, nonfiction texts provide an important opportunity to build the knowledge base upon which reading comprehension depends. A recent review by Cervetti and Hiebert (2015) provides an engaging but detailed discussion of the relationship between preexisting knowledge and comprehension of new texts.

Informational text is written in an expository style. The information is organized into topics (rather than chronologically, as most stories are written). This type of text is often dense, packed with interesting details as well as major concepts. The writing may be terse, with limited explanation or elaboration. The text is often interrupted by illustrations, graphics, or headings. Paragraphs and/or chapters may follow a main idea and supporting detail structure, or be organized into other structures such as cause and effect or compare and contrast.

To help readers navigate a dense structure, and to highlight the most useful information, informational texts contain *obvious text features that make it easier for the reader to learn* from and enjoy the book. If they have been taught how to use them, text features help the reader by indicating important information or providing clarification. The function of each text features is listed below.

1. *Features that signal important ideas:* titles, headings, table of contents, bold print.
2. *Features that provide additional clarifying information:* illustrations, text boxes (such as those used throughout this book), glossary, captions, charts, maps.

In reading a nonfiction text, the reader may need to understand all the discipline-specific vocabulary in order to understand and learn from the text, which is why many informational texts include a glossary (and/or text boxes). In nonfiction, the illustrations and graphics often provide additional and important information that is not included in the text, so full understanding of nonfiction depends upon careful study of all the visual information sources.

Understanding the Reading Process:
How Do Readers Understand Fiction?

Fiction is defined as a story that is at least partly imaginary, with characters, setting, and plot. Often, the main character encounters a conflict and then a series of events (the plot) occur as the character addresses the conflict. The character may learn or change during the story; there may be a lesson or message from the author. We encourage teachers to carefully consider the language they use to define fiction. If students don't understand what fiction is, their misconception(s) may be obstacles to constructing meaning with text.

Fiction is not "fake or untrue"; if this definition is used, students may be confused by the realistic parts of realistic fiction, or the historical figures and events in some historical fiction. Having been told that fiction is "made up," we've encountered readers who feel free to ignore the author's words and make up their own story! Similarly, students may be confused if they are taught that "fiction is made up by the author," since folktales typically were made up long ago, and were only written down by an author.

Fiction is most often written in a *narrative* form—that is, it is a report of connected events, presented as a continuous stream of information. Some fiction will include breaks in the stream of information (e.g., a change of setting) that readers may find challenging. Fiction is often chronological, although it may include challenging flashbacks. In fiction, the author may use sophisticated vocabulary words (sometimes called Tier Two words, discussed in Chapter 12) to enrich the story. Some fiction includes illustrations that serve as the illustrator's visualization of the settings, characters, and events. These illustrations support understanding, but in some stories, the text can be understood without attention being paid to the illustrations.

While fiction has structure, the elements (e.g., the setting) are not presented in bold print or signaled by headings, the way the important ideas are signaled in nonfiction. The structure of a story must be gleaned through careful reading, so readers may comprehend better if they have learned to attend to these elements.

In most fiction, the main character faces a *conflict* to be resolved. Often, the author begins the book by providing the reader with some background or "setup," and then introduces the conflict. The conflict may stem from the character's goal, task, or mission. Or a character may be in conflict with another character, the setting, or him- or herself. Often, there are episodes within the story in which the character responds to the situation and takes action to resolve the conflict(s). The outcome from taking that action often leads to another episode.

In most fiction, early in the story the author provides clues to the *setting* (where and when the story takes place). Some stories could occur anywhere, so there is little detail about the setting. In other stories, the setting is *integral* (Watson, 1991) to the story because the setting poses a challenge that a character must overcome or limits how a character can resolve the conflict. When the setting is integral, attending to it helps the reader to understand and anticipate the character's actions. These actions are often critical events in the building story.

In most fiction, the author introduces the major *characters* early in the story. Depending upon the sophistication of the text, the author may provide information about the characters' physical attributes, qualities, feelings, relationships, and/or goals. Attending to the main character will help readers to understand the conflict and episodes in the story (Roser, Martinez, Furhken, & McDonnold, 2007). The main character's qualities, attributes, and feelings often determine how the character will respond to the conflict. Attending to the main character's qualities, attributes, and feelings will allow readers to anticipate and/or understand the character's actions. Major characters may change or learn as a result of their experiences in addressing the conflict. Thus, attending to the many dimensions of the characters will help readers to understand the entire narrative.

To successfully understand the text they are reading, many readers of fiction have learned to read to identify the conflict(s) that the main character(s) have to resolve. They have learned that there may be episodes in resolving the conflict(s). Such readers have learned to attend to the main character(s) through the episodes in the story, using what they know about the character(s) to understand the characters' responses and actions. They have also learned to attend to the setting, if it influences the character(s) or conflict resolution(s).

Instructional Decision Making:
Using Noticing and Naming While Reading Nonfiction and Fiction

When planning instruction for readers with very limited sight vocabulary, teachers may find that there simply isn't sufficient time for explicit instruction about nonfiction and fiction structures. In these instances, teachers can use conversation during reading to provide readers with useful information about fiction and nonfiction, preparing students for more explicit instruction that will occur when additional instructional time is available.

Nonfiction

Spending time reading nonfiction is a first step in coming to understand how it is organized. Prior to the adoption of the CCSS (National Governors Association Center for Best Practices & Council of Chief State School Officers, 2010), most reading instruction did not include sufficient opportunities to read or even listen to informational text (Duke, 2000). However, recently, publishers of children's trade books have produced many nonfiction series that can be read by readers with limited oral reading accuracy skills. Because many such texts are now available, we encourage teachers to engage readers with such texts as often as possible, as they allow students to develop knowledge while simultaneously consolidating their knowledge of word identification strategies, high-frequency words, and decoding elements.

As described in Chapter 11, in our ISA-X research projects, students read multiple informational texts about the same topic at the start of each thematic text set. As students developed knowledge about the topic, the texts became more challenging. During the conversations that occurred as students read these texts, teachers could lay the groundwork for strategic use of text features by informally sharing how they thought about genre and used text features during reading:

> "I'm noticing that this book has a lot of facts about bears. I'm thinking that this is an informational book—so I don't expect that there will be much of a story—but I expect I'll have a chance to learn a lot about bears!"

> "Wow! This book is telling us about a lot of things that Paul Revere did."

> "I'm going to start by reading this chapter title because titles usually tell me something important about the chapter."

> "I'm not exactly sure what this word means. I'm glad the author included a glossary. Let's use the glossary to help us understand more about what the author is telling us."

The process of reading multiple informational texts about the same topic very naturally led our readers to make the following observations about the texts' common features:

> "All of these books contain *facts* about rivers."

> "All of these books have a *table of contents*."

> "The *illustration* shows us what the word *meander* means."

It also led students to report differences they observed:

"In this book, the *glossary* has pictures and not words."

In these informal conversations, the teacher could continue to prepare students for strategic use of these text features, by rephrasing student comments:

"Yes, our purpose in reading these informational texts is to learn *facts* about rivers."

"The *table of contents* tells the reader what the book will be about."

Fiction

The opportunity to listen to and/or read many well-structured stories allows the construction of a story schema (Goldman & Rakestraw, 2000; Mandler & Johnson, 1977). Drawing students' attention to the critical elements of a story through teacher modeling has been shown to be a helpful way to enhance struggling readers' learning from experience with stories (Alves, Kennedy, Brown, & Solis, 2015; Boon, Paal, Hintz, & Cornelius-Freyre, 2015).

Most students receive some instruction regarding character, setting, and plot in the primary grades. In our experience, readers in intervention at the intermediate level and beyond may have had some introduction to story elements, but will have had much less opportunity to (1) strategically use the story elements to support comprehension, and (2) learn to attend to more subtle aspects of character and setting to support comprehension. Specifically, they may not:

- Look for and follow the main character's conflict, which is the key to the organization of the events in the story.
- Attend to all dimensions of the major characters (attributes, qualities, feelings, relationships, and goals) and how these influence the actions that the characters take.
- Attend to how the setting may influence the story's conflict.

As a group reads and discusses fictional texts, teachers can set the stage for students to use genre features by informally sharing their thinking and noticing readers' thinking:

"Readers often read the first few pages of a story carefully because they know the author is going to start telling them what the important characters are like. Knowing what the characters are like helps readers to understand what the characters do in the story."

"[Student] has noticed that [character] has a conflict here, and [student] is predicting that the story will explain how [character] solves that problem. Noticing that conflict is likely to help [student] to understand the story."

Promoting Students' Schema for Specific Genre

As described in Chapter 11, in our research projects, students read a small set of examples of one genre as a part of a thematic text set. The process of reading multiple texts from the same genre provided an opportunity for the teachers to engage readers in making observations about their common features, thus developing the readers' schema for a specific genre.

Before reading the first in a group of folktales, the teacher might say:

> "Folktales are stories that often have special characters. As we read today, let's see what we notice about the characters and how they act. Noticing the characters will help us understand this folktale. What's really useful is that what we notice and learn about this and other folktales can help us to more easily understand other folktales."

During reading and discussion, the teacher might say:

> "I'm noticing that this animal can talk. This is definitely *not* like some of the other things we read. I'm wondering whether this is something that we'll see mostly in folktales."

> "Is anyone noticing anything unusual about the characters in this folktale?"

After reading, the teacher might say:

> "So, we noticed that the characters in this folktale could do things that don't happen in real life. Can anyone share an example that they noticed while reading?"

Once the group has a set of examples that can be drawn upon, the teacher can then help readers to see how this information is helping them to comprehend what they are reading.

Before reading, the teacher might say:

> "We've read three folktales. In these three folktales [name the folktales], what did we notice about the characters? [Students: 'The animals could talk, the animals communicated with other kinds of animals.'] So, you noticed that folktales usually have characters with unusual powers or abilities, like animals that can talk. When we read folktales, we can use this knowledge that the characters are unusual to help us to understand the book. Today we're going to read this folktale. What are you expecting now that you know a little more about folktales?"

During reading and discussion, the teacher might say:

> "You know that in folktales characters sometimes use magic, so you're thinking now that this character will use magic to solve his or her problem. Let's see if it works that way this time."

"You figured out the part that was confusing to you by using your knowledge of the characters' special powers in folktales."

After reading, the teacher might summarize:

"Knowing that characters in folktales often have special powers helped us as readers to anticipate and understand what happened in this folktale."

In future lessons, the teacher can release responsibility to students by asking more general questions before, during, and after reading:

"What have we learned about folktales that will help us understand this book?"

"If we use what we know about folktales, it will be easier to understand this book."

Summary

In this chapter, we discussed some of the processes used by readers who actively engage in meaning construction while reading and how teachers can guide readers to engage in those processes. Learning to set purposes, question, and make predictions can help readers to approach text with an eye toward gathering information and learning. We also discussed the utility of understanding the characteristics and structures of fiction and nonfiction texts, as these structures serve as schemas that can enable more effective processing of the information presented in texts.

In the next and final chapter, we present a thematic unit on bees with the goal of illustrating both how a thematic unit might be structured and how the comprehension-fostering activities and instructional goals described throughout Part III might be addressed. The purpose of building knowledge and vocabulary about the topic and, perhaps more importantly, helping students learn to engage with text for the purpose of constructing meaning and building knowledge at the same time can help students to see themselves as capable and enthusiastic readers.

CHAPTER 16

Sample Thematic Text Set

In Chapter 11, we asserted that knowledge development is one important way to foster students' comprehension and also their reading accuracy. Based on this premise, in the ISA-X research projects, we had students read texts that were thematically related as one way to develop knowledge and vocabulary while also addressing other reading objectives in a way that was responsive to students' individual needs.

In this chapter, we provide an example of such a thematic text set. First, we describe what might be a characteristic group of third- or fourth-grade students

---

Books in the Honey Bees Text Set

Ashley, S. (2004). *Bees*. Pleasantville, NY: Gareth Stevens.

Barton, B. (1995). *Buzz, buzz, buzz*. New York: Simon & Schuster Children's Publishing.

Bell, C. (2010). *Bee-wigged*. London: Walk Books.

Dickmann, N. (2010). *A bee's life*. Chicago: Capstone Global Library.

Giles, J., & Lowe, I. (2000). *Speedy Bee*. Austin, TX: Harcourt Achieve.

Giles, J., & Lowe, I. (2007). *Speedy Bee's dance*. Austin, TX: Harcourt Achieve.

Haydon, J. (2004). *Facts about honey bees*. Austin, TX: Harcourt Achieve.

Leaf, M. (1936). *The story of Ferdinand*. New York: Grosset & Dunlap.

Mortensen, L., & Arbo, C. (2009). *In the trees, honey bees*. Nevada City, CA: Dawn.

Schaefer, L. M. (1999). *Honey bees and hives*. Mankato, MN: Capstone Press.

Smith, A. (2001). *The bear and the bees*. Austin, TX: Harcourt Achieve.

Tagliaferro, L. (2004). *Bees and their hives*. Mankato, MN: Capstone Press.

---

who are still developing their sight vocabulary and developing their word-solving skills and strategies. We then illustrate how a set of texts about honey bees could be used to foster knowledge development and address multiple reading objectives for these readers. We provide an overview of the text set and the instructional objectives that will be addressed with this set of books for a particular group of students. The main portion of the chapter is a "sample unit" that illustrates what the teacher might say and do to address the selected intervention goals. At the end of the chapter, we briefly note how this unit might be adapted for students with different needs from those of the hypothetical group. The website for this text contains a Statue of Liberty and Immigration text set that may be used with middle school age students (see the box at the end of the table of contents).

Instructional Decision Making: Addressing Multiple Objectives Using the Honey Bees Text Set

We designed this text set for use with third graders, and in this example, we describe how we would use the text set with a hypothetical group of third and/or fourth graders reading at an early to mid-second-grade level (guided reading levels around I, J, or K). We estimate that the text set would be read in 12–14 half-hour sessions that also include word-level instruction.

The readers in this group have learned to use all of the word identification strategies (described in Chapter 5) except for "Break the word into smaller parts," which will be taught during the sessions when the honey bee texts are read. To be responsive to the needs of the readers in this group, the teacher also plans to review the vowel part *ar*, as some readers in the group are still consolidating knowledge of this part, and to teach the part *aw*. This knowledge will be linked to the strategy "Look for parts you know." The theme texts provide opportunities for readers to practice using these strategies (and decoding elements) interactively with the meaning-based strategies that this group of students already uses well.

While reading this text set, the teacher encourages students to *enjoy reading* through his or her language, by engaging students in discussion, and by encouraging students to reflect on what they are learning and enjoying as they read. *Ample reading time* will enable students in this group to practice identifying unfamiliar words and to build their sight vocabulary. The teacher makes use of daily rereading of theme texts and frequent partner reading (with partners matched in reading accuracy level) to allow students to read more.

The teacher analyzes each text and decides whether it offers students opportunities to successfully practice their word identification strategies, paying careful attention for opportunities to practice the strategies just being learned. The teacher plans to engage the students as a group when he or she expects they will need more support in reading a particular text, and in partner reading when the texts allow students to function more independently.

The informational and fiction books in this text set include new Tier Two and Tier Three vocabulary words. Some are honey bee specific (e.g., *hive, honeycomb*); others have more general utility (e.g., *cell, colony, enormous, fierce, guard, lonesome, queen, worker*). In many cases, students will use the illustrations and context to learn about the meaning of these words. In other cases, the teacher will briefly explain what the word means. In order to keep a focus on building readers' sight vocabulary, the teacher's objective is simply for students to become more word conscious—that is, to be curious to learn what these words mean, and to enjoy learning and using new words.

As described in the next section, different parts of the text set are used to address different instructional objectives. Not every text provides opportunities to address every objective, but the set, as a whole, allows a fairly comprehensive and responsive approach to instruction. Figure 16.1 summarizes the objectives addressed by each group of texts.

	Informational text with one to two sentences and a photograph on each page	Informational text with photographs and longer paragraphs	Short fiction with one to two sentences and an illustration on each page	Poem/informational text	Longer fiction
Enjoy reading	✓	✓	✓	✓	✓
Build content knowledge and vocabulary	✓	✓	✓	✓	
Use illustrations and the author's words and ideas to build knowledge	✓	✓		✓	
Spend ample time reading		✓	✓		✓
Strategically identify unfamiliar words		✓			✓
Build word consciousness	✓	✓		✓	✓
Develop fluency	✓		✓		
Use knowledge to support comprehension		✓	✓	✓	✓
Ask questions and read for answers	✓	✓	✓	✓	✓

FIGURE 16.1. Objectives addressed by each subgroup of texts.

Short Informational Texts

In the first part of the text set, the readers in our group will develop knowledge about honey bees as they read and discuss three short informational texts on the topic. These texts include one or two sentences of text and a photograph on each page. These books might be considered to be well within these readers' independent reading level, except that they contain lots of new vocabulary and knowledge about bees. These books will be read in a small-group format with teacher support as students build knowledge about the new topic of bees, and reread during future sessions to foster fluency. The teacher's objectives for these books include helping readers to enjoy reading and become more aware of interesting new vocabulary words.

To focus the group's attention on the central conceptual knowledge of how bees survive, the teacher asks this as a guiding question as readers begin the short fiction texts. This question also serves as a model of the process of asking questions and reading for answers, which the teacher expects that students will engage in throughout the text set. As or after students read, the teacher records what the group is learning about how bees survive, and periodically encourages students to reflect on all that was learned.

One of the teacher's objectives in reading these texts is for readers to use both the photographs and the ideas that the author has written about as ways to build new knowledge, as the teacher has observed that these students do not yet reliably do this. The teacher briefly models *using the illustrations and written information*; the teacher also encourages students to do this through his or her comments before and as they read. The teacher periodically provides feedback about how noticing and using the illustrations as well as the written ideas and information helped students to learn more about how bees survive.

To foster knowledge development, the teacher demonstrates what it means to find and mark specific facts in informational text. Students then have multiple opportunities to learn facts by practicing this with the support of a partner.

To maximize reading time, and to keep attention focused on learning new information, the teacher decides to record information about bees for the group on chart paper, rather than ask students to individually write this information.

Longer Informational Texts

In the next part of the text set, readers read two informational texts that contain longer paragraphs (and plenty of photographs). These texts are written at the readers' instructional level. Having read the first group of texts in this text set, these readers will have already acquired some knowledge and vocabulary about bees. Reading the longer informational texts offers opportunities for students to (1) practice puzzling through and identifying unfamiliar words by using their word identification strategies, and (2) learn more about bees. Because they have some knowledge, the group will be encouraged to develop their own guiding question prior to reading and to read for answers. The teacher expects that students will continue to ask questions during reading. These books will be read with partners to increase time spent reading while providing some support for students as they build knowledge and identify unfamiliar words. The books will be reread in subsequent sessions to build sight vocabulary and fluency and to reinforce the knowledge students are acquiring.

As they read these books, students will practice using both the photographs and the author's written information and ideas as ways to learn new knowledge. Students will also practice marking new facts they are learning, and strategically puzzling through unfamiliar words. Once again, the teacher feels that these books are appropriate ways to address the instructional objectives of helping readers to enjoy reading and become more aware of interesting new vocabulary words.

Short Fiction

After reading the five informational texts about bees, students have the opportunity to use their knowledge of bees to support comprehension of two short stories. These stories include one or two sentences and an illustration on each page, and feature the same bee character that engages in many of the same activities as real worker bees. New knowledge about bees is introduced in the second story; the teacher prompts a question that will encourage students to look for that information. The teacher expects that these books will (1) be enjoyed by readers, (2) not offer many unfamiliar words for students to solve, and (3) include new information. Students will use these books to practice reading fluently to a partner, and discuss with their partner the knowledge they are using and building.

Poem/Informational Text

The next text is included because it allows students to see the value of knowledge, because they will be reading text that requires inference on the part of the reader. *In the Trees, Honey Bees* (Mortensen & Arbo, 2009) alternates between short, dense rhymes and informational paragraphs. Each page also includes vivid drawings of the world from a honey bee's perspective. The teacher anticipates that if he or she reads the rhymes to the group, they will be able to use the illustrations and their honey bee knowledge to interpret the rhymes. The group can then read the informational paragraphs to confirm their interpretation of the text. The teacher expects the group to be motivated by this display of their expertise. The teacher also expects students to enjoy the reading, interesting vocabulary, and detailed illustrations, and to continue to ask questions and seek answers to questions as they learn.

Longer Fiction

In the last part of the text set, students read four longer works of fiction that include bees as characters. The teacher expects that these books will (1) be enjoyed by readers, (2) offer ample unfamiliar words for students to solve, and (3) offer opportunities for students to be exposed to new vocabulary. The first has only one sentence per page—the teacher judges that students can read this successfully with the support of a partner. The last three fiction books have longer passages on each page and will be read in a group format so that the teacher can provide needed support for word identification strategy use and briefly teach the meaning of new vocabulary.

In these texts, the teacher will model asking, "I wonder what the character will do next?" and expects that students may ask questions as well. Students can use their knowledge of bees to support comprehension of these texts. In the first three texts, bees act in predictable ways. In the final text, the bee does its best to reject the role of "stinger," and instead is social. The teacher reminds students that they have knowledge they can use to help them to understand the text. Students are encouraged, at the end of each text, to reflect on how their knowledge about bees helped them to understand the stories. They also reflect on the utility of their word identification strategies. To provide additional opportunities for student thinking, students will write a brief response after reading each text.

Of course, a teacher might well select different objectives with a real group of students, and would adjust his or her comments and questions accordingly. A teacher might also address these same objectives but at a different pace, accelerating or decelerating the expectation for student independence. The unit in this chapter is one possible way that the text set could be used. At the end of the chapter, we provide some suggestions for alternative approaches.

Lesson Format

As we described in Chapter 2, a typical ISA-X intervention session begins with instruction on and/or practice with one or more word identification strategies, decoding elements, and/or high-frequency words. Students often engage in rereading during this time, allowing the teacher to target instruction or practice to individuals or smaller groups of students. If the lesson includes Word Work to allow students to learn or practice a new decoding element, students would then read a text that provides practice with the decoding element, such as a Ready Reader, unless the theme book for the day provides appropriate opportunities to practice the decoding element.

Theme books would be read and discussed after this portion of the session, which focuses primarily on words in isolation. The strategies and decoding elements that are addressed will frequently be those that the students can apply in their reading of new text in that same session. The intervention session would close with opportunities to reflect on what was learned from the books read; students might respond in writing or through discussion. On occasion, students would reflect on what they have learned about themselves as readers.

In the sample unit that follows, we only briefly summarize what might happen in the Word Work portion of the intervention session. More detailed lesson examples are provided in Chapters 6, 7, and 9.

Sample Unit to Address Selected Goals Using the Honey Bees Text Set

Part I. Short Informational Texts

Instruction Focused on Words in Isolation

On the days when the group is reading the short informational texts, during the first segment of the session students reread texts from previous sessions while the teacher reviews high-frequency words with individual students in the group. The teacher elects to omit word identification strategy and decoding instruction during these sessions to allow more time for the text set introduction, text set reading, and discussion. After the first session, students who are not involved in Word Work with the teacher can be encouraged to reread the theme texts to develop fluency.

Sample Motivational Language to Introduce Part I and an Upcoming Challenging Text

"I have an exciting book that I will share with you soon called *In the Trees, Honey Bees*. The author and illustrator of this book teach about bees in an interesting way. On each page, they use short rhymes and detailed illustrations to show readers some aspect of a bee's life. In a way, the book is like a puzzle and it can be fun to use the clues in the words and the pictures to figure out what they are trying to teach. To do that, though, it helps to know a lot about bees.

"Over the next few sessions, we are going to read lots of books about bees so we can become experts on how bees live. Then, we will read *In the Trees, Honey Bees* together to see whether we can match what we have learned to what the author and illustrator are sharing."

TEXT: *Honey Bees and Hives* (Schaefer, 1999)

Background for the Teacher

This text describes how honey bees live in hives that have a honeycomb structure. Honey bees store pollen, make honey, and lay eggs in the hive. Some honey bees feed the young and others guard the hive.

The text gives students the opportunity to learn new facts and vocabulary about honey bees by using both the text and the illustrations as sources of information. In order to maximize time spent reading, the teacher can record this information on chart paper, rather than expecting students to spend time writing. As students read, they may start to raise questions about why the honey bees do what they do. The teacher can record the questions on sticky notes so they can be saved and revisited across texts.

Prior to Reading

- **Support knowledge acquisition by modeling a central guiding question.** For example:

  "When readers read informational texts, they often find themselves interested and have questions that they want to learn the answers to as they read. Honey bees are really small, and I'm wondering, 'How do honey bees survive? How do they stay alive, and even if they do die, there are always more honey bees.' As we read today, let's see what new information this book teaches us about what honey bees do to survive."

Leading Questions

At the beginning of a thematic unit students may not have enough knowledge related to the topic of the unit to generate productive questions. Therefore, it is useful for the teacher to articulate a question that will serve as a point of departure for the unit. In posing a question, it is useful for the teacher to share the thinking that led to the question (e.g., "Honey bees are really small. I wonder how they survive?").

As discussed in the previous chapter, the ultimate goal is that the students will use their developing knowledge to generate their own questions.

- **Model using the text and illustrations to gain information.** For example:

  "This book is *Honey Bees and Hives* by Lola Schaefer. As we read it together, we are going to use both the author's words and the pictures to gather some facts. I will record what we learn on this chart paper. Listen as I read the first page. 'Honey bees live in hives.' So right away, this book tells us that honey bee homes are called hives. I'm going to look carefully at this picture to see what a hive looks like. It seems like a lot of bees live together in that hive. Now, I am going to write down the information we've just learned on our chart paper. Let's read the next page and see what we can learn."

Note: As students read the first text, they may stop and record something for each page because all the information is new. As they move into later texts, encourage students to read larger chunks of text before pausing to note information that is new or different. This will help students process and paraphrase rather than simply repeat information.

During Reading

GROUPING

Whole group; students take turns reading.

THE TEACHER'S ROLE

- Continue **modeling** using both the text and the pictures together to gain information.

  "Studying this picture helps me understand what the author means by honeycomb."

- **Support** students' use of both the text and the photographs to gain information.

  "Good observation about the photograph. How does that fit with what you are reading here?"

- **Support** word consciousness.

  "We're learning some interesting new vocabulary about bees."

- **Support** word solving. The teacher provides or confirms the pronunciation of unfamiliar vocabulary as students are reading.

- **Response:** As the group reads and finds facts, the teacher records the facts on chart paper.

Word-Solving Support
for Words That Are Not in Readers' Spoken Vocabulary

Note that because students will be encountering words that are not yet in their spoken vocabulary, it is appropriate for the teacher to provide pronunciations or confirm the students' attempts. However, students should nevertheless be encouraged to look all the way through the unfamiliar word so that once its pronunciation is established, the word is more likely to be stored in memory in a way that will make it more accessible upon future encounters. The next time that students encounter these words, it is expected that they will be able to confirm the words on their own.

After Reading

- **Encourage readers to reflect** on what was learned.

  "What have we learned so far about what honey bees do that helps them to survive?"

- **Follow up** on student-generated questions as needed.

- **Link** the learning the group has just done to what they will do in the future.

  "When we read our next book, we will use what the author has written and the photographs to see what new information we can learn."

TEXT: *Bees and Their Hives* (Tagliaferro, 2004)

Background for the Teacher

This text explains that honey bees build hives made of wax cells that form the honeycomb. The queen's job is to lay eggs; when the eggs hatch, worker bees feed the young. This text also mentions that guard bees protect the hive.

The text gives students the opportunity to gather more general information and vocabulary about honey bees. As students read, they have the chance to add to what they learned from the first book. To allow for more reading time, the teacher can record the new information on chart paper. The new text may also answer some student-generated questions or raise new ones.

Prior to Reading

- **Support knowledge acquisition by modeling a central guiding question.** For example:

  "Honey bees do many unique things to help them survive. I wonder what new information about honey bees can be learned from this book?"

- **Model looking for new information in the reading and/or illustrations.** For example:

  "When readers want to learn about a topic, one thing they might do is read lots of books on that topic. We are reading lots of books about honey bees. As we read each new book, we need to ask ourselves, 'What am I learning that is new or different from what I read in the other book(s)?'

  "Our next book is *Bees and Their Hives* by Linda Tagliaferro. Let's read the first page right now and see what it teaches about bees. 'Bees live in hives. Bees build hives in trees or logs.' That pretty much matches what we learned in our last book. The picture also looks just like one we saw in our first book. Let's check out the next page. 'Bees work for about two weeks to make a hive.' That's new information. We can add that to our chart. Let's keep reading and see what else we can learn from reading and studying the pictures in this book."

Note: This book will most likely be read in the same session as the first text so the introduction can be short and students can move right into reading.

During Reading

GROUPING

Whole group; students take turns reading.

THE TEACHER'S ROLE

- Continue **modeling** finding new information.

    "The first book had information on honeycombs but it didn't mention they were made out of wax."

- **Support** reading for enjoyment.

    "It looks like that really surprised you. What are you thinking about that?"

- **Support** word consciousness.

    "Dante has noticed another new vocabulary word about bees."

- **Support** word solving. The teacher provides or confirms pronunciation of unfamiliar vocabulary as students are reading and encourages the students to confirm the pronunciation of words that are likely to be part of their spoken vocabulary.

- **Response:** As the group reads and finds facts, the teacher records the facts on chart paper.

After Reading

- **Encourage readers to reflect** on what was learned.

    "What have we learned so far about what honey bees do that helps them to survive?"

- **Reflect** on the usefulness of using both the text and the illustrations to learn information.

    "As readers, we can gather information by reading what the author has written and studying the pictures to learn what each new book has to teach us. That's how we become experts."

- **Follow up** on student-generated questions as needed.

- **Link** the learning the group has done to what they will do in the future.

    "By the time we read *In the Trees, Honey Bees,* we'll know all sorts of information."

TEXT: *A Bee's Life* (Dickmann, 2010)

Background for the Teacher

This informational text is about the bee life cycle. It describes how the queen lays eggs and larva hatch from the eggs. Other bees feed the larva, which then turn into different kinds of bees: worker bees (who get food and make honey for the hive), drones, and the queen.

This text gives students the opportunity to continue to learn new facts and vocabulary about bees by using both the text and the illustrations as sources of information. Some information is new and some has already been encountered. To allow for maximum reading time, the teacher can record the new information on chart paper. As students read, they may start to raise questions about why the bees do what they do. The teacher can record the questions on sticky notes so they can be saved and revisited across texts.

Students will read this text with a partner so they can continue to gather facts and compare information across texts with more independence. As students read, they are encouraged to mark new key details with sticky notes. When the group comes back together at the end of the session, students can return to the places in the text that contain new information for the chart.

Prior to Reading

- **Support knowledge acquisition by modeling a central guiding question.** For example:

  "Honey bees do many unique things to help them survive. I wonder what new information about honey bees can be learned from this book?"

- **Model marking the source of new information.** For example:

  "So far, we've been sharing new information as soon as we find it. We have been able to look right back at the text and see exactly what the author said or the illustrations showed. When readers share information it is important to go back and point out the place where it was found. For now we are just going to focus on gathering information from our sources.

  "We are going to read the next book in partnerships and then come back and share the new information we find with the group. When you and your partner find information that is new or different in the book, mark the page with a sticky note. By marking the page, you can go right back to the information during our discussion.

  "Listen and watch as I read these pages and look for new information. 'A queen bee lays eggs in the cells.' That sounds familiar. 'A larva hatches from each egg.' That sounds new. I don't remember reading about larva in the last book. I'm not even exactly sure what a larva is. I am going to put my sticky note here because this is new information that I want to go back to when we share with the group.

As I continue reading, I am going to be looking for an answer to my new question, 'What is a larva?' and I'll continue to look for answers to any other questions I have."

During Reading

GROUPING

Partner reading (the teacher moves among the groups) followed by whole-group discussion.

THE TEACHER'S ROLE

- Continue **modeling** preparing to refer back to specific places in the text.

  "You've found a new fact. Let's put a sticky note there and bring it up with the group."

- **Support** students' use of both the text and illustrations to learn new information.

  "So that picture makes you think _____. Let's read the words and see what the author says."

- **Support** reading for enjoyment.

  "I noticed you're really enjoying that part of the book. What is it that you are enjoying?"

- **Support** word consciousness.

  "Have you noticed all the vocabulary we're learning about bees?"

- **Support** word solving. The teacher provides or confirms pronunciation of unfamiliar vocabulary as students are reading and encourages students to confirm the pronunciation of words that are likely to be part of their spoken vocabulary.

After Reading

- **Response:** Students come back together as a group and return to specific pages in the text to share the new information they have learned in this text. The teacher adds the new information to the chart.

  "Good thing we marked the new facts with sticky notes. Now we can go right back to the information we want to discuss."

- **Encourage readers to reflect** on what was learned.

  "What new information have we learned about what bees do that helps them to survive?"

- **Reflect** on the usefulness of marking new information in the text.

  "Going back to the text today helped us make sure we were writing accurate information on our chart."

- **Follow up** on student-generated questions as needed.

- **Link** the learning the group has just done to what they will do in the future.

  "We'll use sticky notes as we read the next book so we can quickly get back to important information in the text."

Part II. Longer Informational Texts

TEXT: *Bees* **(Ashley, 2004)**

Instruction Focused on Words in Isolation

Now that students have learned some information related to the theme, the teacher can devote time to learning a new decoding element. For our sample group, it would be appropriate for the teacher to begin the session by conducting a Word Work activity on a part that students need to learn, and then to engage students in reading a short text (such as a Ready Reader) that provides practice with that part. Students not directly engaged in this teacher-led instruction can continue to reread theme texts to build sight vocabulary and fluency and reinforce the knowledge they are building.

Background for the Teacher

This informational text gives students the opportunity to gather more specific information on bees. *Bees* (Ashley, 2004) covers many topics: bee parts, getting nectar and pollen from flowers, different bee jobs, the bee life cycle, and the structure of the hive.

Now that students have some knowledge about bees, the teacher will help them to ask the guiding question prior to reading, and encourage them to read for answers. It is expected that students may ask additional questions as they read.

This text provides opportunities for students to practice using a range of word identification strategies as they encounter challenging words like *covered, grocery, hatches, insect, laying, quickly,* and *thousand.* Prior to beginning the reading, the teacher will provide a reminder to students to use their word identification strategies.

Before students read this text with a partner, the teacher can use the illustrations to briefly explain the meaning of some new bee vocabulary: *abdomen, colony,* and *thorax.* Students can then practice identifying these words having been taught their meaning.

Students can read this text and gather facts from it with a partner. Partner reading allows for more independence and reading time. As students read, they can be encouraged to mark key details with sticky notes. When the group comes back together at the end of the session, students can return to the places in the text that contain new information for the chart.

Prior to Reading

- **Support knowledge acquisition by having students ask a central guiding question.** For example:

  "Honey bees do many unique things to help them survive. What are you wondering about that you'll look for information about as you read today?"

- **Use motivational language to prompt reading for new information.** For example:

  "You and your partner will continue reading interesting informational text and gathering information about honey bees. As you read, ask yourself, 'Does this match something we have already learned or is it new or different?' Be sure to look for new or different information both as you read and in the illustrations. You can mark those places with sticky notes so we can all go back to those places during our whole-group discussion. I bet we learn some more really cool stuff that bees do."

- **Introduce new vocabulary.** For example:

  "Before you start reading with your partner, let's look at some new and interesting words this author uses to teach readers about bees. Turn to page 9. On this page, the author is teaching readers the parts of a bee's body. The first label says *head.* That's a body part you already know. Put your fingers under the next label. This word is *thorax.* Say, 'thorax.' Follow the arrow with your finger and you can see that it is pointing to the middle part of the bee's body. The thorax is the middle section. The third label is the word *abdomen.* Say, 'abdomen.' The abdomen is the back end of a bee's body. So this photo teaches us that the bee's body has three parts. Say the parts with me as I point to each label: 'head, thorax, abdomen.' Now turn to page 10. The word in bold on this page is pronounced 'colony.' Say, 'colony.' When you read this page with your partner, the two of you can use the author's words to figure out what a colony is."

- **Prompt use of word identification strategies.** For example:

  "Remember that you have lots of strategies on your resource (Figure 5.1) that you can use if you come to a word you don't know yet. If you use strategies as you are reading with your partner, use a sticky note to mark the word so you can share what you did to solve it with the group."

During Reading

GROUPING

Partner reading (the teacher moves among the groups) followed by whole-group discussion.

THE TEACHER'S ROLE

- **Support** students' use of the text and illustrations to develop knowledge.

  "What are you learning from the text on this page? What are you learning from the pictures?"

- **Support** reading for enjoyment.

  "Wow, you've marked a lot of new information! You've learned a lot from reading that book."

- **Support** word consciousness.

  "Now that everyone has read through page 12, let's stop and talk about the word *colony*. What have you learned about the meaning of this word?"

- **Support** word identification strategy use.

  "What strategies could you use to help you puzzle through that word?"

After Reading

- **Response:** Students come together as a group and discuss and react to what has been learned in the text. Students return to specific places in the text to pull out new facts about bees. The teacher adds the new facts to the chart.

  Students share words that were identified using word identification strategies.

- **Reflect** on word identification strategy use.

  "You were able to identify an unfamiliar word using some of our strategies."

- **Reflect** on the value of reading.

"Wow! Look at all the information we've learned from reading these books about bees. We've really become experts by reading and thinking about how bees survive."

- **Follow up** on student-generated questions as needed.
- **Link** the learning the group has just done to what they will do in the future.

"Next, you're going to read another interesting book about bees and learn even more."

TEXT: *Facts about Honey Bees* (Haydon, 2004)

Instruction Focused on Words in Isolation

The students in this group have been using the strategy "Break the word into smaller parts" to break off -*ing* endings. Now they are ready to learn how to extend this strategy, and the theme text they will be reading contains many compound words. For these reasons, the teacher opts to begin the session by showing students how to break apart compound words and having them practice using the strategy interactively (with meaning-based strategies) to identify compound words in sentences that the teacher has written. Then students will be encouraged to use this strategy, along with the others they know, as they read the theme text.

Background for the Teacher

Facts about Honey Bees (Haydon, 2004) has short chapters that address different topics. This text describes the bee's body parts and the processes of getting nectar and pollen from flowers. It explains that when bees collect pollen from flowers, they also help plants to make seeds and reproduce. Different bee jobs are described, and it is pointed out that the colony works together to survive.

The text contains several compound words (*beehive, honeycomb, beekeeper, beeswax, teamwork*), providing students with the opportunity to practice breaking compound words into smaller parts. The teacher can prompt the use of this and other word identification strategies, and ensure that students have their Tips for Breaking Apart Words card available as a resource (see Figure 9.9 on p. 194).

Now that students have some knowledge about bees, the teacher can help them to ask the guiding question prior to reading, and encourage them to read for answers. It's expected that students may ask additional questions as they read.

Partner reading and fact gathering can be used to increase reading time and student independence. As students read, they can be encouraged to mark key details with sticky notes. When the group comes back together at the end of the session, students can return to the places in the text that contain new information for the chart.

Prior to Reading

- **Support knowledge acquisition by having students ask a central guiding question.** For example:

  "Honey bees do many unique things to help them survive. What are you wondering about that you'll look for information about as you read today?"

- **Use motivational language to prompt reading for new information.** For example:

  "You and your partner will continue reading interesting informational text and gathering information about honey bees. Be sure to look for new or different information as you read and in the illustrations. You can mark those places with sticky notes so we can all go back to those places during our whole-group discussion. Let's continue to learn about bees!"

- **Prompt use of word identification strategies.** For example:

  "Remember to bring your strategy resource (Figure 5.1) with you when you read with your partner. Today you have a new way to use 'Break the word into smaller parts' by breaking compound words into the two words that make up the compound word. When you use strategies as you are reading with your partner, mark the word so you can share it with the group."

During Reading

GROUPING

Partner reading (the teacher moves among the groups) followed by whole-group discussion.

THE TEACHER'S ROLE

- **Support** reading for enjoyment.

  "You've learned even more about bees by reading that book."

- **Support** questioning.

  "That's an interesting question! I'll write it down and we'll see whether the book gives you an answer—or maybe one of our other books will."

- **Support** word identification strategy use.

  "What strategies could you try to help you puzzle through that word?"

After Reading

- **Response:** Students come together as a group and discuss and react to what has been learned in each text. Students return to specific places in the text to pull out new facts about bees. The teacher adds the new facts to the chart.
- **Reflect** on word identification strategy use.

Students share words that were identified using word identification strategies and discuss which strategies they used.

> "We were able to identify unfamiliar words using our strategies. And our new way of using the strategy to break the word into smaller parts really came in handy for puzzling through compound words today!"

- **Reflect** on the value of reading.

> "Reading and thinking about informational books has helped us to become experts about how bees survive."

- **Follow up** on student-generated questions as needed.
- **Link** the learning the group has just done to what they will do in the future.

> "Next, you're going to have a chance to use what you've learned as you read some stories that have bees as characters."

Part III. Short Fiction Texts

TEXTS: *Speedy Bee* **(Giles & Lowe, 2000)**
and *Speedy Bee's Dance* **(Giles & Lowe, 2007)**

Instruction Focused on Words in Isolation

If the teacher judges that students would benefit from practicing the new application of the strategy they learned in the previous session, the teacher can conduct a consolidation lesson regarding "Break the word into smaller parts." The teacher can provide students with the opportunity to practice using the strategy interactively (with meaning-based strategies) to identify compound words in sentences that the teacher has written.

Background for the Teacher

In *Speedy Bee* (Giles & Lowe, 2000), the baby bees are hungry. Speedy Bee is a worker bee that searches and finds flowers to get food for the baby bees. In *Speedy Bee's Dance* (Giles & Lowe, 2007), Speedy Bee communicates the location of flowers to other worker bees by dancing. Then lots of worker bees visit the flowers to get food for the hungry baby bees.

These short fiction books give students the opportunity to use the information they have learned to reflect on how the bees act in the story. As students read, they can look for places where the story bees are similar to real-life bees. They can also look for places in which the bees act in ways that weren't discussed in the informational texts.

These texts are written at students' independent level, so offer few opportunities for word solving. The teacher encourages students to read these books with partners and to practice reading to their partner with expression that conveys the author's message.

The teacher can have the partnerships come together as a whole group after reading both books so that the pairs can share what they have learned.

Prior to Reading

- **Introduce the transition to fiction.** For example:

  "We've been reading informational text about honey bees. Today you have a chance to apply what you've learned about honey bees as you read two stories about bees."

- **Support the use of acquired knowledge by stating the guiding question.** For example:

  "Today we're reading with a different question in mind. Since we know so much about honey bees, we can ask ourselves, 'How are the honey bees in this fiction book like the honey bees in the informational text? Did they act in ways that matched or didn't match what we've read about so far?'

  "I have another question about the title of our second book, *Speedy Bee's Dance*. I'm wondering what that title might mean, because in the books we've read there haven't been any dancing bees. As you read the story, see whether you can figure out what the author means by that title."

- **Provide instructions for partner work.** For example:

  "We're going to read each book twice, and practice reading to our partner in a way that really conveys the author's message. Pay special attention to the dialogue in the book.

  "In addition to reading with expression, we're reading to think about the author's message. Read the book together once to think about the story as a whole. Read it a second time with the guiding questions in mind. Use sticky notes to mark places in the text where the story bees act like real bees. Be ready to share your findings with the whole group."

During Reading

Partner reading (the teacher moves among the groups) followed by whole-group discussion.

- **Support** student use of relevant knowledge.

    "What is Speedy Bee doing here? Does that fit with what you've learned about bees?"

- **Support** fluency.

    "You're using different voices to show that different characters are speaking. That really communicates the author's message, doesn't it?"

- **Support** reading for enjoyment.

    "So we just learned more about how the bees find the flowers with nectar."

After Reading

- **Discuss and react** to the events in the text, focusing first on enjoyment of the stories.

    "What do you think of the story?"
    "What was your favorite part?"
    "Who has a different favorite part?"
    "Did Speedy Bee act like the bees we've read about?"

- **Reflect** on the usefulness of knowledge.

    "Paying attention to the ways Speedy Bee acted like a real bee really helped us understand why she was doing what she was doing in these books."

- **Link** the learning the group has done to what they will do next.

    "We studied bees in informational text and that helped us understand Speedy Bee. Next, we'll get to use what we know as we read a poem about bees."

Part IV. Poem/Informational Text

TEXT: *In the Trees, Honey Bees* (Mortensen & Arbo, 2009)

Instruction Focused on Words in Isolation

Because of the challenge posed by the theme book, on this day the teacher opts not to introduce new content related to words in isolation. She encourages students to reread the longer informational texts and to continue practicing their word identification strategies. While the other students are rereading, the teacher can use instructional time efficiently by engaging individual students in practicing their high-frequency words.

Background for the Teacher

This mixed-genre text alternates between short, dense rhymes and information about bees. The rhymes (e.g., "Blossoms out. Dancing scout," pp. 2–3) require the reader to make inferences (in this example, to infer that the scout bee sees flowers and then goes back to the hive to communicate by dancing the location of the flowers). To support the reader in making the inferences, the text includes large, detailed illustrations, drawn from the point of view of a honey bee. Each page also includes a paragraph that provides information that will help the reader to make these inferences. Much of this information will have already been learned earlier in the text set, so readers can be expected to make some of these inferences as they first encounter the rhymes. The book discusses the processes of getting nectar and pollen from flowers, and the bee life cycle. Bee jobs are described in detail.

The rhymes in this book give students the opportunity to draw on all they have learned about bees to understand challenging text. To illustrate to students the value of their knowledge, the teacher will read the poem portion of the book (skipping the informational paragraphs) aloud to the students, stopping at each page to have students share their interpretation of what the rhymes and illustrations are showing about bees. If students are uncertain, the teacher will encourage them to check the group's chart of ideas from the informational texts.

After the group has had the chance to form their own ideas about what the rhymes and illustrations are working together to show, the informational paragraphs can be read to confirm the group's interpretation. The teacher can call upon students in the group to read paragraphs with familiar information and the teacher can read paragraphs with novel vocabulary or information.

Prior to Reading

- **Model the use of prior knowledge to make inferences, and state the value of knowledge to readers.** For example:

  "We have been reading to become experts on bees. Here's our chance to see how much we've learned so far. Today we are going to read this picture book that I told you about at the beginning of our bee topic. We'll read to see whether we can match what we've already learned to what this author and illustrator show about the life of a bee. The author has written short rhymes that are like puzzles. As we read, we will need to use the author's words and the pictures together to figure out what is being said in these rhymes. The author and illustrator use carefully chosen words and detailed drawings to show a lot about the life of bees. Let's think about all we have learned so far and use that to help us think about what is being shown.

  "Listen as I try it on the first page. 'Morning light, warm and bright. In the trees, honey bees.' What stands out to me is the tree. The tree takes up the whole illustration and the author uses the word *tree*. We learned that bees make hives in trees in several of our books. I think the author is telling us that honey bees live in trees. The bees in the trees are waking up because its morning. Let's turn to the next page. After you have a chance to look at the picture and listen to the words, turn to a partner and talk about what you think the author is saying."

During Reading

GROUPING

Whole group; the teacher reads page by page and engages the group in discussion.

THE TEACHER'S ROLE

- **Support** students in using learned information about bees to understand what the poem is saying.

  "Look at this illustration of bees flying away from the hive. The words say 'sisters fly through the sky.' Is there anything we learned that might help us to understand who the sisters are in the poem? [We read that worker bees are all female.] So you think the poet is talking about worker bees here? Let's read the informational text to see whether our interpretation of the poem matches the author's thinking."

- **Reflect** on the value of information; support word consciousness.

  "Great thinking! You knew from what we learned by reading that the worker bees feed the larva, and recognized the workers and the larva in the illustration. When the poem said, 'Lots of food. Hungry brood,' you figured out that brood must be the larva, even though this is the first time we've seen them called brood. We sure are learning a lot of new words in the reading and thinking we have been doing."

- **Support** reading for enjoyment.

   "Wow. I sure wouldn't want to be that bear robbing the honey!"

- **Response:** Students discuss as they listen and then reflect on how the knowledge they gained from the informational text made it easier to figure out the poem's meaning.

After Reading

- **Discuss and react** to the text, focusing first on enjoyment.

   "What do you think of this author's way of telling about bees?"

- **Encourage reflection** on the usefulness of knowledge.

   "Go back into the poem and find a place where you used what we learned by reading about bees to understand what the poet was saying. Who wants to share how using their knowledge helped them to understand the poem?"

- **Link** the learning the group has done to what it will do next.

   "We've learned a lot about bees and how they act in the real world. Now, we get to look at bees as characters in stories. We are going to use all we have learned so far with some new questions in mind.

Part V. Longer Fiction

TEXT: *Buzz, Buzz, Buzz* (Barton, 1995)

Instruction Focused on Words in Isolation

In this group there are two students who are still learning the *ar* vowel part. The teacher notices that the theme book includes some words containing *ar*, so during the word-learning part of the intervention session the teacher elects to do a consolidation Word Work lesson with the two students for whom it is appropriate. During this time the other students can reread theme texts to build sight vocabulary and fluency and reinforce/consolidate knowledge.

Background for the Teacher

In this circular story, a bee stings a bull and triggers a chain of events that cause problems across the whole farm. This book is funny, and at a level that students can read it with a partner. Students can use knowledge about bees to help them understand the story. While reading, students can practice interactive use of word identification strategies to solve unfamiliar words including words containing the *ar* part in *barked, barn, farmer,* and *hard.*

Prior to Reading

- **Use motivational language to introduce fiction reading.** For example:

  "We have been spending time becoming experts on bees through reading. We used informational texts and some fiction texts to learn about how bees live. Now we are going to shift our focus a bit and use what we've learned to help us understand the bees that are characters in stories. We are going to read four more stories with bees as characters. As we read, we will think about the bee as a character. We will ask ourselves, 'What does this bee do?' and 'Based on our knowledge, is this what we would expect a bee to do?'"

- **Introduce the reading.** For example:

  "Today we have a chance to read and enjoy another story that has a bee as a character. When we read *Speedy Bee's Dance,* we noticed some things about Speedy Bee. We noticed that her dance showed the other bees where to find the flowers. That helped us figure out that she was helpful to her whole hive. As we read *Buzz, Buzz, Buzz* today, we are going to pay attention to the bee. We will talk about what the bee does and that will help us to understand the story.

  "As you read, you'll get to use your word identification strategies to help you puzzle through some words. Remember that you have resources, including your strategy list (Figure 5.1) and the key words we've been using recently (Figure 9.5).

  "As a reader, you may notice words that you don't know the meaning of. Remember that you can use the illustrations and the sentence to help you figure out the word's meaning. You can also ask your partner or me [the teacher] for assistance if the illustrations and words aren't helpful."

- **Engage readers in creating one or more guiding questions.** For example:

  "Looking at the bee on the cover of this book and thinking about the bees we've seen and read about in the informational texts, what questions do you have?"

- **Provide instructions for partner work.** For example:

  "Read this story together. Partners, if you are not the one who is reading out loud, remember to follow along in your book and to give your partner time to solve words independently, and be ready to recommend strategies if your partner asks for recommendations. As you read, pay careful attention to what the bee is like. When you are done, we will come together as a group to talk about the bee character."

During Reading

GROUPING

Partner reading followed by whole-group discussion.

THE TEACHER'S ROLE

- **Support** students' attention to using knowledge.

  "What are you noticing about the bee?"

- **Support** word identification strategy use.

  "You saw the *ar* part and that helped you to read that word. 'Looking for parts you know' is helping you to read and enjoy this story."

- **Support** reading for enjoyment.

  "Wow. Look at his face! What do you think he'd say right now?"

After Reading

- **Discuss and react** to the events in the text, focusing first on enjoyment of the story.

  "What do you think of the story?"

  "What was your favorite part?"

  "Who has a different favorite part?"

- **Encourage students to reflect** on the usefulness of the word identification strategies.

  "Are there strategies that were especially helpful to you as you read today?"

- **Reflect** on the usefulness of bee knowledge.

  "Paying attention to the bee helped us understand the whole story. He was just one small character, but he sure had a big impact."

- **Response:** After discussion, students will write and share a brief response to the prompt, "Do you think the bee will act the same at the end of the story as he did at the beginning?"

- **Link** the thinking the group has done to what it will do next.

  "I wonder what the bees will do in the next story."

TEXT: *The Bear and the Bees* (Retold by Smith, 2001)

Instruction Focused on Words in Isolation

Students in this group have been learning vowel parts and then using that knowledge to expand the way they use the strategy "Look for parts you know." The teacher notices that one part that students have not yet learned, *aw*, will be encountered in the theme book. In this session, the teacher elects to do a Word Work lesson to introduce the *aw* vowel part and then encourages students to look for this part as they read the theme book.

Background for the Teacher

In this retelling of an Aesop's fable, the bear gets stung by a bee and lets his anger get the best of him. Students can use knowledge about bees to help them understand the story. While reading, students can practice interactive use of word identification strategies to solve unfamiliar words including words containing the *aw* part in *clawed, crawled, paw,* and *saw*.

Prior to Reading

- **Introduce the reading.** For example:

  "Today you get to read and enjoy another story that has a bee as a character. As you read *The Bear and the Bees* today, pay attention to the bee. We will talk about what the bee does and that will help us to understand the story.

  "As you read, you may encounter some puzzling words. If you need them, I've posted the strategy list (Figure 5.1) and the key words we've been using recently— like *aw* and *ar*. [The teacher points to the two most recently used key words on Figure 9.5.] You can use these parts you've been learning when you look for parts you know.

  "We'll also notice what the bees do and whether it is what we would expect."

During Reading

GROUPING

Whole-group reading and discussion; students take turns doing the reading.

THE TEACHER'S ROLE

- **Support** students' use of knowledge about bees to help understand the text.

  "What are you noticing about the bees? Is this what you would expect?"

- **Support** use of word identification strategies.

  "What strategies could you use to help you puzzle through that word?"

The teacher is alert for evidence of interactive use of "Look for parts you know" and "Break words into smaller parts," combined with meaning-based strategies.

- **Model** questioning.

  "I wonder what the bear will do next?"

- **Support** reading for enjoyment.

  "I can't wait to see what's going to happen when he digs into that log."

- **Support** word consciousness.

  The teacher is prepared to briefly define the words *plodded, crossly, grump,* and *ground squirrel* when they are encountered during reading.

After Reading

- **Discuss and react** to the events in the text, focusing first on enjoyment of the story.

  "What do you think of the story?"
  "Who thought something different?"

- **Reflect** on the usefulness of the word identification strategies.

  "You were able to puzzle through some words today using your word identification strategies. Does anyone want to share how they identified a word?"

- **Response:** Students will write and share a brief response to the prompt "Do you think the bear will act differently next time?"
- **Link** the thinking the group has done to what it will do next.

  "We are becoming expert bee watchers. As we read our next stories, we will continue to watch for what they do and are like."

TEXT: *The Story of Ferdinand* (Leaf, 1936)

Instruction Focused on Words in Isolation

Students in this group have learned the strategy "Break the word into smaller parts." Earlier in this text set they learned and practiced using this strategy with compound words. The teacher notices that *Ferdinand* includes words containing the *-est* suffix. In this session, the teacher elects to briefly show students examples of words that include the *-est* suffix, and to demonstrate how to break off this suffix as another application of the strategy "Break the word into smaller parts." The teacher then encourages students to practice using this strategy interactively (with meaning-based strategies) to identify words containing *-est* in sentences that the teacher has prepared. Students will have further opportunity to practice this strategy when reading the theme text.

Background for the Teacher

This picture book tells the story of a gentle bull that is momentarily turned into a fierce beast by a bee sting. Students can use knowledge about bees to help them understand the story. This text contains lots of interesting vocabulary to foster word consciousness. While reading, students can practice interactive use of word identification strategies to solve unfamiliar words, including words containing the -est suffix in *biggest, fastest, fiercest, largest, proudest,* and *roughest.*

Prior to Reading

- **Introduce the reading.** For example:

    "Today we have a chance to read and enjoy another story that has a bee as a character. As we read *The Story of Ferdinand,* we are going to pay special attention to the bee. We will talk about what the bee does and that will help us to understand the story.

    "As you read, you may encounter some puzzling words. I've posted the strategy list (Figure 5.1) as usual. I know you already know and use a lot of these strategies, but the list will be here in case there's one you can't remember, along with the key words we've been using recently (Figure 9.5). You can use these parts you've been learning when you look for parts you know. If you come to any words that have the *-est* suffix, you'll be able to break off that part of the word to help you puzzle through the word.

    "The author uses lots of interesting vocabulary in this book. If there is a word you notice that you want to learn more about, you can try to figure out what the word means using the rest of the sentence and the illustration—and perhaps an earlier sentence or two. If that doesn't work, please ask. I'm sure everyone in the group will be interested in learning the words also."

During Reading

GROUPING

Whole-group reading and discussion; students take turns doing the reading.

THE TEACHER'S ROLE

- **Support** students' use of knowledge about bees to help understand the text.

    "What are you noticing about the bee? Is this what you would expect?"

- **Support** use of word identification strategies.

    "What strategies could you use to help you puzzle through that word?"

The teacher is alert for evidence of interactive use of "Look for parts you know" and "Break the word into smaller parts," in combination with meaning-based strategies.

- **Model** questioning.

  "I wonder what Ferdinand will do next?"

- **Support** reading for enjoyment.

  "Take a look at this illustration. What would that bee say if he could talk right now?"

The teacher should consider reading the bullring pages out loud to the group to ensure that they are understood.

- **Support** word consciousness.

  "Trevon noticed a word to learn. _____ means _____."

The teacher is prepared to briefly define the words *fierce, lonesome,* and *snorting,* when they are first encountered during reading. These words appear multiple times in the story.

After Reading

- **Discuss and react** to the events in the text, focusing first on enjoyment of the story.

  "What do you think of Ferdinand?"
  "Who thought of something different?"

- **Reflect** on the value of knowledge.

  "What did the bee do? Why was that important here?"

- **Reflect** on the usefulness of the word identification strategies.

  "You were able to puzzle through some words today using your word identification strategies. Does anyone want to share how they identified a word?"

- **Response:** Students will write and share a brief response to the prompt, "Do you think that Ferdinand will act differently in the future?"
- **Link** the thinking the group has done to what it will do next.

  "We are becoming expert bee watchers. As we read our next stories, we will continue to watch for what they do and are like."

TEXT: *Bee-Wigged* (Bell, 2010)

Instruction Focused on Words in Isolation

Students in this group have been learning and practicing the vowel parts *ar* and *aw*, and then looking for these parts as they use the strategy "Look for parts you know." The teacher judges that some students would benefit from additional practice with these parts so elects to do a consolidation Word Work lesson focused on the parts *ar* and *aw*. There are opportunities to apply knowledge of both parts during the reading of the theme book. Students who do not need the consolidation activity can reread theme books to develop fluency and sight vocabulary.

Background for the Teacher

In this picture book, Jerry the Bee can't make any friends because all the people he meets are afraid he will sting them. This is a funny story that shows students that fictional bees can be quite different from real bees. This text contains lots of interesting vocabulary to foster word consciousness. Students can use what they know about bees as they react to Jerry's behavior. While reading, students can practice interactive use of word identification strategies to solve unfamiliar words.

Prior to Reading

- **State the guiding question.**

  "What does this bee do? Based on your knowledge, is this what you'd expect?"

- **Prompt for use of word identification strategies.**

  "What are some things you can do if you encounter puzzling words today?"

- **Prompt questioning.**

  "You look like you're wondering about something. Do you have a question to share?"

- **Prompt word consciousness.**

  "If you hear a word you want to learn more about, remember to ask."

During Reading

GROUPING

Whole-group reading and discussion; students take turns doing the reading.

THE TEACHER'S ROLE

- **Support** students' use of knowledge about bees to help understand the text.

   "What are you noticing about Jerry? Is this what you would expect from a bee?"

- **Support** use of word identification strategies.

   "Breaking that longer word into smaller parts helped you figure it out."
   "Would you like to ask someone to recommend a different strategy?"

- **Model** questioning.

   "I wonder what Jerry will do next?"

- **Support** reading for enjoyment.

   "I was totally surprised by _____."

- **Support** word consciousness.

   "That's a great word, isn't it?"

   The teacher is prepared to briefly define the words *enormous, generous, complimented, inspired, remarkable, ecstatic,* and *honor* when they are encountered during reading.

After Reading

- **Discuss and react** to the events in the text, focusing first on enjoyment of the story.

   "The first time I read this book, I had no idea the wig was an animal! Did that catch anyone else by surprise?"
   "What do you think about how Jerry was treated at the beginning? Were people right to be scared of such a big bee?"

- **Reflect** on word identification strategy use.

   "Today, when Max came to the word *started,* he checked the key word resource (Figure 9.5) to help him remember the sound for *ar* and that helped him solve the word."

- **Conclude unit.**

> "We've learned so much about bees by reading. Today we read about *making friends with a bee.* Based on all you know about bees, would you make friends with a bee? Why or why not? Turn and talk to your partner, and then we'll share our ideas."

Summary

In this chapter, we illustrated what it might look like to use a set of thematically related texts to develop readers' knowledge, motivation, word-solving abilities, vocabulary, and comprehension—that is, we have sought to portray intervention that is comprehensive and responsive, which is typical of ISA-X intervention sessions.

Our goal is to provide teachers with a multiday, multitext example of how ISA-X instruction would be designed and delivered for intermediate and middle school readers who have yet to attain the level of reading accuracy expected at their grade level. We expect that teachers would modify the use of this text set as appropriate for their readers and encourage them to use this example as a model in developing thematic text sets on other topics (see also Chapter 11 and Gelzheiser et al., 2014, for guidance on developing text sets). Finally, we note that with different groups of students, this text set could be used to address other objectives appropriate to different students, such as to help them:

- Learn to value reading as a way to learn interesting things.
- Develop self-efficacy.
- Learn word meanings sufficiently well to use the words in spoken and written language.
- Compare and contrast different texts (critical comprehension).
- Make predictions about how the bee characters and other characters will act.
- Learn to use glossaries.
- Notice what characters are doing and how that influences the story.
- Attend to what the characters are like and how that influences the story.
- Learn guidelines for discussion.
- Learn to initiate conversation.
- Learn to respond to one another's ideas.

Glossary of Terms
as They Are Used in This Book

accuracy: The ability to read printed words correctly without errors, rereading, self-correcting, or teacher prompting.

acquisition: The period of time when a learner is beginning to develop new skill(s), strategies, or knowledge; an acquisition lesson is designed to help the student to learn something previously unknown.

automatic: Done largely without conscious thought or effort—for example, identifying a written word with seemingly little effort.

autonomy: When the learner is self-directed rather than guided by the teacher.

blend (spoken language): To say two individual sounds (phonemes) so that there is no separation between them.

blend (written language): See *consonant blend*. Examples include *sl, br,* and *sn*.

coarticulation: The process by which the sound that a speaker is producing is influenced or altered by the sounds around it. For example, in the *tr* blend, the sound of the *t* is influenced by the sound of the *r* such that the sound of the *t* is hard to discern. Unless students know the conventional spelling of a word, they will often spell a *tr* blend as *chr* (*trip* vs. *chrip*).

coherence: Logical and consistent understanding of information. For example, to achieve coherence, a reader may need to think about the author's words and ideas until they all fit together to communicate a sensible message.

compound word: A word formed by combining two shorter words that each retain their meaning. Examples include *snowshoe, bedtime,* and *doorstep*.

341

comprehension: The act of reading and thinking about the meaning of what is being read; using the author's words and the reader's knowledge to construct an understanding of a text.

comprehension—critical: The reader's thinking involves comparing or evaluating texts and/or reflecting on the author's intentions.

comprehension—inferential: The reader's thinking involves using background knowledge and intepretation to construct understanding of the author's message.

comprehension—literal: The reader's thinking is focused on understanding information that has been stated directly in the text.

concept: An abstract idea generalized from specific examples. For example, the concept of a "river" is formed by generalizing the features of many different rivers.

confirm: To verify the accuracy of (an unfamiliar word's identity).

consolidation: The process of converting new skills, strategies, or knowledge into something that is well-known and remembered and can be applied.

consonant: A letter representing a consonant sound (these are speech sounds characterized by constriction of the mouth or throat). All of the letters of the alphabet are consonants except *a, e, i, o, u,* and, in some cases, *y.*

consonant blend: Two to three adjacent consonant letters that are in the same syllable. When read, the sound of each letter is pronounced in sequence and without a separation between them. Each of the consonants' sounds can be discerned (at least to some extent). Examples include *sl, br,* and *sn.*

consonant digraph: Two adjacent consonant letters that together represent a single sound. Examples include *sh, ch,* and *ph.*

(continuent) consonant: A consonant sound that can be stretched out or elongated without distortion. Examples include /f/, /m/, and /s/.

(nasal) consonant: A consonant sound that is produced by air flowing through the nose (nasal passage) instead of through the mouth. Examples include /m/ and /n/.

(stop) consonant: A consonant sound that cannot be stretched out or elongated without distortion. Examples include /b/, /d/, and /k/.

(unvoiced) consonant: A consonant sound that is produced without the vibration of the vocal chords. Examples include /p/, /s/, and /t/.

(voiced) consonant: A consonant sound that is produced, in part, by the vibration of the vocal chords. Examples include /b/, /d/, and /z/.

culminating text: A final, longer, and more challenging text in a thematic text set.

decoding element: Frequently used letter or letter group that represents a sound or sequence of sounds. Examples include *a, oi,* and *tion.*

digraph: Two adjacent letters that represent a single sound. Examples include *ch, ow,* and *ar.*

discussion: Students share with one another what they are thinking (clues from the author, relevant knowledge) as they construct meaning during reading. Readers respond to one another in a discussion format and build understanding together.

distinctive feature: One of the attributes or characteristics that helps to define a concept.

engagement: Involvement in the process of constructing the meaning of a book or other text.

explicit instruction: Instruction that states what is being learned, why the learning is useful and important, and when the learner will use it. If a procedure is being taught, explicit instruction shows the learner how to execute the procedure. Explicit instruction also involves presenting new information/material in small steps and providing guided practice and continued practice, perhaps over multiple sessions, until students have achieved a level of success.

expository: A style of writing that uses a topical (rather than chronological) organization. Paragraphs and/or chapters may follow a main idea and supporting detail structure.

eye–voice span: The span of words between where the reader's eyes are focused and what the reader is reading aloud. Knowledge of what's coming next in the reading helps the reader to apply appropriate intonation.

feedback: Information about an action or process provided to the learner with the goal of improving performance.

fiction: Stories that are at least partly imaginary, usually with characters, setting, and plot.

figure of speech: An expression that has a different meaning from the literal meaning of the words it contains.

fluency: Oral reading that is smooth, flowing (without hesitation), and with expression that is consistent with the author's message.

front-loading: The practice of a teacher telling students facts that will be useful in understanding the text before a text is read.

gradual release of responsibility: The teacher provides less support as the learner gains competence.

high-frequency word: One of the 300–500 words that occur most often in children's books.

illustration: A picture, photograph, or other graphic feature that serves to clarify or decorate text.

independent level: Text that a reader can read with greater than 95% accuracy and strong comprehension. There is no universally agreed-upon cutoff for what constitutes an independent level relative to comprehension.

independent reader: A reader who is not dependent upon a teacher or another reader to identify words or construct text meaning while reading; an independent reader becomes strategic when necessary and engages in meaning construction while reading.

inference: The process of reaching a logical conclusion based on evidence presented in the text and on the reader's (pre)existing knowledge. Readers make inferences when they understand or learn something that is not explicitly stated in the text.

inflectional ending: Letters added to a word to show plurals, verb tense, or the comparative form of an adjective.

informational text: Nonfiction written to convey factual information, often with text features such as headings and glossaries.

instructional level: Text that a reader can read with 70–95% accuracy and comprehension. Definitions of instructional level vary, depending upon the expert and on whether the focus is on comprehension or accuracy.

interactive strategy use: Using, as needed, multiple information sources in a mutually supportive manner to identify a written/printed word that is, initially, unknown.

key word: A word intended to help readers to remember the sound(s) made by a letter or group of letters. Examples include the word *apple* (along with a picture of an apple) to help readers remember one of the sounds represented by the letter *a*.

knowledge: Information stored in an individual's long-term memory.

morpheme: A unit of meaning in a word. For example, the word *want* has one morpheme, *wanted* has two, and *unwanted* has three.

morphology: The study of meaningful word-forming elements in our language. These elements include root words, prefixes, and suffixes.

motivation: What gets one going, keeps one engaged, and moves one forward in any task that requires effort.

multisyllabic word: A word with more than one syllable. Examples include *singing, imagine,* and *constitution*.

narrative: Text written as a report of connected events that are usually presented as a continuous stream of information often in chronological order.

nonfiction: Text presented as factual by the author, with the purpose of providing the reader with accurate information about a topic (informational text) or person (biography) or other subject (e.g., a "how-to" book).

open-ended question: A question that cannot be answered with a yes/no or other single-word answer.

orthography: The conventions for how words are spelled and how sounds are represented using letters.

partner reading: Two students alternating reading aloud to each other and supporting each other's thinking; may also be called buddy reading.

prediction: What the reader thinks (based on the reader's background knowledge and clues from the author's text and/or the text's illustrations) that the author will have happen in narrative text.

prefix: A meaningful word part (morpheme) attached to the beginning of a word or base to produce a related word. Examples include *pre-*, *un-*, and *re-*.

prosody: During oral reading, grouping the words into meaningful phrases that serve to convey the author's intended meaning, and using the correct intonation to communicate that meaning.

purpose setting: The reader establishes a meaning-related reason for engaging in reading.

questioning: Readers' goal for understanding of a text takes the form of asking their own questions as they read, then reading for answers.

reading: Identifying words and constructing meaning from continuous text. Reading may occur silently or orally; students may read alone, to a partner, or to a group.

repeated reading: Reading a text multiple times and attempting to read more accurately and fluently on each successive reading.

rereading: Purposeful reading of a complete text or meaningful portion of a text that has previously been read.

resource: A concise list of strategies and/or key words available to the reader to assist in the recall of useful information. Texts that have been read also serve as resources.

responsive instruction: The goals of instruction and the teacher's level of support are chosen based on the current capabilities of the learner.

schema: Knowledge that is structured and organized. Having a schema related to a text's topic enables the reader to more readily comprehend the text.

self-efficacy: Confidence in one's ability to achieve a goal or accomplish a task.

sight vocabulary: The body of words that a reader can identify automatically and in all contexts when they are seen in print.

silent reading: Quiet rereading, or reading of novel text, without peer or teacher support. In the context of the ISA-X, this occurs after students have acquired strategies and knowledge and are ready to practice/use these independently.

strategy: A tactic employed for the purpose of achieving a goal—for example, breaking apart a long word with the goal of being able to identify the word.

(code-based) strategy: Analyzing individual letters and/or groups of letters within an unknown word in order to identify it.

(meaning-based) strategy: Using information from the pictures and/or the context to support the identification of an unknown word.

suffix: A meaningful word part attached to the end of a root word or base to produce a related word or an inflectional form of a word. Examples include *-ing*, *-ly*, and *-s*.

syllable: A unit of spoken language that includes a single vowel sound; a syllable may also include consonant sounds before and/or after the vowel.

syntax: The system of rules that govern the formation of grammatical sentences and phrases.

(literary) syntax: The type of sentence structure found more often in written than in spoken language.

thematic text set: Several carefully sequenced nonfiction and fiction trade books on a single science or social studies topic.

think-aloud model: The part of explicit instruction in which the teacher shares how he or she carries out a mental procedure.

vocabulary: Knowledge of words' meanings stored in the reader's long-term memory.

(Tier Two) vocabulary: Sophisticated, generally useful words that may be encountered more often in books than in conversation. Examples include *abandon, commence,* and *investigate.*

(Tier Three) vocabulary: Sophisticated words used in narrow contexts—for example, science content words. Examples include *colony, chrysalis,* and *hive.*

vowel: A letter representing speech sounds in which the mouth and/or throat are not constricted. The letters *a, e, i, o, u,* and, in some cases, *y,* are used to represent vowel sounds. Two-letter combinations can also be used to represent vowel sounds. Examples include *aw* and *oa.*

wide reading: Students read a lot of unfamiliar (novel) text.

word consciousness: Attentiveness to word meanings and interest in learning the meanings of new words.

word identification: The process of naming a written word.

word learning: The process by which a word is added to a reader's sight vocabulary. For many words, word learning requires word solving (see next definition) on multiple occasions. Word learning has occurred when a reader stores in memory a complete representation of a word enabling the reader to identify the word effortlessly and in all contexts on future encounters.

word solving: The act of using strategies in an effort to identify an unknown word encountered while reading.

written response: A reader's thoughts about a text that are recorded in writing by the student or the teacher. Examples include bulleted lists and phrases, paragraphs, and longer summary works.

References

Adams, M. J. (1990). *Beginning to read.* Cambridge, MA: MIT Press.

Adams, M. J. (2009). The challenge of advanced texts: The interdependence of reading and learning. In E. H. Hiebert (Ed.), *Reading more, reading better* (pp. 163–189). New York: Guilford Press.

Adams, M. J. (2011). The relation between alphabetic basics, word recognition, and reading. In S. J. Samuels & A. E. Farstrup (Eds.), *What research has to say about reading instruction* (4th ed., pp. 4–24). Newark, DE: International Reading Association.

Allington, R. (2009a). If they don't read much . . . 30 years later. In E. H. Hiebert (Ed.), *Reading more, reading better* (pp. 30–54). New York: Guilford Press.

Allington, R. (2009b). *What really matters in fluency.* Boston: Allyn & Bacon.

Allington, R. L., McCuiston, K., & Billen, M. (2015). What research says about text complexity and learning to read. *The Reading Teacher, 68*(7), 491–501.

Allington, R. L., & McGill-Franzen, A. (2010). Why so much oral reading? In E. H. Hiebert & D. R. Reutzel (Eds.), *Revisiting silent reading: New directions for teachers and researchers* (pp. 45–56). Newark, DE: International Reading Association.

Almasi, J. F., & Garas-York, K. (2009). Comprehension and discussion of text. In S. E. Israel & G. G. Duffy (Eds.), *Handbook of research on reading comprehension* (pp. 470–493). New York: Routledge.

Almasi, J. F., McKeown, M. G., & Beck, I. (1996). The nature of engaged reading in classroom discussions of literature. *Journal of Literacy Research, 28*(1), 107–146.

Alves, K. D., Kennedy, M. J., Brown, T. S., & Solis, M. (2015). Story grammar instruction with third and fifth grade students with learning disabilities and other struggling readers. *Learning Disabilities: A Contemporary Journal, 13*(1), 73–93.

Anderson, R. C. (1984). The role of readers' schema in comprehension, learning, and memory. In R. C. Anderson, J. Osborn, & R. Tierney (Eds.), *Learning to read in American schools: Basal readers and content texts* (pp. 243–257). Hillsdale, NJ: Erlbaum.

Armbruster, B. B. (1984). The problem of inconsiderate text. In G. G. Duffy, L. R.

Roehler, & J. Mason (Eds.), *Comprehension instruction: Perspectives and suggestions* (pp. 202–217). New York: Longman.

Assor, A., Kaplan, H., Kanat-Maymon, Y., & Roth, G. (2005). Directly controlling teacher behaviors as predictors of poor motivation and engagement in girls and boys: The role of anger and anxiety. *Learning and Instruction, 15*(5), 397–413.

Baddeley, A. D., & Hitch, G. (1974). Working memory. In G. A. Bower (Ed.), *The psychology of learning and motivation* (pp. 47–89). New York: Academic Press.

Bandura, A. (1997). *Self-efficacy: The exercise of control.* New York: Freeman.

Barth, A. E., Tolar, T. D., Fletcher, J. M., & Francis, D. (2014). The effects of student and text characteristics on oral reading fluency of middle-grade students. *Journal of Educational Psychology, 106*(1), 162–180.

Beck, I. L., & McKeown, M. G. (2001). Text talk: Capturing the benefits of read-aloud experiences for young children. *The Reading Teacher, 55*(1), 10–20.

Beck, I. L., McKeown, M. G., Hamilton, R. L., & Kucan, L. (1997). *Questioning the author: An approach for enhancing student engagement with text.* Newark, DE: International Reading Association.

Beck, I. L., McKeown, M. G., & Kucan, L. (2013). *Bringing words to life: Robust vocabulary instruction* (2nd ed.). New York: Guilford Press.

Bentum, K. E., & Aaron, P. G. (2003). Does reading instruction in learning disability resource rooms really work?: A longitudinal study. *Reading Psychology, 24*, 361–382.

Bloom, P. (2000). *How children learn the meanings of words.* Cambridge, MA: MIT Press.

Boon, R. T., Paal, M., Hintz, A. M., & Cornelius-Freyre, M. (2015). A review of story mapping instruction for secondary students with LD. *Learning Disabilities: A Contemporary Journal, 13*(2), 117–140.

Bowers, P. N., Kirby, J. R., & Deacon, S. H. (2010). The effects of morphological instruction on literacy skills: A systematic review of the literature. *Review of Educational Research, 80*, 144–179.

Brophy, J. E., & Good, T. L. (1970). Teachers' communication of differential expectations for children's classroom performance: Some behavioral data. *Journal of Educational Psychology, 61*(5), 365–374.

Buly, M. R., & Valencia, S. W. (2002). Below the bar: Profiles of students who fail state reading assessments. *Educational Evaluation and Policy Analysis, 24*(3), 219–239.

Cain, K. (1999). Ways of reading: How knowledge and use of strategies are related to reading comprehension. *British Journal of Developmental Psychology, 17*(2), 293–309.

Cain, K., & Oakhill, J. (2011). Matthew effects in young readers: Reading comprehension and reading experience aid vocabulary development. *Journal of Learning Disabilities, 44*, 431–443.

Carlisle, J. F., & Goodwin, A. P. (2013). Morphemes matter: How morphological knowledge contributes to reading and writing. In C. A. Stone, E. R. Silliman, B. J. Ehren, & G. P. Wallach (Eds.), *Handbook of language and literacy: Development and disorders* (2nd ed., pp. 265–282). New York: Guilford Press.

Carney, R. N., & Levin, J. R. (2002). Pictorial illustrations still improve students' learning from text. *Educational Psychology Review, 14*(1), 5–26.

Catts, H. W., Hogan, T. P., & Adolf, S. M. (2005). Developmental changes in reading and reading disabilities. In H. W. Catts & A. G. Kahmi (Eds.), *Connections between language and reading disabilities* (pp. 25–40). Mahwah, NJ: Erlbaum.

Cervetti, G., & Hiebert, E. H. (2015). Knowledge, literacy, and the Common Core. *Language Arts, 92*(4), 256–269.

Cervetti, G. N., Jaynes, C. A., & Hiebert, E. H. (2009). Increasing opportunities to acquire knowledge through reading. In E. H. Hiebert (Ed.), *Reading more, reading better* (pp. 79–100). New York: Guilford Press.

Ciullo, S., Lembke, E. S., Carlisle, A., Thomas, C. N., Goodwin, M., & Judd, L. (2016). Implementation of evidence-based literacy practices in middle school response to intervention. *Learning Disability Quarterly, 39*(1), 44–57.

Clymer, T. (1963). The utility of phonic generalizations in the primary grades. *The Reading Teacher, 16*(4), 252–258.

Connor, C. M., Morrison, F. J., Fishman, B., Giuliani, S., Luck, M., Underwood, P. S., et al. (2011). Testing the impact of child characteristics × instruction interactions on third grader's reading comprehension by differentiating literacy instruction. *Reading Research Quarterly, 46*(3), 189–332.

Coxhead, A. (2000). A new academic word list. *TESOL Quarterly, 34*(2), 213–238.

Coxhead, A. (2011). The academic word list 10 years on: Research and teaching implications. *TESOL Quarterly, 45*(2), 355–362.

Coyne, M. D., Simmons, D. C., Hagan-Burke, S., Simmons, L. E., Kwok, O.-M., Kim, M., et al. (2013). Adjusting beginning reading intervention based on student performance: An experimental evaluation. *Exceptional Children, 80*(1), 25–44.

Crosson, A. C., & Lesaux, N. K. (2010). Revisiting assumptions about the relationship of fluent reading to comprehension: Spanish-speakers' text-reading fluency in English. *Reading and Writing, 23,* 475–494.

Cunningham, A. E. (2006). Accounting for children's orthographic learning while reading text: Do children self-teach? *Journal of Experimental Child Psychology, 95,* 56–77.

Cunningham, A. E., & Stanovich, K. E. (1998). What reading does for the mind. *American Educator, 22*(1–2), 8–15.

Currie, N. K., & Cain, K. (2015). Children's inference generation: The role of vocabulary and working memory. *Journal of Experimental Child Psychology, 137,* 57–75.

Deci, E. L., & Ryan, R. M. (1985). *Intrinsic motivation and self-determination in human behavior.* New York: Plenum Press.

Dolch, E. W. (1936). A basic sight vocabulary. *Elementary School Journal, 36*(6), 456–460.

Duff, D., Tomblin, J. B., & Catts, H. (2015). The influence of reading on vocabulary growth: A case for a Matthew effect. *Journal of Speech, Language and Hearing Research, 58*(3), 853–864.

Duffy, G. G. (2009). *Explaining reading: A resource for teaching concepts, skills, and strategies* (2nd ed.). New York: Guilford Press.

Duke, N. K. (2000). 3.6 minutes per day: The scarcity of informational texts in first grade. *Reading Research Quarterly, 35*(2), 202–224.

Duke, N. K., & Bennett-Armistead, V. S. (2003). *Reading and writing informational text in the primary grades: Research-based practices.* New York: Scholastic.

Duke, N. K., Cartwright, K. B., & Hilden, K. R. (2013). Difficulties with reading comprehension. In C. A. Stone, E. R. Silliman, B. J. Ehren, & G. P. Wallach (Eds.), *Handbook of language and literacy: Development and disorders* (2nd ed., pp. 451–468). New York: Guilford Press.

Duke, N. K., Pearson, P. D., Strachan, S. L., & Billman, A. K. (2011). Essential elements of fostering and teaching reading comprehension. In S. J. Samuels & A. E. Farstrup (Eds.), *What research has to say about reading instruction* (4th ed., pp. 51–93). Newark, DE: International Reading Association.

Dweck, C. S. (2007). *Mindset*. New York: Ballantine Books.

Eccles, J., & Wigfield, A. (2002). Motivational beliefs, values, and goals. *Annual Review of Psychology, 53*, 109–132.

Ehri, L. C. (2005a). Development of sight word reading: Phases and findings. In M. S. Snowling & C. Hulme (Eds.), *The science of reading: A handbook* (pp. 135–154). Oxford, UK: Blackwell.

Ehri, L. C. (2005b). Learning to read words: Theory, findings, and issues. *Scientific Studies of Reading, 9*, 167–188.

Ehri, L. C. (2014). Orthographic mapping in the acquisition of sight word reading, spelling memory, and vocabulary learning. *Scientific Studies of Reading, 18*, 5–21.

Ehri, L. C., Nunes, S., Stahl, S., & Willows, D. (2001). Systematic phonics instruction helps students learn to read: Evidence from the National Reading Panel's meta-analysis. *Review of Educational Research, 71*, 393–447.

Ehri, L. C., & Saltmarsh, J. (1995). Beginning readers outperform older disabled readers in learning to read words by sight. *Reading and Writing: An Interdisciplinary Journal, 7*(3), 295–326.

Englert, C. S., & Thomas, C. C. (1987). Sensitivity to text structure in reading and writing: A comparison between learning disabled and non-learning disabled students. *Learning Disability Quarterly, 10*(2), 93–105.

Fisher, D., & Frey, N. (2012). Close reading in elementary schools. *The Reading Teacher, 66*(3), 179–188.

Fisher, D., & Frey, N. (2015). Selecting texts and tasks for content area reading and learning. *The Reading Teacher, 68*, 524–529.

Fisher, D., & Ivey, G. (2006). Evaluating the interventions for struggling adolescent readers. *Journal of Adolescent and Adult Literacy, 50*(3), 180–189.

Flynn, L. J., Zheng, X., & Swanson, H. L. (2012). Instructing struggling older readers: A selective meta-analysis of intervention research. *Learning Disabilities Research and Practice, 27*(1), 21–32.

Foorman, B., Beyler, N., Borradaile, K., Coyne, M., Denton, C. A., Dimino, J., et al. (2016). *Foundational skills to support reading for understanding in kindergarten through 3rd grade* (NCEE 2016-4008). Washington, DC: National Center for Education Evaluation and Regional Assistance, Institute of Education Sciences, U.S. Department of Education. Retrieved from *http://whatworks.ed.gov.*

Francis, D. J., Santi, K. L., Barr, C., Fletcher, J. M., Varisco, A., & Foorman, B. R. (2008). Form effects on the estimation of students' oral reading fluency using DIBELS. *Journal of School Psychology, 46*, 315–342.

Fry, E. B., & Kress, J. (2006). *The reading teacher's book of lists* (5th ed.). New York: Wiley.

Gaskins, I. W. (2011). Interventions to develop decoding proficiencies. In A. McGill-Franzen & R. L. Allington (Eds.), *Handbook of reading disability research* (pp. 289–306). New York: Routledge.

Gaskins, I., Ehri, L. C., Cress, C., O'Hara, C., & Donnelly, K. (1996). Procedures for word learning: Making discoveries about words. *The Reading Teacher, 50*, 312–327.

Gelzheiser, L. M. (2005). Maximizing student progress in one-to-one programs: Contributions of texts, volunteer experience and student characteristics. *Exceptionality, 13,* 229–243.

Gelzheiser, L., Hallgren-Flynn, L., Connors, M., & Scanlon, D. (2014). Reading thematically related texts to develop knowledge and comprehension. *The Reading Teacher, 68*(1), 53–63.

Gelzheiser, L. M., Scanlon, D., & Hallgren-Flynn, L. (2010). Spotlight on RTI for adolescents: An example of intensive middle school intervention using the interactive strategies approach—extended. In M. Y. Lipson & K. K. Wixson (Eds.), *Approaches to response to intervention (RTI): Evidence-based frameworks for preventing reading difficulties* (pp. 211–230). Newark, DE: International Reading Association.

Gelzheiser, L. M., Scanlon, D. M., Vellutino, F. R., & Deane, G. D. (2017). *The effects of a comprehensive and responsive intervention on the reading comprehension of intermediate grade struggling readers.* Manuscript in preparation.

Gelzheiser, L. M., Scanlon, D., Vellutino, F., Hallgren-Flynn, L., & Schatschneider, C. (2011). Effects of the interactive strategies approach—extended: A responsive and comprehensive intervention for intermediate-grade struggling readers. *Elementary School Journal, 112*(2), 280–306.

Gersten, R., Fuchs, L. S., Williams, J. P., & Baker, S. (2001). Teaching reading comprehension strategies to students with learning disabilities: A review of research. *Review of Educational Research, 71*(2), 279–320.

Goatley, V. J., Brock, C. H., & Raphael, T. E. (1995). Diverse learners participating in regular education "book clubs." *Reading Research Quarterly, 30*(3), 352–380.

Goldman, S. R., & Rakestraw, J. A. (2000). Structural aspects of constructing meaning from text. In M. L. Kamil, P. B. Mosenthal, P. D. Pearson, & R. Barr (Eds.), *Handbook of reading research* (Vol. 3, pp. 311–336). Mahwah, NJ: Erlbaum.

Good, R. H., & Kaminski, R. A. (2002). *Dynamic indicators of basic early literacy skills* (6th ed.). Eugene, OR: Institute for the Development of Educational Achievement.

Good, T. L., Slavings, R. L., Harel, K. H., & Emerson, H. (1987). Student passivity: A study of question asking in K–12 classrooms. *Sociology of Education, 60*(3), 181–199.

Gough, P. B., & Tunmer, W. E. (1986). Decoding, reading and reading disability. *Remedial and Special Education, 7,* 6–10.

Graham, S., & Hebert, M. (2011). Writing to read: A meta-analysis of the impact of writing and writing instruction on reading. *Harvard Educational Review, 81*(4), 710–744.

Graves, M. F. (2006). *The vocabulary book: Learning and instruction.* New York: Teachers College Press.

Greenberg, E., Dunleavy, E., & Kutner, M. (2007). *Literacy behind bars: Results from the 2003 National Assessment of Adult Prison Literacy Survey.* Washington, DC: National Center for Education Statistics, U.S. Department of Education.

Guthrie, J. T., & Humenick, N. M. (2004). Motivating students to read: Evidence for classroom practices that increase reading motivation and achievement. In P. McCardle & C. Chhabra (Eds.), *The voice of evidence in reading research* (pp. 329–354). Baltimore: Brookes.

Guthrie, J. T., & Klauda, S. L. (2016). Engagement and motivational processes in reading. In P. Afflerbach (Ed.), *Handbook of individual differences in reading: Reader, text, and context* (pp. 41–53). New York: Routledge.

Guthrie, J. T., Wigfield, A., Barbosa, P., Perencevich, K. C., Taboada, A., Davis, M. H., et al. (2004). Increasing reading comprehension and engagement through concept-oriented reading instruction. *Journal of Educational Psychology, 96*(3), 403–423.

Hasbrouck, J., & Tindal, G. A. (2006). Oral reading fluency norms: A valuable assessment tool for reading teachers. *The Reading Teacher, 59*(7), 636–644.

Hebert, M., Bohaty, J. J., Nelson, J. R., & Brown, J. (2016). The effects of text structure instruction on expository reading comprehension: A meta-analysis. *Journal of Educational Psychology, 92,* 609–629.

Hernandez, D. J. (2011). *Double jeopardy: How third grade reading skills and poverty influence high school graduation.* Baltimore, MD: The Annie E. Casey Foundation.

Hiebert, E. H., & Martin, L. A. (2009). Opportunity to read: A critical but neglected construct in reading instruction. In E. H. Hiebert (Ed.), *Reading more, reading better* (pp. 3–29). New York: Guilford Press.

Hirsch, E. D. (2003). Reading comprehension requires knowledge—of words and the world. *American Educator, 27*(1), 10–13.

Hoff, E. (2006). How social contexts support and shape language development. *Developmental Review, 26,* 55–88.

Individuals with Disabilities Education Improvement Act, 20 U.S.C. section 1400 (2004).

International Literacy Association. (2016). *Dyslexia* (Research advisory). Newark, DE: Author.

Inhoff, A. W., Solomon, M., Radach, R., & Seymour, B. A. (2011). Temporal dynamics of the eye–voice span and eye movement control during oral reading. *Journal of Cognitive Psychology, 33,* 543–558.

Jeong, J., Gaffney, J. S., & Choi, J. O. (2010). Availability and use of informational texts in second-, third-, and fourth-grade classrooms. *Research in the Teaching of English, 44*(4), 435–456.

Johnston, P. H. (2004). *Choice words: How our language affects children's learning.* Portland, ME: Stenhouse.

Kempe, C., Eriksson-Gustavsson, A., & Samuelsson, S. (2011). Are there any Matthew effects in literacy and cognitive development? *Scandinavian Journal of Educational Research, 55*(2), 181–196.

Kendeou, P., & O'Brien, E. J. (2016). Prior knowledge: Acquisition and revision. In P. Afflerbach (Ed.), *Handbook of individual differences in reading: Reader, text, and context* (pp. 151–163). New York: Routledge.

Kieffer, M. J., & Stahl, K. D. (2015). Complexities of individual differences in vocabulary knowledge. In P. Afflerbach (Ed.), *Handbook of individual differences in reading: Reader, text and context* (pp. 120–137). New York: Routledge.

Kim, W., Linan-Thompson, S., & Misquitta, R. (2012). Critical factors in reading comprehension instruction for students with learning disabilities: A research synthesis. *Learning Disabilities Research and Practice, 27*(2), 66–78.

Kintsch, W., & Rawson, K. A. (2005). Comprehension. In M. J. Snowling & C. Hulme (Eds.), *The science of reading: A handbook* (pp. 209–226). Malden, MA: Blackwell.

Kucan, L., & Palincsar, A. S. (2013). *Comprehension instruction through text-based discussion.* Newark, DE: International Reading Association.

Kuhn, M. R., & Levy, L. (2015). *Developing fluent readers: Teaching fluency as a foundational skill.* New York: Guilford Press.

Kuhn, M. R., & Schwanenflugel, P. J. (2009). Time, engagement, and support: Lessons from a 4-year fluency intervention. In E. H. Hiebert (Ed.), *Reading more, reading better* (pp. 141–162). New York: Guilford Press.

Kuhn, M. R., & Stahl, S. A. (2003). Fluency: A review of developmental and remedial practices. *Journal of Educational Psychology, 95*(1), 3–21.

Laing, E., & Hulme, C. (1999). Phonological and semantic processes influence beginning readers' ability to learn to read words. *Journal of Experimental Child Psychology, 73*(3), 183–207.

Leach, J. M., Scarborough, H. S., & Rescorla, L. (2003). Late-emerging reading disabilities. *Journal of Educational Psychology, 95*(2), 211–224.

Lightner, S. C., & Wilkinson, I. A. G. (2016). Instructional frameworks for quality talk about text: Choosing the best approach. *The Reading Teacher, 70*(4), 435–444.

Loftus, S. M., & Coyne, M. D. (2013). Vocabulary instruction within a multi-tier approach. *Reading and Writing Quarterly, 29*(1), 4–19.

Malloy, J. A., & Gambrell, L. B. (2011). The contribution of discussion to reading comprehension and critical thinking. In R. L. Allington & A. McGill-Franzen (Eds.), *Handbook of reading disabilities research* (pp. 253–262). Mahwah, NJ: Erlbaum.

Maloch, B. (2002). Scaffolding student talk: One teacher's role in literature discussion groups. *Reading Research Quarterly, 37*(1), 94–112.

Mandler, J. M., & Johnson, N. S. (1977). Remembrance of things parsed: Story structure and recall. *Cognitive Psychology, 9*(1), 111–151.

Martin-Chang, S. L., Levy, B. A., & O'Neil, S. (2007). Word acquisition, retention, and transfer: Findings from contextual and isolated word training. *Journal of Experimental Child Psychology, 96*, 37–56.

Mason, L., Tornatora, M. C., & Pluchino, P. (2013). Do fourth graders integrate text and picture in processing and learning from an illustrated science text?: Evidence from eye-movement patterns. *Computers and Education, 60*(1), 95–109.

McKenna, M. C., Kear, D. J., & Ellsworth, R. A. (1995). Children's Attitude Towards Reading: A national survey. *Reading Research Quarterly, 30*, 934–956.

McKeown, M. G., Beck, I. L., & Blake, R. G. (2009). Rethinking reading comprehension instruction: A comparison of instruction for strategies and content approaches. *Reading Research Quarterly, 44*(3), 218–253.

McRae, A., & Guthrie, J. T. (2009). Promoting reasons for reading: Teacher practices that impact motivation. In E. H. Hiebert (Ed.), *Reading more, reading better* (pp. 55–76). New York: Guilford Press.

Meichenbaum, D., & Biemiller, A. (1998). *Nurturing independent learners: Helping students take charge of their learning.* Cambridge, MA: Brookline Books.

Meisinger, E. B., Bradley, B. A., Schwanenflugel, P. J., Kuhn, M. R., & Morris, R. D. (2009). Myth and reality of the word caller: The relation between teacher nominations and prevalence among elementary school children. *School Psychology Quarterly, 24*(3), 147–169.

Menon, S., & Hiebert, E. H. (2011). Instructional texts and the fluency of learning disabled readers. In A. McGill-Franzen & R. L. Allington (Eds.), *Handbook of reading disability research* (pp. 57–67). New York: Routledge.

Meyer, B. J. (1987). Following the author's top-level organization: An important skill for reading comprehension. In R. J. Tierney, P. L. Anders, & J. Nichols Mitchell (Eds.),

Understanding readers' understanding: Theory and practice (pp. 59–76). Hillsdale, NJ: Erlbaum.

Miller, B., McCardle, P., & Hernandez, R. (2010). Advances and remaining challenges in adult literacy research. *Journal of Learning Disabilities, 43*(2), 101–107.

Müller, B., Richter, T., Križan, A., Hecht, T., & Ennemoser, M. (2015). Word recognition skills moderate the effectiveness of reading strategy training in grade 2. *Learning and Individual Differences, 40,* 55–62.

Murphy, P. K., Wilkinson, I. A., Soter, A. O., Hennessey, M. N., & Alexander, J. F. (2009). Examining the effects of classroom discussion on students' comprehension of text: A meta-analysis. *Journal of Educational Psychology, 101*(3), 740–764.

Nagy, W. E., & Anderson, R. C. (1984). How many words are there in printed school English? *Reading Research Quarterly, 19,* 357–366.

Nagy, W. E., & Herman, P. A. (1987). Breadth and depth of vocabulary knowledge: Implications for acquisition and instruction. In M. G. McKeown & M. E. Curtis (Eds.), *The nature of vocabulary acquisition* (pp. 19–36). Hillside, NJ: Erlbaum.

Nagy, W. E., Herman, P., & Anderson, R. C. (1985). Learning words from context. *Reading Research Quarterly, 20,* 233–253.

National Assessment of Educational Progress. (2002). Oral Reading Fluency Scale. Retrieved from *https://nces.ed.gov/nationsreportcard/studies/ors/scale.aspx.*

National Assessment of Educational Progress. (2015). The nation's report card: Mathematics and reading assessment. Retrieved from *www.nationsreportcard.gov/reading_math_2015/#reading/acl?grade=4.*

National Governors Association Center for Best Practices & Council of Chief State School Officers. (2010). *Common Core State Standards for English language arts and literacy, history/social studies, science, and technical subjects.* Washington, DC: Author.

National Reading Panel. (2000). *Teaching children to read: An evidence-based assessment of the scientific research literature on reading and its implications for reading instruction: Reports of subgroups.* Washington, DC: National Institute of Child Health and Human Development.

Neuman, S. B., & Celano, D. C. (2012). Worlds apart: One city, two libraries, and ten years of watching inequality grow. *American Educator, 36*(3), 13–23.

O'Connor, R. E. (2014). *Teaching word recognition* (2nd ed.). New York: Guilford Press.

O'Connor, R. E., Gutierrez, G., Knight-Teague, K., Checca, C. J., Sun, J., & Ho, T. (2013). Variations in practice time reading aloud: 10 versus 20 minutes. *Scientific Studies of Reading, 17,* 134–162.

O'Connor, R. E., Swanson, H. L., & Geraghty, C. (2010). Improvement in reading rate under independent and difficult text levels. *Journal of Educational Psychology, 102,* 1–19.

O'Connor, R. E., White, A., & Swanson, H. L. (2007). Repeated reading versus continuous reading: Influences on reading fluency and comprehension. *Exceptional Children, 74,* 31–46.

Paris, S. G., & Hamilton, E. E. (2009). The development of children's reading comprehension. In S. E. Israel & G. G. Duffy (Eds.), *Handbook of research on reading comprehension* (pp. 32–53). New York: Routledge.

Paris, S. G., Wasik, B., & Turner, J. C. (1991). The development of strategic readers. In

R. Barr, M. L. Kamil, P. B. Mosenthal, & P. D. Pearson (Eds.), *Handbook of reading research* (Vol. 2, pp. 609–640). Hillsdale, NJ: Erlbaum.

Pearson, P. D., & Gallagher, M. C. (1983). The instruction of reading comprehension. *Contemporary Educational Psychology, 8*(3), 317–344.

Perfetti, C. A. (1985). *Reading ability.* New York: Oxford University Press.

Perfetti, C. A. (1994). Psycholinguistics and reading ability. In M. Gernsbacher (Ed.), *Handbook of psycholinguistics* (pp. 849–894). San Diego, CA: Academic Press.

Perfetti, C. A., Landi, N., & Oakhill, J. (2005). The acquisition of reading comprehension skill. In M. J. Snowling & C. Hulme (Eds.), *The science of reading: A handbook* (pp. 227–247). Malden, MA: Blackwell.

Pike, M. M., Barnes, M. A., & Barron, R. W. (2010). The role of illustrations in children's inferential comprehension. *Journal of Experimental Child Psychology, 105*(3), 243–255.

Pintrich, P. R., & Schunk, D. H. (2002). *Motivation in education: Theory, research and application.* Columbus, OH: Merrill.

Pressley, M., & Allington, R. L. (2014). *Reading instruction that works: The case for balanced teaching* (4th ed.). New York: Guilford Press.

Pressley, M., Wood, E., Woloshyn, V. E., Martin, V., King, A., & Menke, D. (1992). Encouraging mindful use of prior knowledge: Attempting to construct explanatory answers facilitates learning. *Educational Psychologist, 27*(1), 91–109.

Prochnow, J. E., Tunmer, W. E., & Chapman, J. W. (2013). A longitudinal investigation of the influence of literacy-related skills, reading self-perceptions, and inattentive behaviours on the development of literacy learning difficulties. *International Journal of Disability, Development and Education, 60*(3), 185–207.

Quinn, J. M., Wagner, R. K., Petscher, Y., & Lopez, D. (2015). Developmental relations between vocabulary knowledge and reading comprehension: A latent change score modeling study. *Child Development, 86*(1), 159–175.

Quirk, M., & Beem, S. (2012). Examining the relations between reading fluency and reading comprehension for English language learners. *Psychology in the Schools, 49*(6), 539–553.

Rasinski, T. V. (2004). Creating fluent readers. *Educational Leadership, 61*(6), 46–51.

Rasinski, T., Samuels, S. J., Hiebert, E. H., Petscher, Y., & Feller, K. (2011). The relationship between a silent reading fluency instructional protocol on students' reading comprehension and achievement in an urban school setting. *Reading Psychology, 32,* 75–97.

Recht, D. R., & Leslie, L. (1988). Effect of prior knowledge on good and poor readers' memory of text. *Journal of Educational Psychology, 80*(1), 16.

Reutzel, D. R., Jones, C. D., Fawson, P. C., & Smith, J. C. (2008). Scaffolded silent reading: A complement to guided repeated oral reading that works! *The Reading Teacher, 62,* 194–207.

Rimbey, M., McKeown, M., Beck, I. L., & Sandora, C. (2016). Supporting teachers to implement contextualized and interactive practices in vocabulary instruction. *Journal of Education, 196*(2), 69–87.

Rodgers, E., D'Agostino, J. V., Harmey, S. J., Kelly, R. H., & Brownfield, K. (2016). Examining the nature of scaffolding in an early literacy intervention. *Reading Research Quarterly, 51*(3), 345–360.

Rose, T. L. (1986). Effects of illustrations on reading comprehension of learning disabled students. *Journal of Learning Disabilities, 19*(9), 542–544.

Roser, N., Martinez, M., Fuhrken, C., & McDonnold, K. (2007). Characters as guides to meaning. *The Reading Teacher, 60*(6), 548–559.

Sakiey, E., & Fry, E. (1984). *3,000 instant words.* Providence, RI: Jamestone.

Samuels, S. J. (2006). Reading fluency: Its past, present, and future. In T. Rasinski, C. Blachowicz, & K. Lems (Eds.), *Fluency instruction: Research-based best practices* (pp. 7–20). New York: Guilford Press.

Samuelstuen, M. S., & Bråten, I. (2005). Decoding, knowledge, and strategies in comprehension of expository text. *Scandinavian Journal of Psychology, 46*(2), 107–117.

Scanlon, D. M., Anderson, K. L., & Sweeney, J. M. (2010). *Early intervention for reading difficulties: The interactive strategies approach.* New York: Guilford Press.

Scanlon, D. M., Anderson, K. L., & Sweeney, J. M. (2017). *Early intervention for reading difficulties: The interactive strategies approach* (2nd ed). New York: Guilford Press.

Scanlon, D. M., Gelzheiser, L. M., Vellutino, F. R., Schatschneider, C., & Sweeney, J. M. (2008). Reducing the incidence of early reading difficulties: Professional development for classroom teachers versus direct interventions for children. *Learning and Individual Differences, 18*(3), 346–359.

Scanlon, D. M., Vellutino, F. R., Small, S. G., Fanuele, D. P., & Sweeney, J. M. (2005). Severe reading difficulties—Can they be prevented?: A comparison of prevention and intervention approaches. *Exceptionality, 13*(4), 209–227.

Schilling, S. G., Carlisle, J. F., Scott, S. E., & Zeng, J. (2007). Are fluency measures accurate predictors of reading achievement? *Elementary School Journal, 107*(5), 429–448.

Schultheiss, O. C., & Brunstein, J. C. (2005). An implicit motive perspective on competence. In A. J. Elliot & C. S. Dweck (Eds.), *Handbook of competence and motivation* (pp. 31–51). New York: Guilford Press.

Schunk, D. H., Meece, J. L., & Pintrich, P. R. (2012). *Motivation in education: Theory, research, and applications* (4th ed.). Upper Saddle River, NJ: Pearson.

Schunk, D. H., & Rice, J. M. (1987). Enhancing comprehension skill and self-efficacy with strategy value information. *Journal of Reading Behavior, 19*(3), 285–302.

Schwanenflugel, P. J., & Kuhn, M. R. (2016). Reading fluency. In P. Afflerbach (Ed.), *Handbook of individual differences in reading: Reader, text, and context* (pp. 107–119). New York: Routledge.

Shanahan, T. (2014). Should we teach students at their reading levels? *Reading Today, 32*(2), 14–15.

Share, D. L. (1995). Phonological recoding and self-teaching: Sine qua non of reading acquisition. *Cognition, 55*(2), 151–218.

Short, E. J., & Ryan, E. B. (1984). Metacognitive differences between skilled and less skilled readers: Remediating deficits through story grammar and attribution training. *Journal of Educational Psychology, 76*(2), 225.

Simmons, D. (2015). Instructional engineering principles to frame the future of reading intervention research and practice. *Remedial and Special Education, 36*(1), 45–51.

Sitton, R. A., & Forest, R. G. (1992). *The quick-word handbook for beginning writers.* North Billerica, MA: Curriculum Associates.

Snow, C., & O'Connor, C. (2016). Close reading and far-reaching classroom discussion: Fostering a vital connection. *Journal of Education, 196*(1), 1–8.

Solis, M., Ciullo, S., Vaughn, S., Pyle, N., Hassaram, B., & Leroux, A. (2012). Reading comprehension interventions for middle school students with learning disabilities: A synthesis of 30 years of research. *Journal of Learning Disabilities, 45*(4), 327–340.

Stahl, S. A., & Fairbanks, M. M. (1986). The effects of vocabulary instruction: A model-based meta-analysis. *Review of Educational Research, 56*(1), 72–110.

Stahl, S. A., & Heubach, K. M. (2005). Fluency-oriented reading instruction. *Journal of Literacy Research, 37*(1), 25–60.

Sternberg, R. J. (1987). Most vocabulary is learned from context. In M. G. McKeown & M. E. Curtis (Eds.), *The nature of vocabulary acquisition* (pp. 89–106). Hillsdale, NJ: Erlbaum.

Swanson, E. A., Wexler, J., & Vaughn, S. (2009). Text reading and students with learning disabilities. In E. H. Hiebert (Ed.), *Reading more, reading better* (pp. 210–230). New York: Guilford Press.

Tan, A., & Nicholson, T. (1997). Flashcards revisited: Training poor readers to read words faster improves their comprehension of text. *Journal of Educational Psychology, 89*, 276–288.

Treiman, R., Sotak, L., & Bowman, M. (2001). The role of letter names and letter sounds in connecting print to speech. *Memory and Cognition, 29*, 860–873.

Trisler, A., & Cardiel, P. H. (1989). *Words I use when I write.* Cambridge, MA: Educators Publishing Service.

Tunmer, W. E., & Nicholson, T. (2011). The development and teaching of word recognition skill. In M. L. Kamil, P. D. Pearson, E. B. Moje, & P. P. Afflerbach (Eds.), *Handbook of reading research* (Vol. 4, pp. 405–431). New York: Routledge.

Unrau, N., & Schlackman, J. (2006). Motivation and its relationship with reading achievement in an urban middle school. *Journal of Educational Research, 100*(2), 81–101.

Valencia, S. W. (2011). Reader profiles and reading disabilities. In R. L. Allington & A. McGill-Franzen (Eds.), *Handbook of reading disabilities research* (pp. 25–35). Mahwah, NJ: Erlbaum.

Van den Branden, K. (2000). Does negotiation of meaning promote reading comprehension?: A study of multilingual primary school classes. *Reading Research Quarterly, 35*(3), 426–443.

Van Ryzin, M. J. (2010). Motivation and reading disabilities. In A. McGill-Franzen & R. L. Allington (Eds.), *Handbook of reading disability research* (pp. 242–252). New York: Routledge.

Vansteenkiste, M., Lens, W., & Deci, E. L.(2006). Intrinsic versus extrinsic goal contents in self-determination theory. *Educational Psychologist, 41*(1), 19–31.

Vaughn, S., Wexler, J., Roberts, G., Barth, A. A., Cirino, P. T., Romain, M. A., et al. (2011). Effects of individualized and standardized interventions on middle school students with reading disabilities. *Exceptional Children, 77*(4), 391–407.

Vellutino, F. R. (1987). Dyslexia. *Scientific American, 256*, 34–41.

Vellutino, F. R., & Scanlon, D. M. (2002). The interactive strategies approach to reading intervention. *Contemporary Educational Psychology, 27*(4), 573–635.

Vellutino, F. R., Scanlon, D. M., Sipay, E., Small, S., Pratt, A., Chen, R., et al. (1996). Cognitive profiles of difficult-to-remediate and readily-remediated poor readers: Early intervention as a vehicle for distinguishing between cognitive and experiential deficits as basic causes of specific reading disability. *Journal of Educational Psychology, 88*(4), 601–638.

Vellutino, F. R., Tunmer, W. E., Jaccard, J. J., & Chen, R. (2007). Components of reading ability. *Scientific Studies of Reading, 11*(1), 3–32.

Wanzek, J., & Kent, S. C. (2012). Reading interventions for students with learning disabilities in the upper elementary grades. *Learning Disabilities: A Contemporary Journal, 10*(1), 5–16.

Wanzek, J., & Roberts, G. (2012). Reading interventions with varying instructional emphases for fourth graders with reading difficulties. *Learning Disability Quarterly, 35*(2), 90–101.

Wanzek, J., Vaughn, S., Scammacca, N. K., Metz, K., Murray, C. S., Roberts, G., et al. (2013). Extensive reading interventions for students with reading difficulties after grade 3. *Review of Educational Research, 83*(2), 163–195.

Watson, J. J. (1991). An integral setting tells more than when and where. *The Reading Teacher, 44*(9), 638–646.

Weiner, B. (1980). The role of affect in rational (attributional) approaches to human motivation. *Educational Researcher, 9*(7), 4–11.

Wigfield, A., Gladstone, J., & Turci, L. (2016). Beyond cognition: Reading motivation and reading comprehension. *Child Development Perspectives, 10*(3), 190–195.

Wigfield, A., & Guthrie, J. T. (1997). Relations of children's motivation for reading to the amount and breadth of their reading. *Journal of Educational Psychology, 89*(3), 420–432.

Williams, J. P. (2015). Reading comprehension instruction: Moving into a new era. In P. D. Pearson & E. H. Hiebert (Eds.), *Research-based practices for teaching Common Core literacy* (pp. 79–92). New York: Teachers College Press.

Willingham, D. T. (2009). *Why don't students like school?: A cognitive scientist answers questions about how the mind works and what it means for the classroom.* San Francisco: Jossey-Bass.

Ziegler, J. C., & Goswami, U. (2005). Reading acquisition, developmental dyslexia, and skilled reading across languages: A psycholinguistic grain size theory. *Psychological Bulletin, 131*(1), 3–29.

Zwaan, R. A. (1994). Effect of genre expectations on text comprehension. *Journal of Experimental Psychology: Learning, Memory, and Cognition, 20*(4), 920–933.

Children's Books

Ashley, S. (2004). *Bees.* Pleasantville, NY: Gareth Stevens.

Atwell, D. (1999). *River.* New York: Houghton Mifflin.

Barton, B. (1995). *Buzz, buzz, buzz.* New York: Simon & Schuster Children's Publishing.

Bauer, D. M. (2006). *Niagara Falls.* New York: Aladdin Paperbacks.

Bell, C. (2010). *Bee-wigged.* London: Walk Books.

Bruchac, J., & Bruchac, J. (2001). *How chipmunk got his stripes: A tale of bragging and teasing.* New York: Puffin Group.

Dalgliesh, A. (1954). *The courage of Sarah Noble.* New York: Aladdin Paperbacks.

Dickmann, N. (2010). *A bee's life.* Chicago: Capstone Global Library.

Giles, J., & Lowe, I. (2000). *Speedy Bee*. Austin, TX: Harcourt Achieve.

Giles, J., & Lowe, I. (2007). *Speedy Bee's dance*. Austin, TX: Harcourt Achieve.

Haydon, J. (2004). *Facts about honey bees*. Austin, TX: Harcourt Achieve.

Hillert, M. (1963). *The three little pigs*. Parsipanny, NJ: Modern Curriculum Press.

Hoena, B. (2008). *The legend of Sleepy Hollow*. North Mankato, MN: Capstone.

Leaf, M. (1936). *The story of Ferdinand*. New York: Grosset & Dunlap.

Lobel, A. (1971). *Frog and Toad together*. New York: Harper & Row.

Mattern, J. (2007). *The legend of Sleepy Hollow*. New York: Scholastic.

McCloskey, R. (1957). *Time of wonder*. New York: Puffin Books.

McPhail, D. (2001). *Jack and Rick*. New York: Houghton Mifflin Harcourt.

Mortensen, L., & Arbo, C. (2009). *In the trees, honey bees*. Nevada City, CA: Dawn.

Murphy, F. (2002). *George Washington and the general's dog*. New York: Random House.

Nichols, C. (2006). *Off to sea*. New York: Sterling.

Nickel, S. (2011). *Race on the river*. Mankato, MN: Capstone.

Riehecky, J. (2008). *China*. Minneapolis, MN: Learner.

Schaefer, L. M. (1999). *Honey bees and hives*. Mankato, MN: Capstone Press.

Short, L. (1999). *The Short books*. Jenison, MI: Short Books.

Smith, A. (2001). *The bear and the bees*. Austin, TX: Harcourt Achieve.

Standiford, N. (1992). *The headless horseman*. New York: Random House.

Tagliaferro, L. (2004). *Bees and their hives*. Mankato, MN: Capstone Press.

Van Leeuwen, J. (1982). *Amanda pig and her big brother Oliver*. New York: Puffin Group.

Index

S